Tax for
Australians

9th Edition

T0363585

by Jimmy B. Prince

Tax for Australians For Dummies®, 9th Edition

Published by

John Wiley & Sons, Australia Ltd

Level 4, 600 Bourke Street

Melbourne, Vic 3000

www.dummies.com

Copyright © 2024 John Wiley & Sons Australia, Ltd

The moral rights of the author have been asserted.

ISBN: 978-1-394-23741-8

A catalogue record for this book is available from the National Library of Australia

Cover image: © fizkes/Adobe Stock Photos

Typeset by Straive

Printed in Singapore

M WEP316750 151024

Contents at a Glance

Table of Contents

Introduction

Australian income tax law can be very complicated and difficult to understand. You may need to thumb through two income tax assessment Acts equivalent in size to four telephone books, thousands of income tax rulings and a library full of legal books to find the right answer!

The dominant purpose of the income tax legislation is to raise revenue by levying a tax on taxable income. The tax Acts point out that assessable income minus deductions equals taxable income, and then tell you the rules you need to follow to calculate your assessable income and allowable deductions. The Acts also tell you who must pay income tax and how to work out how much income tax you must pay.

Generally, you have a choice of two ways to solve your tax liability problems: You can either pay a registered tax agent or solicitor who specialises in income tax law, or you can try to find out the answer yourself. If you pay someone, you quickly find that the meter starts ticking the moment you walk through the door or pick up the phone. Although seeking professional advice is highly recommended and encouraged, you need never underestimate your own abilities. If you use basic research skills that you acquired during your student days plus the skills you use to do your job, you may be pleasantly surprised at how adept you are at taking on responsibility for your own tax journey.

So, if you have a winning edge — the skills to do basic research — why not have a go? If you can't solve your problem or you lack confidence, at least you tried. And if you do seek professional advice, you're in a position to have a meaningful conversation (especially if the fee is substantial!). As a student once said to me, 'I'll at least be in a position to verify and check the facts out myself and not feel like a fool!'

About This Book

This 2023–24 edition of *Tax for Australians For Dummies* caters to tax beginners and is also useful as a quick reference for the more tax-savvy readers. As well as helping you come to terms with the basic principles of income tax law, it also appeals to students who plan to study tax law, because it closely follows the content of a standard course syllabus. This book explains in simple terms core tax concepts that you need to be aware of when dealing with Australian tax issues. Throughout this book, case studies reinforce core tax principles. Also, you have the option of checking out technical information such as references to major Tax Office fact sheets and income tax rulings that tax professionals use and rely on to solve tax issues. This level of information is useful to readers who are studying income tax law or who wish to understand how the Tax Office comes to certain tax conclusions in its own interpretation of the tax laws.

To keep things consistent and easy to follow, here are a couple of the conventions this book uses:

>> Tax terms appear in italics and are closely preceded or followed by an easy-to-understand definition.

>> When I reference tax office publications or provide websites of interest, I include the address in a special typeface like this: www.ato.gov.au.

Foolish Assumptions

I wrote this book with some assumptions in mind. I assume that

>> You're in one or more of the following categories: Accountant or adviser on tax, employee, employer, investor, retiree, self-employed, taxation student or working in the tax industry.

>> You want simple facts on the complex subject of tax in an easy-to-use format.

>> You want to have on hand the many ways to minimise your tax while keeping the Tax Office happy.

>> You're likely to be aged 18 years and upwards.

Icons Used in This Book

Some people are more visual than others. That's where icons come in handy. This book uses several icons in the page margin and each has a little titbit of information associated with it. Here's what each icon means.

CHECK THE NET

If you're keen and eager to discover more about tax, this icon points you to handy websites to help you quickly solve tax issues that may come your way.

REMEMBER

Everyone can use a friendly reminder. The Remember icon is a quick and easy way to identify some of the more important tax points that you may want to make note of throughout the book.

TECHNICAL STUFF

Sometimes I get carried away with the technical stuff. You may find this level of information really interesting, or you may be bored to tears. Skip it if you wish or use it if you want a more complete understanding of your tax issue.

TIP

Tips include tax information that can help you save time or cut down on frustration.

WARNING

Text flagged with the Warning icon can keep you out of trouble. Serious legal issues encourage you to watch your tax step.

Where to Go From Here

Tax for Australians For Dummies may not be the exciting novel that you read from cover to cover. Rather, you can dip in and out to suit the occasion (tax return time) or when your interest level is piqued (due to a change in personal circumstance or making plans for your retirement).

Each chapter is designed to give you a good overview of a specific tax topic you may be interested in, with case studies to reinforce the learning process. If you're after a crash course on how Australians are generally taxed, flip to Part 1. The chapters in Part 2 cover tax issues relating to individuals, Part 3 is all about tax and your precious investments, Part 4 talks about business taxation, and Part 5 has all your long-term tax queries covered. For a quick rundown on clever but legal ways to minimise tax and common mistakes to avoid, check out Part 6. If you wish to brush up on a particular tax term, you can flip to the Glossary for a quick prompt.

While sitting in a comfortable chair or at your desk with a cup of coffee (and a suitable device nearby to access the internet), within a matter of minutes you can come to terms with specific issues such as assessable income, deductions, superannuation and business structures, to name a few. And, if you're cramming for an exam or you're not sure about a particular issue, *Tax for Australians For Dummies* can quickly steer you in the right direction — and save you much time and heartache!

1

How You're Taxed in Australia

Figure out the formula used in Australian income tax law.

Find out how Australian residents are taxed differently from non-residents and why it's so important that you're aware of your residential status.

Discover the different types of tax returns and which ones you need to lodge.

Understand what happens if your tax affairs are audited.

Chapter **1**

Understanding the Australian Tax System

I f you find tax a — excuse the pun — taxing subject, you're not alone. Most people are confused by taxes and, of course, would rather not pay them. However, we all know the cliché: Death and taxes are the only sure things in life. So, put another way, you probably need to take some time to understand taxation.

This chapter goes over some basic info that you need to understand in order to lodge your tax return in Australia. I explain the basics of the Australian tax system, tell you how to work out sources of income, and examine what tax you need to pay if you're setting up as a company.

Explaining the Australian Tax System

In Australia, two income tax assessment Acts are used by the federal government to levy tax on taxable income. They're equivalent in size to four telephone books and are the *Income Tax Assessment Act 1936* and the *Income Tax Assessment Act 1997*. (The reason for two Acts is because the 1936 Tax Act is gradually being replaced with the more user-friendly 1997 Tax Act.)

Understanding Your Income Tax Rates

For resident individuals, tax is levied on worldwide income on a progressive basis, referred to as *marginal tax rates*. Your marginal tax rate can vary between 0 per cent and 45 per cent (marginal tax rates are detailed in Chapter 5). This rating system means the more income you earn, the greater the amount of tax you're liable to pay.

Australia has numerous federal, state and territory, and local government taxes that you need to deal with.

TECHNICAL
STUFF

The Australian Taxation Office (Tax Office or commonly abbreviated to just ATO) is the federal government authority responsible for administering Australia's tax laws. To help you meet your legal requirements, the Tax Office regularly issues free-of-charge fact sheets, income tax rulings, tax determinations and interpretative decisions to explain tax issues that need clarification. You can access these fact sheets and tax rulings by visiting the Tax Office's website (www.ato.gov.au). I reference many of these useful resources through this book too!

TIP

If you want to quickly know your tax obligations in a nutshell, visit the Tax Office website (www.ato.gov.au) and check out 'Tax in Australia: what you need to know'. See also 'Australian business taxes' on the Australian Trade and Investment Commission website (globalaustralia.gov.au).

Federal taxes

The most important federal taxes include the following:

>> *Capital gains tax* (CGT) is paid on gains you make when you sell assets you own and on the occurrence of certain CGT events. Your main residence is exempt from tax and some other concessions may potentially be available (see Chapters 11 and 17 for more).

>> *Customs duty* is paid on certain goods you import into Australia (for example, cameras, perfume, alcohol and cigarettes).

>> *Excise duty* is levied on certain goods manufactured in Australia, such as alcohol and tobacco. (The hefty hike in excise duty on cigarettes is enough to make you quit smoking for good!)

>> *Fringe benefits tax* (FBT) applies to certain benefits you may receive (for example, your employer provides you with a car for private use). See Chapter 16.

>> *Fuel tax* is levied on petrol.

>> *Goods and services tax* (GST) is applied to most purchases and sales. See Chapter 15.

>> *Income tax* is paid on income you derive from worldwide sources. See Chapters 5 to 7.

>> The *Medicare levy* is used to help fund the Australian health system. The rate is 2 per cent of your taxable income.

>> *Withholding tax* is paid on certain income derived by a non-resident (see Appendix A).

In the 2023–24 tax year, if you earned below $24,276 as an individual or $40,939 as a couple/family, you were exempt from paying the Medicare levy. *Note:* For each dependent child, the family threshold increases by $3,760. For single seniors and pensioners, the threshold is $38,365 and for families it's $53,406.

WARNING

If you don't have private health insurance, you may be liable to pay a Medicare levy surcharge (MLS) if you earn more than a certain amount. For the 2023–24 tax year, the levy is 1.0 per cent if your taxable income (for the purposes of calculating your MLS) is between $93,001 and $108,000 for individuals or between $186,001 and $216,000 for couples/families. The MLS increases (in stages) to 1.5 per cent if you're an individual earning more than $144,001, or couples/families earning more than $288,001. *Note:* The family threshold for the MLS increases by $1,500 for each dependent child after the first child. For more details see Tax Office fact sheet 'Medicare levy surcharge income, thresholds and rates' on the Tax Office website (www.ato.gov.au).

State and local taxes

Following are some of the taxes levied by states:

>> *Gambling tax* is levied on certain gambling transactions (such as licence fees and poker machines).

>> *Land tax* is paid on some property holdings.

>> *Payroll tax* is levied on wages and fringe benefits an employer pays employees.

>> *Stamp duty* applies to certain transactions, particularly when you buy a property.

In a local context, *property valuation* and *rates* charges fund local government services (such as rubbish collection).

Taxing Major Income Streams

Income is normally derived from three major sources:

>> Income from personal exertion, such as salary and wages, bonuses and commissions you earn as an employee, and any allowances you receive (see Chapter 5)

>> Income from property and investments, such as interest, dividends, rent, annuities and royalty payments (see Chapters 8 to 10)

>> Income from carrying on (or running) a business, such as profits you earn from your business activities (see Chapter 12)

Taxing your treasures: CGT assets

You may be liable to pay capital gains tax (CGT) on profits you make when you sell CGT assets such as shares, real estate and collectables. However, just 50 per cent of the capital gain you make is liable to tax if you own the CGT asset for more than 12 months. This concept is discussed in more detail in Chapter 11.

TIP

Under the CGT provisions, your main residence is exempt from tax. If you're temporarily absent from Australia, the good news is your main residence continues to be exempt for an indefinite period if the property isn't used to earn assessable income. Alternatively, if you lease the property while you're away, your main residence is exempt from tax for up to six years (for more details, see Chapter 6).

Bringing home the money: International sources of income

As an Australian resident, you're required to disclose income you earn from worldwide sources, and non-residents are required to disclose income that only has an Australian source. Unfortunately, the tax Acts don't provide a statutory definition of *source*. So it basically boils down to a 'practical hard matter of fact'. Generally, three key tests are used to determine the origin or 'source' of income:

>> The place where you perform the services

>> The place where you sign the contract to perform those services

>> The place of the payment

CHECKING YOUR RESIDENCY STATUS

Your residency status determines the amount of tax you're liable to pay, because different tax rules and tax rates apply to residents and non-residents.

A resident of Australia is a person who normally lives in Australia and has a permanent home and job in Australia (commonly known as the *residency test*). In most cases, determining residency is relatively

(continued)

(continued)

straightforward (for instance, you're physically present in Australia for 183 days of the tax year or more). But this determination can become a little cloudy if you're absent from Australia for a long time and you still maintain some 'continuity of association' with Australia.

Your personal circumstances can change from year to year, so a number of tests may be used to check whether you're a resident. The main tests are

- Do you intend to live in Australia?
- Are you physically present in Australia?
- How long do you stay in Australia each financial year?
- Do you have a family home in Australia?
- Do you have business and family ties in Australia?
- Are your personal assets located in Australia?

As a general rule, if you're out of the country for more than two years and you sever your economic and social ties with Australia (for example, you quit your job and your family goes with you), you're most likely going to be treated as a non-resident for income tax purposes (for more details see Tax Office fact sheet 'Residency — the domicile test' on the Tax Office website (www.ato.gov.au)). Of course, after you leave Australia, you can still change your mind and come back in the future. On the other hand, if you migrate to Australia, you're generally considered a local for tax purposes from the date of your arrival, which means you're taxed as a resident from day one, and you gain all the tax concessions available to residents.

If you become a resident of Australia part way during the financial year, you can't claim the full *tax-free threshold*. (The tax-free threshold is the maximum amount of income you can receive that isn't taxed — see Chapter 5.) You need to pro rata the amount. You can claim one-twelfth of the amount for each month you're in Australia including the month you arrive. For example, if you arrive in Australia on 13 October 2023, at the time of writing your tax-free threshold is $13,650 ($18,200 / 12 × 9 months).

The Tax Office has published Taxation Ruling 'TR 98/17' regarding the residency status of certain individuals entering Australia (such as migrants, academics, students studying in Australia, visitors on holiday and workers with prearranged employment contracts). You can download a copy from the Tax Office website (www.ato.gov.au).

Ordinarily, your source of income is where you perform the services. For example, if you earn salary and wages, the source of income is the place where you perform the work, while the source of business profits is where you carry on the business activities.

WARNING

If you're a resident of Australia deriving foreign employment income such as salary and wages, you need to include the amount you earn overseas in your Australian tax return and pay tax here. If you pay foreign tax while working overseas, you can claim a foreign income tax offset in respect of the foreign tax that you pay. However, this rule harbours an exception. Foreign employment income derived by charity workers, the military and police, and people working on approved projects of national importance is exempt from tax in Australia. This exemption applies on the proviso that you work overseas for more than 90 days and you're liable to pay foreign tax on the income you earn. If you don't pay tax on income you earn overseas, the bad news is you have to include it in your Australian tax return and pay tax here. Unfortunately, you can't win all the time!

TECHNICAL
STUFF

If you want more info about foreign employment income visit the Tax Office website (www.ato.gov.au) and check out Tax Office fact sheets 'Exempt income from foreign service', 'Working on an approved overseas project' and 'Australian resident foreign and worldwide income'.

If you earn foreign income such as dividends, interest and royalties, and withholding tax is deducted from the payment, you need to include both the foreign income and withholding tax as part of your assessable income, and you can ordinarily claim a foreign tax credit for the foreign tax you pay. You need documentary evidence to substantiate your claim for a foreign tax credit (for example, notice of assessment and receipt of payment). For more details visit the Tax Office website (www.ato.gov.au) and check out the fact sheet 'Foreign and worldwide income'.

TECHNICAL
STUFF

The Tax Office has issued Taxpayer Alert 'TA 2012/1 Non-disclosure of foreign source income by Australian tax residents' warning Australian resident taxpayers of their obligations to disclose their worldwide income. You can get a copy from the Tax Office website (www.ato.gov.au).

Taxing a Company

A company is a separate legal entity. It must apply for a tax file number (see Chapter 13) and lodge a company tax return at the end of the financial year, disclosing the company's taxable net income or loss (see Chapter 3). Companies with an annual aggregated turnover (sales) of more than $50 million are liable to pay a 30 per cent flat rate of tax on taxable net income (derived). The rate reduces to 25 per cent for small or medium size business companies with an annual aggregated turnover (sales) of up to $50 million. The good news is that a company isn't liable to pay a 2 per cent Medicare levy. By the way, if you want to be a company director, you'll need to apply for a 'Director Identification Number'. (See the Australian Business Registry Services website — abrs.gov.au — for more details.)

WARNING

If a company derives predominantly passive investment income (such as interest, dividends, rent, royalties and net capital gains), it could be liable to pay a 30 per cent rate of tax. This could arise if more than 80 per cent of its assessable income is passive investment income.

A company can also be a resident or non-resident of Australia. Under Australian income tax law, a company is a resident of Australia if it incorporates in Australia. If this scenario isn't the case, a company can still be a resident for tax purposes if

>> It runs a business in Australia.

>> Its central management and control is in Australia.

>> Its voting power is controlled by shareholders who are residents of Australia.

A company's central management and control is usually where the company directors ordinarily meet to manage and run the company's ongoing business operations, and make the big decisions regarding the company's general policies and transactions it will enter. (For more info, check out Tax office fact sheet 'Working out your residency' and more particularly the bit relating to companies) and Taxation Ruling 'TR 2018/5 Income tax: central management and control test of residency'. In Chapter 12, I guide you through choosing a company structure. Chapters 13 to 17 go into the tax issues that arise when running a small business, covering GST, FBT and CGT.

IN THIS CHAPTER

» **Understanding the tax formula**

» **Identifying assessable income**

» **Working out exempt income**

» **Dissecting the general deduction provisions**

» **Including possible tax offsets**

Chapter **2**

Taxing Australians: The Formula You Need to Know

ncome tax law is like doing a jigsaw puzzle: You need to figure out where all the bits and pieces fit together. The Australian tax system uses a tax formula to work out whether you're liable to pay tax or get a tax refund. The tricky part is coming to terms with all the rules and regulations that you need to obey.

In this chapter, I guide you through the key components that make up the tax formula and explain the statutory regulations you need to follow.

Doing Your Sums

Tax is levied on taxable income. At the end of each financial year (which commences on 1 July and ends on 30 June), Australian residents are required to disclose the taxable income they derive from all sources in and out of Australia. (Non-residents are required to disclose only taxable income they derive from sources in Australia — refer to Chapter 1 and Appendix A for more.)

The Australian tax system uses the following tax formula to calculate your taxable income:

Assessable income minus allowable deductions equals taxable income

The system then sets out the rules you need to follow to determine your taxable income. Figure 2-1 shows an overview of the various elements that make up this tax formula.

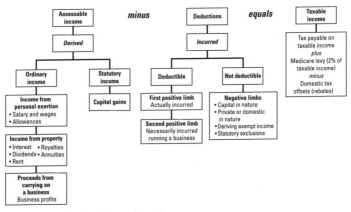

FIGURE 2-1: Charting the tax formula.

Declaring What You Earn: Assessable Income

Assessable income is income that you're liable to pay Australian income tax on. Assessable income is a combination of two key components: Ordinary income and statutory income.

You're considered by the Tax Office to have derived (earned) assessable income when you receive a payment or when you can legally demand payment for the services you've provided. The following classes of assessable income are considered to have been derived when they're paid to you:

>> Business profits (if you use the cash or receipts basis to recognise your income — for more details see Chapter 13)

>> Dividends (see Chapter 9)

» Interest (see Chapter 8)

» Rent (see Chapter 10)

» Salary and wages and directors fees (see Chapter 5)

You're liable to pay tax only on assessable income you derived during the year of income. This liability means that payments you haven't earned aren't taxed. You're considered to have derived or earned the amount as soon as you instruct someone as to how the income should be applied on your behalf (for instance, you instruct your employer to pay a bill on your behalf rather than giving the income to you).

If you run a business and use the accruals or earnings basis to recognise your income, you're considered to have derived your business profits when you have a legal right to demand payment — for instance, at point of sale. (See Chapter 13 for more.) Further, if you receive a payment before providing the services, you're considered to have derived this amount when the services have been completed.

TIP

If you receive a compensation payment for loss of income, the amount you receive is ordinarily treated as assessable income. For example, one of your clients compensates you for loss of business profits due to the cancellation of a commercial contract you entered into in the ordinary course of running your business.

CHECK
THE NET

The Tax Office provides fact sheets and tax rulings to help you understand the meaning of assessable income. The main ones ('Assessable income for business' and 'Income you must declare') are available from the Tax Office website (www.ato.gov.au).

REMEMBER

A payment you receive can be capital or income in nature. Capital is often likened to a fruit tree (such as a rental property or business premises that you own), while income is the fruit that the tree produces (such as rent you receive from your rental property or business profits you derive from your business premises). A capital receipt (such as a capital gain you make on sale of your rental property or business premises) is ordinarily liable to tax under the capital gains tax (CGT) provisions. (Check out Chapter 11 for more on CGT.)

Ordinary income

Ordinary income can cover a broad category of potential receipts. The Tax Act doesn't tell you what ordinary income means, so you need to follow the general principles associated with identifying the characteristics of ordinary income.

Ordinary income is generally divided into three categories:

>> **Income from personal exertion:** Particularly salary and wages, tips, bonuses and commissions you earn as an employee, and any allowances you receive. Income derived from this source is taxed at your marginal tax rates (see Chapter 5). If you're a resident of Australia, you may qualify for certain domestic tax offsets (rebates).

>> **Income from property:** Such as interest, dividends, rent, annuities and royalty payments. If you're a resident of Australia, income derived from this source is taxed at your marginal tax rates. Further, if you receive a dividend, you may qualify for a dividend franking credit tax offset (see Chapter 9). If you're a non-resident, certain payments you receive (for instance, interest and dividends) are liable only to withholding tax (see Appendix A).

>> **Proceeds from carrying on (running) a business:** This includes the profits you earn from your business activities. Income earned from this source is taxed at your marginal tax rates. However, if you run a small- or medium-size business in a company structure, you pay a 25 per cent flat rate of tax if your company's annual aggregated turnover (sales) does not exceed $50 million. (If your company's annual aggregated turnover is more than $50 million, the tax rate is 30 per cent; see Chapter 12.)

CHECK THE NET

For more info on ordinary income, check out the fact sheet 'Assessable income' available from the Tax Office website (www. ato.gov.au).

WARNING

Assessable income, particularly ordinary income, can also arise from an isolated commercial transaction outside the scope of what you normally do for a living; for example, if you're a fashion designer and decide to build a block of flats. This tax liability is on the proviso that the intention or purpose of entering into the transaction is to make a profit or gain. Any profit or gain you make is treated as assessable income. Conversely, if you make a loss, you can claim a tax deduction. Because this area of the law is complex, you're best to seek advice from a registered tax agent or solicitor. (For more details, see the Tax Office's Taxation Ruling 'TR 92/3 Whether profits on isolated transactions are income' and 'TR 92/4 Whether losses on isolated transactions are deductible' — these deal with profits and losses from isolated transactions.)

Statutory income

Statutory income is assessable income that's liable to tax because it's specifically listed in the Tax Act. This tax liability may arise, for example, if you make a net capital gain on the sale of a CGT asset or the occurrence of some other CGT event (see Chapter 11), or you receive a franking credit attached to a dividend (see Chapter 9).

Keeping What You Receive: Exempt Income

Not everything that comes your way has to be shared with the Tax Office — phew! Why? Because certain payments you may receive are exempt from tax. For example, you don't have to pay tax if you receive regular maintenance payments from a former spouse, you're a full-time student in receipt of a scholarship, or you receive certain government pensions or allowances (see Chapter 19). Other payments that are exempt from income tax include certain

>> Compensation payments

>> Defence force allowances (including payments and allowances from part-time service)

>> Educational assistance allowances

>> Family assistance allowances

>> Payments received from one or two students boarding with you under a homestay arrangement organised by the Department of Education (see ATO Interpretative Decision ID 2001/381 for more info)

The good news gets even better because certain organisations are also exempt from tax. These can include registered employer associations, non-profit societies for the encouragement of music, charitable institutions, non-profit sports clubs, public educational institutions and non-profit hospitals. Because these organisations don't pay tax on income derived, more money is available to help fund their activities! For more info, check out the Tax Office instruction guide 'Tax basics for non-profit organisations (NAT 7966)'. You can download a copy from the Tax Office website (www.ato.gov.au).

A number of specific payments are also exempt from tax, so you need to know which ones are assessable or exempt. As a general rule, exemption depends on why you received the payment. The confusing bit is that a payment can come from many different sources, for example:

>> An income-earning activity, such as employment or from running a business

>> An isolated commercial transaction with a view to making a profit or gain

>> Investment activities

>> Gifts from friends and relatives

>> A deceased estate

>> A hobby or pastime

>> A big win at the casino or races

>> Proceeds on the sale of CGT assets

It may be difficult to work out which of these payments are assessable or exempt. To make matters even more confusing, if the payment is a capital receipt, it can be liable to tax under the CGT provisions (see Chapter 11).

Income has the following characteristics:

>> Income is a periodical cash receipt (or benefit that can be converted into cash); it's recurrent and regular and you rely upon it to meet your living costs (for example, pension payments).

>> Income usually arises if a sufficient connection exists between an income-earning activity and the payment (such as a salary or business profits). If a sufficient connection isn't present, the receipt is most likely exempt from tax.

The following payments are examples of receipts that are normally exempt from tax because they fail the sufficient connection test:

>> Money you receive from windfall gains such as lottery, gambling and betting wins.

>> Personal gifts you receive from friends and relatives.

>> Pocket money you give to your children.

>> Proceeds from a hobby or pastime. However, if you're getting $5,000 from selling your homegrown fruit and vegetables, for example, you may be liable to tax because you may be considered to be running a business if you're doing this on a regular basis.

>> Money you inherit.

>> Certain compensation payments (such as for losing an eye or limb).

CHECK THE NET

If you have a home-based hobby and you sell products or services online (for example, you collect postage stamps and you regularly buy and sell them on eBay) you need to know whether your activities are a hobby or a business. For more details visit the Tax Office website (www.ato.gov.au) and read fact sheet 'Business or hobby'. Also check out fact sheet 'Is your hobby a business?' on the business.vic.gov.au website.

TECHNICAL STUFF

If you receive a non-cash benefit from a business relationship (for instance, you're a motor mechanic and customers give you a tray of meat instead of cash for fixing their car), the value of the non-cash business benefit you receive is ordinarily brought to account as assessable income if the benefit exceeds $300 (otherwise, it's exempt). For more info, check out Taxation Ruling 'IT 2668 Income tax: barter and countertrade transactions' on the Tax Office website (www.ato.gov.au).

If you like horse racing, regularly buy lotto tickets in the hope of hitting the jackpot, or play poker, I've got some good news for you! The proceeds from gambling and betting are normally exempt from tax, unless you can prove you're running a business of gambling and betting. Before you start sending thank-you letters to the Tax Office, though, the reason the Tax Office isn't keen to tax your winnings is because if it treats your activities as a business, any gambling and betting losses you incur become a tax-deductible expense. And, because losing generally trumps winning, the Tax Office isn't eager to subsidise your bad habits!

Whether a sufficient connection exists to make gambling proceeds assessable is a question of fact. As a general rule, proving this connection to the Tax Office is extremely difficult because activities involving an element of chance are normally considered to be no more than a hobby or pastime and not a business. Unless you're connected with the racing industry (for example, you're a bookmaker, trainer or horse breeder), you're unlikely to succeed in your attempt to convince the Tax Office.

TECHNICAL STUFF

If you want to know more about whether your horse-racing activities are a business or a hobby, check out Taxation Ruling 'TR 2008/2 Horse racing, training and breeding activities' on the Tax Office website (www.ato.gov.au).

Reducing Your Tax Bill: General Deductions

You must satisfy a number of conditions to claim a general deduction (referred to as the *general deduction provisions*). You can also claim certain specific deductions, which I talk about in Chapter 14.

The general deduction provisions set out the following rules for claiming a tax deduction. You can deduct from your assessable income any loss or outgoing to the extent that either

>> The loss or outgoing is incurred in gaining or producing your assessable income.

>> The loss or outgoing is necessarily incurred in carrying on (running) a business for the purpose of gaining or producing your assessable income.

However, be warned that you can't deduct a loss or outgoing under the general deduction provisions to the extent that it's

>> A loss or outgoing of capital, or of a capital nature.

>> A loss or outgoing of a private or domestic nature.

>> A provision of the Tax Act, which prevents you from deducting it.

When you examine the nuts and bolts that make up the general deduction provisions, two positive limbs allow you to claim a tax deduction and four negative limbs prevent you from claiming a tax deduction.

Further, you can claim a deduction only to the extent to which it's incurred in gaining or producing your assessable income. This means you're allowed to separate the parts of expenditure that may be partly allowable for deriving assessable income and partly not allowable because they're private or domestic in nature. For example, this could arise if you use your car partly for the purposes of deriving assessable income (such as using your car for only two days a week to earn income). Under these circumstances, two-sevenths of your car expenses are deductible, while the balance would be private or domestic in nature. The general deduction provisions also point out you can only claim expenditure that has been incurred in gaining or producing assessable income.

To comply with the deduction part of the tax formula (refer to Figure 2-1), you need to come to terms with the following key concepts:

>> First positive limb

>> Second positive limb

>> The negative limbs

>> Meaning of incurred

Checking out the first leg: First positive limb

The *first positive limb* sets out the rules for claiming a tax deduction. It applies to individuals who derive personal exertion income, such as salary and wages, and income from property, such as interest, dividends and rent. (If you're not running a business, you must rely only on the first limb to claim a tax deduction.)

The first positive limb points out that you can deduct from your assessable income any loss or outgoing to the extent that it's incurred in gaining or producing your assessable income. To claim a tax deduction under this limb, you need to demonstrate that the loss or outgoing was incurred in the actual course of gaining or producing your assessable income, and that it must be incidental and relevant to that end. Further, for the expenditure to be deductible, a perceived connection between the expenditure and the gaining or producing of your assessable income must be shown to exist. The perceived connection is determined by examining the character of the expense.

To qualify for a tax deduction under the first positive limb:

>> A direct connection must exist between the expenditure and the derivation of your assessable income.

>> The expenditure must be incurred while you're deriving your assessable income.

Examining the next leg: Second positive limb

To claim a tax deduction under the *second positive limb*, you need to demonstrate that you're running a business. The deduction must be incurred in running a business for the purpose of gaining or producing your assessable income.

Check out Chapter 13 for a discussion about whether you're actually running a business. Generally speaking, to qualify for a tax deduction under the second positive limb, the outgoing must be part of the cost of trading operations. This assessment depends on two key conditions:

>> The outgoing was necessarily incurred in running a business.

>> Running the business was for the purpose of gaining assessable income.

Following are examples of outgoings necessarily incurred in running a business:

>> Payments to secure the resignation of two managing directors, having proven to be unsatisfactory.

>> Expenses incurred by a company in defending its commercial reputation.

Being aware of the negatives: Negative limbs

The general deduction provisions of the Tax Act also tell you what loss or outgoing isn't a tax-deductible expense. They point out you can't deduct a loss or outgoing under this section if

>> The loss or outgoing is capital, or of a capital nature.

>> The loss or outgoing is of a private or domestic nature (for example, if you can't show a sufficient connection with earning your assessable income).

>> A provision of the Tax Act prevents you from deducting it; certain expenses such as entertainment expenses and penalties are specifically not tax deductible (see Chapter 14).

>> The loss or outgoing is incurred in relation to gaining or producing exempt income.

Checking out what is capital in nature

Unfortunately, the area of the law concerning whether a loss or outgoing is capital, or of a capital nature, is very complex. Whether the expenditure is capital and not deductible, or tax deductible, can depend on a fine level of judgement. Generally, if an expense is designed to bring into existence a lasting or enduring benefit (such as getting a driver's licence in order to get a job), or is a one-off payment (for example, purchasing your business premises), the expenditure is most likely to be capital in nature and not tax deductible.

Following are examples of the types of expenditure that Tax Office folk consider to be capital in nature and not tax deductible:

>> Undertaking a course of study that has no relevance to your current occupation (such as a motor mechanic studying accountancy; see Chapter 5).

>> Costs associated with trying to find employment. Why? Because these costs are incurred at a point too soon to be deductible.

>> Fees paid to an investment adviser for setting up an investment plan (see Chapter 18).

Ordinarily, two key tests are used to help you determine whether certain expenditure is capital or income in nature. The tests are the nature or character of the expense, and the advantage to be sought by incurring the expense. For example, if an expense arises out of the day-to-day activities of your business or income-producing activity (such as advertising costs and salaries you pay your staff), the expenditure is likely to be tax deductible. On the other hand, if the expenditure is devoted to a structural rather than an operational purpose (such as certain legal costs associated with setting up a business) then the expenditure is of a capital nature and the expenses aren't tax deductible.

TIP

Certain business-related costs that aren't ordinarily a tax-deductible expense (for instance, the cost of feasibility studies and the cost of setting up the business entity) can be written-off over a five-year period. The good news is that professional expenses (such as legal and accounting fees) associated with setting up a new business are tax deductible in the financial year you incur the expense (see Chapter 12). For more info, check out the Tax Office Ruling 'TR 2011/6' and fact sheet 'Depreciation and capital expenses and allowances' at www.ato.gov.au.

TECHNICAL STUFF

Expenses associated with establishing, replacing, enlarging or improving a business structure — as distinct from working or operating expenses — are capital in nature and not tax deductible. Further, the expenditure is capital in nature if the benefit or advantage you're seeking from incurring the expense is likely to provide a long-term lasting or enduring benefit for the business (or profit-yielding structure) you're running, and if the expenditure is a one-off payment and unlikely to be recurring. The following are examples of the types of business expenditure the Tax Office folk consider to be capital in nature and, therefore, not tax deductible:

>> Costs incurred in training a guard dog to protect business premises (ATO ID '2011/18 Income tax: deductions — guard dog expenses'). Why? Because you're gaining an enduring benefit for the business.

>> Costs of acquiring a subscriber base (ATO ID '2004/656 Income tax: capital v. revenue — acquisition of a subscriber base'). Why? Because you're enlarging the business or profit-yielding structure.

>> Legal costs to restrict a potential competitor from operating a similar business to the one you're running on your patch. Why? Because you're preserving and protecting the business or profit-yielding structure.

TIP

Some capital expenses may be deductible over a period of time, while some may be deductible outright under specific provisions of tax law. To find out more, visit the Tax Office website (www. ato.gov.au) and check out fact sheets 'Deductions for small business' and 'Income and deductions for business'.

Checking out what is private or domestic in nature

The fact that an expense is necessary to derive assessable income isn't a test for deductibility. For example, you have to wear clothes in order to go to work, but that fact doesn't necessarily mean that you can claim the cost of your clothes as a tax deduction. This interpretation is because the clothes lack a direct or relevant connection with deriving assessable income. So, if a loss or outgoing isn't incurred in the course of gaining or producing assessable income, or is a prerequisite to earning assessable income, the expenditure is considered to be private or domestic in nature.

Following are examples of expenditure that are deemed by the Tax Office to be private or domestic in nature:

>> **Child-minding expenses for someone to look after your children while you work:** These expenses have no direct or relevant connection to an employment activity. The expense is simply a prerequisite to earning your assessable income. However, although these types of expenses aren't tax deductible, you may qualify for a child care rebate (see Chapter 7).

>> **Expenditure incurred in travelling from home to work:** While you're travelling to work you're not actually performing any duties associated with deriving your assessable income. No direct or relevant connection exists between the travel and the work you do to qualify for a tax deduction. (See Chapter 3 for examples of work-related travelling expenses.)

» **Food and drink:** Living expenses are ordinarily considered to be private or domestic in nature, because they lack the character of a working or business expense. Searching for relevance between eating king prawns and enjoying a few beers at your favourite restaurant and doing your work is fruitless. It would be great if you could! However, if you're travelling on business (such as interstate or overseas), the good news is that travel expenses can include the cost of your meals (see Chapter 3 for more).

» **Hairdressing, cosmetics and other personal grooming:** These types of expenses don't have a direct or relevant connection with an income-earning activity. However, you can take advantage of an exception to this rule if you happen to work under harsh conditions and you're expected to be well groomed — for example, if you're a flight attendant.

» **Purchasing and maintaining conventional clothing:** Unless your clothes are part of a recognised work uniform, they lack a direct and relevant connection with an employment activity. These costs are incurred in order for you to be able to commence an employment activity (they're incurred because you can't go to work naked!).

» **Relocation expenses:** You can't ordinarily claim moving and travel costs relating to taking up new employment, or if you're transferred to another employment location (even if your employer asks you to do so). They're considered to be a prerequisite to earning assessable income.

CHECK THE NET

To find out more about expenses that aren't deductible, visit the Tax Office website (www.ato.gov.au) and check out fact sheet 'Non-deductible expenses'.

TIP

If you're required to work outdoors (for instance, you're a physical education teacher), you can claim a tax deduction for expenses such as sunscreen, hats and glasses to protect yourself from the sun and prevent skin cancer.

Figuring out when something is incurred

Under Australian income tax law, to claim a tax deduction you need to establish that the expenditure has been incurred. Ordinarily, you're considered to have incurred an expense when you have a legal obligation to make a payment for certain goods or services you receive. This obligation normally arises at the time you receive an invoice.

When you incur an expense, you can claim a tax deduction. One interesting point to keep in mind is that you don't have to make an actual payment to claim a tax deduction — no proof of payment or actual disbursement needs to be established for an expenditure to be incurred. The only condition is that you're definitely committed and you have a legal obligation to pay the bill.

The mechanics of figuring out whether an expense has been incurred becomes an issue only at the end of each financial year. This point in time is when you have to decide whether the expense is deductible in the current financial year or in the following financial year.

CASE STUDY: DETERMINING WHEN AN EXPENSE IS INCURRED

William runs a business and has an item of plant and equipment that's due for a general overhaul in three months. The overhaul is going to cost $10,000. William can't claim a tax deduction at this point in time because

- Presently, the proposed expenditure isn't an existing liability.
- William isn't definitely committed to making the payment.
- The expenditure is no more than impending, threatened or expected — no matter how sure William is about which year of income that the loss or expenditure is going to be incurred in the future.

However, when William's plant and equipment is serviced and he receives a bill for $10,000, he's considered to have incurred the expense. This consequence is the case even if William hasn't paid the amount, because now he has a presently existing liability and he's definitely committed to paying the bill.

If an expense arises but you're not sure exactly how much it is going to cost, provided you can make a reasonable estimation of the cost and you're committed to making a payment, you may be able to claim a tax deduction. This situation normally arises if you run an insurance business where insurance claims are continually arriving and they haven't been fully processed.

If you want to know more about the meaning of incurred, see Taxation Ruling 'TR 97/7 Meaning of "incurred" — timing of deductions'. You can get a copy from the Tax Office website (www.ato.gov.au).

Looking for Tax Offsets

A *tax deduction* is deducted from your assessable income (refer to the previous section), while a *tax offset* reduces the amount of tax you're liable to pay. However, you can't use tax offsets to reduce your Medicare levy liability — but you can transfer to your spouse some unused tax offsets, such as seniors and pensioners tax offsets (see Chapter 19).

The major tax offsets you're likely to use are listed in Chapters 3 and 7.

Visit the Tax Office website and look for 'Tax offsets' for a comprehensive list of offsets that are relevant to individual taxpayers, and the eligibility tests you need to satisfy to benefit from the offsets.

Chapter **3**

Lodging Your Tax Return: This One Is for the Nation

If you earn income, at the end of each financial year, whether you like it or not, you have a legal obligation to lodge a tax return for individuals with the Tax Office by 31 October (unless you're on a tax agent's lodgement program). This obligation means that you have to disclose the taxable income you derived during the previous financial year. Remember, Australia's financial year commences on 1 July and ends on 30 June. The headache part of the exercise involves the records you have to keep, and grappling with the various tax issues associated with preparing your tax return. To take the pressure off, you can always see a tax agent if you get into difficulty when preparing and lodging your return.

If you run a business in a partnership, company or trust structure (see Chapter 12 for more on these business types), you also have to lodge a tax return disclosing the net profit or loss your business earned during the year of income. You also need to disclose your share of any profits (or losses) that were distributed to you.

In this chapter, I guide you through the process you need to follow to lodge your annual tax return for individuals. I also discuss the process for lodging different types of tax return, such as for a partnership, company, trust or self-managed superannuation fund (SMSF).

WARNING

If you don't lodge your tax return by 31 October, you can be liable to pay a late lodgement penalty (an amount that depends on your taxable income and the period of time the tax return is late by). You can avoid this penalty if you see a tax agent. This exemption exists because tax agents are given an extension of time to lodge tax returns on behalf of their clients.

Preparing Your Individual Tax Return

You can lodge your 'Tax return for individuals (Tax Office reference NAT 2541)' in two ways. You (or your tax agent) can fill out the paper tax form included in 'Individual tax return instructions (NAT 71050)' and post it to your local Tax Office, or you (or your tax agent) can lodge your tax return online using myTax. 'Individual tax return instructions' is a booklet that the Tax Office releases each year to help you correctly fill out your tax return. You can order or download a copy from the Tax Office website: Just visit the ATO Publication Ordering Service (iorder.com.au/publication/main.aspx).

CHECK THE NET

myTax is a free electronic lodgement service provided by the Tax Office that allows you to lodge your tax return online. To take advantage of this online tool, you need to download the Tax Office myTax software package (or app) that permits you to prepare your individual tax return electronically and lodge it over the internet. (*Note:* After your tax return is lodged, you can check the progress of your return online.) myTax returns are usually processed within 12 business days — great news if you're expecting to get a tax refund, which is electronically deposited to your nominated bank account. For more details, visit the Tax Office website (www.ato.gov.au) and read the fact sheets 'How to lodge your tax return' (particularly the bit that deals with lodging your return online using myTax) and 'Check the progress of your tax return'. (*Note:* Before you can lodge online, you need to create a myGov account linked to the Tax Office — see the website my.gov.au for more details.)

If you derive income such as salary and wages, allowances, dividends and interest, and/or Australian government payments, under myTax the Tax Office may notify you that you can quickly complete a pre-filled out tax return online. You can claim certain tax offsets and expenses you incur in deriving your income.

If you're a traditionalist at heart and prefer to lodge a paper tax return, you must sign and date the tax return prior to lodging it to confirm that the information that you disclose is true and correct.

CHECK
THE NET

To help you to prepare your tax return the Tax Office issues (free of charge) a number of publications. The main publications are 'Individual tax return instructions (NAT 71050)'and 'Tax return for individuals (supplementary section) (NAT 2679)', plus some specialist publications such as 'Personal investors guide to capital gains tax (NAT 4152)', 'Rental Properties (NAT 1729)' and 'You and your shares (NAT 2632)'. If you want a copy of any of these publications, you can order or download them from the Tax Office website (www.ato.gov.au).

TIP

If you don't have to lodge a tax return, you need to notify the Tax Office and complete a 'Non-lodgement advice' form. One reason you may not need to lodge a return is if your taxable income is below the seniors and pensioners tax offset (SAPTO) taxable income threshold (see Chapter 19).

Receiving a PAYG payment summary

At the end of the financial year, if you're a salary and wage earner your employer gives you a 'PAYG payment summary — individual non-business (NAT 0046)' statement. This payment summary is a statement that sets out the gross income and allowances you received between 1 July and 30 June, and the total pay-as-you-go (PAYG) withholding tax that was deducted from your pay. You need to include all the relevant details from this payment summary in your tax return.

If you're unable to get a copy of this payment summary from your employer, you need to complete a 'Statutory declaration (NAT 4135)'. You can get a copy of this from the Tax Office website (www.ato.gov.au).

If you want to know more about PAYG payment summaries, visit the Tax Office website and check out the fact sheet 'PAYG payment summary statement'.

Claiming work-related car expenses

Under the car substantiation provisions, you can claim work-related car expenses in two ways, and you can choose the method that gives you the greatest deduction. However, you need to satisfy certain conditions — such as the number of kilometres you travel and whether you keep a record of all your car expenses.

The two methods of claiming a car expense are

» Cents per kilometre method

» Log book method

Using the cents per kilometre method

This method is restricted to the first 5,000 business kilometres you travel. You need to know approximately how many business kilometres you travel each year. You can then claim $0.85 per kilometre (for the 2023–24 tax year). This method is very easy to calculate and you don't need to keep a record of your car expenses. For example, if you travel 4,000 business kilometres, the amount you can claim is $3,400 ($4,000 × $0.85 = $3,400).

If you travel more than 5,000 business kilometres, you can still use the cents per kilometre method, but you can claim only up to a maximum of 5,000 kilometres.

Using the log book method

To use this method, you need to maintain a log book over a period of 12 continuous weeks to work out your business and private kilometres, and keep an accurate record of all your car expenses. The log book used to calculate your business use percentage is valid for five years. For example, if your business use percentage is 50 per cent and your car expenses were $12,000, you can claim $6,000 (50 per cent of $12,000). For more info, check out Tax Office fact sheet 'Logbook method'. You can download a copy from its website (www.ato.gov.au).

Claiming work-related travel expenses

You can claim travel expenses that have a direct or necessary connection with the derivation of your assessable income. But you can't ordinarily claim travel expenses between your home and place of work because they're private or domestic in nature (refer to Chapter 2). The following are examples of the types of business- or work-related travel that are ordinarily a tax-deductible expense:

» Cost of travel between two places of business or work

» Cost of travel between your home and other places if

- You run a home-based business and the travel is for business purposes (for instance, you need to visit your clients or do your banking).

- You need to carry bulky tools to do your work (for instance, heavy industrial equipment).

- You're an itinerant worker and need to travel to different places of work.

- You're a professional sportsperson and you travel to various matches or competitions (both home and away).

By the way — if you're required to travel for work-related purposes (for instance, you travel interstate or overseas to attend a business conference or seminar), travel expenses can also include your cost of meals, accommodation and other incidental costs while you're away performing your work-related duties. But remember, you need to keep a travel record, such as a diary, to substantiate your deductions.

TIP

Work-related car and travel expenses can include outgoings such as short-term car hire, parking fees, bridge and road tolls, taxi fares, and public transport fares.

REMEMBER

Each year the Tax Office issues a Tax Determination, which sets out the latest expense amounts for travel and overtime meal allowance that are considered to be reasonable to claim. For the 2023–24 tax year, the reasonable amount for overtime meal expenses is $35.65. (See Chapter 5 for more details.)

CHECK
THE NET

The Tax Office has issued guidelines of work-related expenses that you can claim if you work in a specific industry (for instance, in the defence or police force, or as an engineer, a nurse or a truck driver). For more info, check out Tax Office fact sheet 'Occupation and industry specific guides'. You can download a copy from its website (www.ato.gov.au).

TIP

Non work-related expenses such as voluntary gifts or donations of $2 or more to approved organisations (such as hospitals) are a tax-deductible expense. For more info, see the Tax Office fact sheets 'Gifts and donations' and 'Shares valued at $5,000 or less'.

Claiming tax offsets (rebates)

You can use tax offsets to reduce your tax payable. But you can't use tax offsets to reduce your Medicare levy liability. The main offsets you can use are listed in the following sections.

Claiming the low income tax offset

Eligibility for the *low income tax offset* is applicable to low income resident individuals. The maximum tax offset you can claim and the relevant income thresholds for the 2023–24 tax year are shown in Table 3-1.

TABLE 3-1 **Eligibility for the Low Income Tax Offset**

Year	2023-24
Maximum tax offset	$700
Taxable income threshold	$37,500
Taxable income upper limit	$66,667

For the 2023–24 tax year, the low income tax offset reduces by 5 cents if your taxable income is between $37,501 and $45,000. If your taxable income is between $45,001 and $66,667 your rebate reduces by a further 1.5 cents for every taxable dollar you earn between $45,001 and $66,667 (refer to Table 3-1).

Claiming the invalid and invalid carer tax offset

If you care for an invalid family member (such as a parent, a spouse or a child aged 16 or older) who is in receipt of a disability support pension or invalidity service pension, you may qualify for an *invalid and invalid carer tax offset* if you satisfy certain conditions. For more info, visit the Tax Office website (www.ato.gov. au) and check out the fact sheet 'Offset for maintaining an invalid or invalid carer'.

Claiming the zone tax offset

If you live or work in a remote part of Australia or you're in the defence forces serving overseas, you may be eligible for a *zone tax offset*. This offset applies to two classifications, known as zone A and zone B. For details regarding eligibility and selected areas within these zones, visit the Tax Office website (www.ato.gov. au) and check out the fact sheet 'Zone and overseas forces tax offsets'. (*Note:* Fly-in fly-out and drive-in drive-out workers are ineligible to claim a zone tax offset.)

TIP

If you receive a lump sum payment (such as salary and wages) that relates to income derived in previous tax years, you may qualify for a *lump sum payment in arrears tax offset* to smooth out any variations in tax payable as a consequence of receiving the previous years' payments. For more info visit the Tax Office website (www.ato.gov.au) and check out fact sheet 'Lump sum payment in arrears tax offsets'.

CHECK
THE NET

Visit the Tax Office website and look for 'Offsets and rebates' for a comprehensive list of offsets that are relevant to individual taxpayers, and the eligibility tests you need to satisfy to benefit from the offsets.

Receiving a Thank-You Note: Notice of Assessment

After you lodge your tax return, the Tax Office calculates the net tax payable (or tax refund) based on the information you submit. As a general rule, a paper tax return is processed within six weeks from the date you lodge it. But if you lodge over the internet using myTax, processing your return normally takes 12 business days. Using myTax may be worth considering if you're expecting a big tax refund and you're keen to get your hands on it. (*Note:* If you're likely to receive a tax refund, you must supply your bank account details when you lodge your 'Tax return for individuals'.)

After your tax return is processed, the Tax Office issues you with a *notice of assessment*, which is a document that summarises the details in your tax return. This document is your official receipt and sets out various details, including the tax on your taxable income, the Medicare levy you have to pay, and the total tax payable or refundable (the most important part!).

You need to keep your notice of assessment to prove that you have lodged your tax return.

If you consider the information set out in your notice of assessment to be wrong, you can lodge an objection or request the Tax Office to fix the error. (Chapter 4 has further information on this.) If an adjustment is made, the Tax Office issues a notice of amended assessment.

If you want to know more about notices of assessment, visit the Tax Office website (www.ato.gov.au) and read the fact sheet 'Your notice of assessment'.

If you end up having to pay the Tax Office and you can't do so by the due date because you're experiencing serious financial hardship (you're unable to provide food, accommodation, clothing, education or medical treatment for you or your family), you should immediately contact the Tax Office. Depending on your personal circumstances, the Tax Office has the power to reduce or release your tax liabilities. For more details see the Tax Office fact sheet 'Application for release from tax debt'.

CASE STUDY: PREPARING YOUR TAX RETURN

During the 2023–24 tax year, Beverley receives a 'PAYG payment summary — individual non-business statement' showing the following amounts:

- Salary: $80,000
- Total PAYG withholding tax: $18,000
- Car allowance: $3,400

She also derived the following amounts:

- $10,000 net profit distribution from a partnership business arrangement
- $100 bank interest from an investment

Beverley's work-related expenses are $1,675 — consisting of $800 union fees, $175 protective clothing and $700 tools of trade (see Chapter 5) — and she keeps receipts to substantiate her deductions. She also made a $200 gift to the Royal Children's Hospital Appeal, which is a tax-deductible expense.

During the 2023–24 tax year, Beverley travels 4,000 business kilometres, and she doesn't keep a log book or a record of her car expenses. Under the 'cents per kilometre' method, Beverley can claim $3,400 ($4,000 × $0.85).

Beverley is liable to pay tax on her taxable income at her marginal tax rates. The tax deducted from her pay (plus tax offsets she can claim) is deducted from the tax payable. She is also liable to pay a 2 per cent Medicare levy (but because she is privately insured and below the income threshold, she doesn't have to worry about the 1 per cent Medicare levy surcharge — refer to Chapter 1).

If Beverley's total tax credits (PAYG tax plus tax offsets) exceed the tax payable plus Medicare levy, the Tax Office refunds her the excess. (Beverley receives a tax refund.) But, if Beverley's total tax credits are less than the tax payable plus the Medicare levy, she must pay the shortfall to the Tax Office.

Beverley's taxable income and tax payable are calculated as follows:

- Beverley is liable to pay tax on the $88,225 taxable income she derives (see calculation below).
- The amount of tax Beverley is liable pay is $19,140.12 (see Chapter 5).
- Beverley is also liable to pay a 2 per cent Medicare levy on the $88,225 taxable income she derives. This amount is $1,764.50 ($88,225 × 0.02 = $1,764.50).
- Beverley can deduct the $18,000 tax withheld from her gross salary or wages from the total amount of tax and Medicare levy she is liable to pay (namely, $19,140.12 plus $1,764.50); therefore, the net tax payable is $2,904.62.

(continued)

(continued)

Tax Return for Individual's Income	Tax Withheld	
Salary or wages	$18,000	$80,000
Car allowance		$3,400
Gross interest		$100
Net partnership distribution		$10,000
TOTAL INCOME		$93,500
Less deductions		
Work-related car expenses		$3,400
Other work-related expenses		$1,675
Gifts or donations		$200
TOTAL DEDUCTIONS		$5,275
TAXABLE INCOME		**$88,225**

Note: Beverley can also claim a small business income tax offset in respect to the partnership income she derived. See chapter 12 and Tax Office fact sheet 'Small business income tax offset' for more info.

Preparing Other Tax Returns

Apart from your individual tax return, you may need to prepare other types of tax return. The following sections outline four different tax returns that may apply to your situation: A partnership tax return, a company tax return, a trust tax return and a self-managed superannuation fund (SMSF) tax return.

Partnership tax return

If you run a business with a partnership, you need to lodge an annual 'Partnership tax return (NAT 0659)' that discloses the partnership net income (or loss) you derived during the financial year. This tax return must be lodged by 31 October unless otherwise included on a tax agent's lodgement program. The partnership isn't liable to pay tax on the net partnership income it derives (see Chapter 12) and the partnership net income (or loss) must be distributed — in accordance with the partnership agreement — to the individual partners. Each partner must disclose the amount distributed in their individual tax return (refer to the sidebar 'Case study: Preparing your tax return') and you must disclose key financial information, such as the partnership's assets and liabilities.

CHECK THE NET

To learn more about lodging a partnership tax return, visit the Tax Office website (www.ato.gov.au) and check out the 'Partnership tax return instructions' fact sheet.

Company tax return

If you set up a company, you need to lodge an annual Company tax return (NAT 0656) that discloses the taxable net income (or loss) the company derived during the financial year. The company tax return must be lodged by 31 October (unless otherwise included on a tax agent's lodgement program). *Note:* Different accounting rules apply to income and deductions under the Corporations Act and Income Tax Act, so the company must reconcile its net profit (or loss), as calculated under company law, with its taxable net income (or loss), as calculated under income tax law. You also need to disclose key financial information such as the company's assets and liabilities, franking account balance, and loans to shareholders and their associates. Because a company is a separate legal entity, the company is liable to pay tax at a flat rate of 30 per cent on the taxable net income it derives; this reduces to 25 per cent if you run a small business company and your annual aggregated turnover (sales) is less than $50 million (see Chapters 1 and 12).

CHECK THE NET

If you want to know more about lodging a company tax return, visit the Tax Office website (www.ato.gov.au) and check out the 'Company tax return instructions' fact sheet.

Trust tax return

If you set up a trust, the trustee (the person in control) must lodge a Trust tax return (NAT 0660) disclosing the net income (or loss) of the trust derived during the financial year. Be sure to lodge the return by 31 October, unless otherwise included on a tax agent's lodgement program. As is the case with partnerships, the trust isn't liable to pay tax on the net income derived. Tax is assessed to the trustee or beneficiaries if they're entitled to receive the trust net income (see Chapters 7 and 12 for more). You also need to disclose key financial information, such as the trust's assets and liabilities.

CHECK
THE NET

If you want to know more about lodging a trust tax return, visit the Tax Office website (www.ato.gov.au) and check out the 'Trust tax return instructions' fact sheet.

SMSF tax return

If you set up a SMSF, you must lodge a Self-managed superannuation fund annual return (NAT 71226) disclosing the taxable income (or loss) derived during the financial year — the first return must ordinarily be lodged by 31 October. The due date for subsequent returns is ordinarily by 28 February after the financial year (unless otherwise included on a tax agent's lodgement program). You also need to disclose member contributions, the fund's assets and liabilities, bank account details, and a statement that the fund had complied with all the rules and regulations.

When you lodge your 2023–24 SMSF annual return, you must pay a $259 (at the time of writing) supervisory levy. Before you can lodge your return, your fund must be audited by an approved qualified auditor to certify that you've complied with all the rules and regulations. A SMSF is liable to pay tax at a flat rate of 15 per cent on the taxable income it derives during the accumulation phase. However, if your super fund is in the pension phase, no tax is payable (see Chapters 18 and 19).

CHECK
THE NET

If you want to know more about lodging a SMSF tax return, visit the Tax Office website (www.ato.gov.au) and check out the 'Self-managed superannuation fund annual return instructions (NAT 71606)' fact sheet.

Neglecting to Lodge Your Prior Years' Tax Returns

If you neglected to lodge a tax return for a number of years (oops!) — for instance, your last three tax returns for individuals — you'll need to download the relevant paper tax return copies from the Tax Office website (www.ato.gov.au) and lodge them with the Tax Office as soon as you can. A registered tax agent can help you to prepare and lodge your outstanding tax returns. You may incur a late lodgement penalty, which isn't ordinarily the case if you're likely to get a tax refund! For more details see Tax Office fact sheets 'Failure to lodge on time penalty' and 'If you don't lodge'.

Chapter **4**

Receiving a Visit: When the Tax Office Comes Knocking

The Australian taxation system works on a self-assessment basis. This means that the onus is on you to declare the correct amount of income you derive each year and claim the correct amount of tax deductions and tax offsets. However, the Tax Office has the authority to check whether you're complying with the tax laws. Penalties apply if you understate your income or overstate your claim for a tax deduction or tax offset.

In this chapter, I explain how self-assessment works and discuss what you should do if your tax affairs are audited. I also explain how you can appeal against a Tax Office decision.

Being Honest with Yourself: Self-Assessment

In 1986, the federal government introduced self-assessment. Under this system, when you lodge a document or submit an income tax return to the Tax Office, the Tax Office basically accepts its contents as being true and correct and, generally speaking, no further action is taken. Apart from correcting any obvious mistakes, the matter ends there.

When you lodge your tax return, you're issued with a notice of assessment based on the information you supply to the Tax Office (refer to Chapter 3). If you find at a later date that you made a mistake on your tax return (for example, you didn't include something on your tax return that you should've), you can ask for an amended assessment or lodge an objection. Lodging an objection is a formal request to correct the error.

TIP

To request an amendment assessment you need to complete the form 'Request for amendment of income tax return for individuals (NAT 2843)'. You can download a copy from the Tax Office website (www.ato.gov.au).

To help you to comply with the tax laws, the Tax Office regularly issues, free of charge, fact sheets, income tax rulings, tax determinations, Tax Office interpretative decisions and other educational material to explain specific issues that need to be clarified and brought to your attention (as illustrated throughout this book). In return, you're required to retain proper records and receipts in accordance with the Tax Act to verify and substantiate what you submit. Further, the Tax Office reserves the right to audit your tax affairs to check you're complying in accordance with the Tax Act.

CHECK
THE NET

One great thing about self-assessment is you can get free advice from the Tax Office. This is especially the case if you happen to come across a complex or tricky issue you're not sure of. You can do this by simply applying for a private ruling. The Tax Office examines your request and gives you a written response on how it would interpret the laws in respect of the issue you raise. To apply for a private ruling, download and complete the appropriate private ruling application form from the Tax Office website (www.ato.gov.au).

If you're contemplating juggling the books or not declaring all the income you derive, don't! The various methods the Tax Office uses to check whether you're complying with the law will eventually find you out. See Tax Office fact sheets 'The cash and shadow economy', 'Personal living expenses' and 'Manual or paper record keeping for businesses' for more info.

Under a temporary amnesty agreement announced on 9 May 2023, small business entities can avoid stiff Tax Office penalties by getting their tax affairs back on track and lodge overdue tax returns, fringe benefit tax returns and business activity statements. But, as they say in the classics, 'conditions apply'. For more details see Tax Office fact sheet 'Small business given unique opportunity to get back on track with tax'.

Getting a Reality Check: Tax Audit

All taxpayers run the risk of an audit, whether you're a business owner or a wage earner. An audit is simply an official examination of your tax records to determine whether you're complying with the Tax Act. Notice that you're going to be audited usually comes via a telephone call or a letter in the mail from the Tax Office. The official conducting the audit is called an *auditor*.

Most business audits take place at the business (or your tax agent's place of business). The Tax Office also conducts desk audits, randomly selecting individuals (especially salary and wage earners) for routine audits and chats about their tax affairs. If your lucky number is pulled out of the barrel, the Tax Office asks you to come in for a visit and produce documentary evidence to verify the accuracy of your tax return. (Who said you've never won a prize in a raffle?!)

If the Tax Office pays your business a visit or invites you to visit, expect questions regarding the contents of your tax return. The auditor compares your records to the information you disclose in your tax return. You may need to produce receipts and other supporting evidence to verify and support your claims. If any mistakes are detected, your tax return is amended.

PRIVILEGED PAPERWORK? RARELY . . .

Whereas the Tax Office, ordinarily, has the right to inspect any of your paperwork that pertains to the Tax Act, under certain circumstances, you may be entitled to claim legal professional privilege for certain documents. In such cases, you don't have to give that information to the Tax Office. Such a case may arise if you run a business and you seek legal advice from a lawyer. Before assuming your paperwork qualifies as privileged, discuss the matter with your tax agent or legal adviser.

WARNING

If you breach the Tax Act, you incur a fine, plus an interest charge on the shortfall. The extent of the penalty depends on the seriousness of your offence, which can range from a 'lack of reasonable care' and being 'reckless' to an 'intentional disregard of a taxation law'. If your offence is extremely serious, you can be prosecuted and civil and criminal penalties may apply (that is, you may need to get your pyjamas and spend some time in the slammer). If you want to know more about this matter, visit the Tax Office website (www.ato.gov.au) and read the fact sheets 'Interest and penalties' and 'Penalties'.

TIP

Preparing for an audit

If you're selected for an audit, follow these steps:

1. **Get your records in order before the audit interview.**

   Review your return so that you can fully explain what you claimed and why, and re-familiarise yourself with what supporting paperwork you've got. If some critical paperwork is missing, obtain a duplicate copy.

2. **If necessary, consult with your tax agent and/or legal adviser about whether your agent should be present.**

   Business owners especially should consider having their tax agent present. Whatever fees you pay (which are tax deductible) to have your tax agent present may be more than offset by the expertise your agent brings to the conversation, and the peace of mind too.

3. **Remember to keep your emotions in check and cooperate appropriately.**

No-one likes to be audited, but keep your emotions in check and don't be belligerent or make false or misleading statements. The Tax Office has a right to full and free access to all buildings, places, books, documents and other papers for the purposes of the Tax Act. This law means you must provide all reasonable facilities and assistance and produce appropriate documents to verify the accuracy of your tax affairs.

TECHNICAL
STUFF

If you're still anxious about the process, visit the Tax Office website (www.ato.gov.au) and check out the fact sheets 'Audits' and 'ATO Charter', which cover info on what happens if you're audited.

Points to keep in mind

If you're an individual, expect the Tax Office to compare the routine interest and dividend information in your tax return with records from the various paying institutions. That kind of mistake is the most common one discovered during a desk audit — an incorrect amount claimed on a form.

If you run a small business, the Tax Office uses small business benchmarks (or business ratios) to check whether you're 'cooking the books' and avoiding your tax obligations. They're also used to compare your business performance against similar businesses in the industry. For more info visit the Tax Office website (www.ato.gov.au) and look for the fact sheets 'Small business benchmarks' and 'Types of small business benchmarks'.

WARNING

The most common tax mistakes associated with running a small business include

>> Failure to correctly apportion your business and private and domestic expenses (refer to Chapter 2)

>> Failure to disclose capital gains on disposal of capital gains tax (CGT) assets (see Chapter 11)

>> Failure to pay fringe benefits tax (FBT) on fringe benefits provided to employees (see Chapter 16)

>> Failure to register for GST if your turnover (sales) is $75,000 or more a year (see Chapter 15)

>> Failure to remit PAYG tax collected from your employees' salary and wages by the due date (see Chapter 13)

>> Failure to remit superannuation guarantee payments to the Tax Office by the due date (see Chapter 13)

>> Incorrectly accounting for assessable income and, more particularly, your cash sales (see Chapter 13)

>> Incorrectly claiming certain business expenses such as repairs, bad debts, borrowing expenses and depreciation (see Chapter 14)

>> Incorrectly valuing your trading stock (see Chapter 13)

>> Over-claiming your business expenses (see Chapter 14)

REMEMBER

Big brother is watching you! To keep yourself honest, under the third-party reporting scheme, certain transactions (such as sales of real estate and shares, and sales through merchant debit and credit services) are reported to the Tax Office. The Tax Office is also targeting people who fail to disclose profits derived on disposal of cryptocurrency. For more info see Tax Office fact sheet 'Data matching' at www.ato.gov.au.

WARNING

If you're a contractor you may need to complete a 'Taxable payments annual report (TPAR)' and report to the Tax Office any payments that you make to contractors for building and construction services. This information is used to check whether building contractors are declaring all the income they derive each year. For more details visit the Tax Office website (www.ato.gov.au) and read the fact sheet 'Building and construction services'.

Mending Your Ways: Amendments and Objections

If your tax return is found to be incorrect, the Tax Office has the power to amend an assessment. Ordinarily, a time limit applies — between two and four years from the date you receive an assessment notice setting out the date any tax you have to pay becomes due and payable. However, in the event of fraud and evasion, the Tax Office has the power and the authority to amend an assessment at any time.

In return, you have the right to seek an amendment or lodge an objection if you're dissatisfied with an assessment or a Tax Office decision (provided you lodge the objection within the prescribed time limit, normally within 60 days of service of the notice of assessment). Further, you have the right to appeal to the Administrative Appeals Tribunal, Small Taxation Claims Tribunal or Tax Appeals Division. You can even appeal as high as the High Court of Australia if your objection is a question of law.

TIP

Under the small business concessions provisions, eligible entities have two years, rather than four, to amend a notice of assessment. The amendment period commences from the date the Tax Office issues the notice of assessment. The Tax Office can amend a notice of assessment to either increase or decrease a tax liability only within the same two-year amendment period. However, this time frame isn't the case in the event of fraud or evasion (which is beyond the scope of this book, so in such a case you're best to seek advice from a professional adviser).

CHECK
THE NET

If you want to know more about amendments, objections and appeals, go to the Tax Office website (www.ato.gov.au) and check out the fact sheet 'Dispute or object to an ATO decision'.

WARNING

If you fail to lodge your annual tax return (oops!), the Tax Office may issue a default assessment based on the taxable income the Tax Office folk estimate you derived for that year, and you may incur a late lodgement penalty. For more details, see the Tax Office publication 'Taxpayers with overdue tax returns' online at www.ato.gov.au.

2

Income from Personal Exertion

Delve into the tax issues of salary and wage earners and identify what tax deductions you can claim.

Discover how your main residence is exempt from tax and identify the tax issues you need to know if you run a home-based business.

Find out all there is to know about how your children are taxed on the income they derive, and discover the benefits you can access if you satisfy certain conditions.

Chapter **5**

Taxing Employees: Working Class Folk

A lingering pain when you work for a living is your legal obligation to share part of your hard-earned cash with the Tax Office. But at least you know it's going to a good cause! And it goes without saying, the more you earn the more it's going to hurt. When you lodge your tax return, the federal government will let you know how your personal tax is spent to help fund public spending activities such as welfare, health care, defence and education.

In this chapter, I explain that if you're an employee, your employer must deduct income tax from the amount you earn and make a contribution to a complying superannuation fund on your behalf. I also go over what happens if your employment is terminated, how to determine your income tax rate, and the conditions you need to satisfy to qualify for a work-related tax deduction.

Earning a Living: Salary and Wages

If you're planning on looking for a job, you need to get a tax file number (TFN) from the Tax Office and quote it to your employer. Your new employer asks you to complete a 'Tax file number declaration form (NAT 3092)' within 14 days of commencing employment. This declaration form covers payments in respect of services you perform and payments of superannuation benefits. (*Note:* You can lodge the relevant info online or by paper to your local Tax Office.) You also need to quote your TFN if you have an account with a financial institution and you derive interest (see Chapter 8).

CHECK THE NET

If you need to apply for a TFN, visit the Tax Office website (www. ato.gov.au) and check out fact sheet 'Australian residents – TFN application'). You can also visit the business.gov.au website (www.business.gov.au), click The Registrations drop-down menu and then click Register for Taxes.

If you don't have a TFN, 45 per cent tax may be deducted from the amount you earn. However, this factor is taken into account when the Tax Office calculates your tax liability and is refunded to you if you pay too much tax.

If you're employed on a full-time, part-time or casual basis, your employer pays you a salary or wage for the work you do. When you receive your pay slip each week, fortnight or month, you find an amount representing the pay-as-you-go (PAYG) withholding tax deducted from your gross pay. The amount of tax you pay depends on how much you earn (and the more you earn, the more tax you pay).

Determining your employment status

Being aware of your employment status for tax purposes is important. Most people working for a living in Australia are classified as employees who earn a salary or wage (income from personal exertion). An employee is a person who receives a salary or wage for work performed under a contract wholly or principally for labour provided. An employee can also be a paid company director, sportsperson, artist or performer. Generally, you're considered to be an employee where a master–service relationship exists. Under this arrangement, you work under a contract wholly or principally for your labour and you're under the control and direction of the person (the boss) who's employing you.

TIP

If you're not sure of your employment status, visit the Tax Office website (www.ato.gov.au) and check out the fact sheet 'How to work it out: employee or contractor'. The Tax Office website also has Tax Rulings available, which you may find useful. Check out 'TR 2001/7 Income tax: the meaning of personal services income', 'TR 2001/8 Income tax: what is a personal services business' and 'TR 2003/10 Income tax: deductions that relate to personal services income'.

Reducing the burden: Receiving an allowance

If you're an employee, your employer may pay you an allowance in addition to the salary or wage you derive. For example, this payment could be a travel allowance or a special allowance unique to your particular industry. Ordinarily, an allowance is paid to compensate you for expenditure you may incur in earning your income. The amount you receive normally forms part of your assessable income (refer to Chapter 2). When you get an allowance, you can usually claim a deduction for expenses you incur in performing your duties.

WARNING

If your employer gives you an allowance, you can't assume that you can automatically claim a tax deduction just because you receive it — you can claim a tax deduction only if you satisfy certain tests (see the section 'Claiming a Tax Deduction: What's On the Menu', later in this chapter).

CONTRACTOR OR EMPLOYEE?

Your employment status is an issue if you run a personal services business (PSB) — for example, if you're an independent contractor and you perform certain tasks similar to that of an employee. If you operate a personal services business, no tax is deducted from your payments and you're not eligible for super guarantee (SG) contributions. Instead, you can claim certain deductions that aren't available to employees, such as running an office. In contrast, if you're an employee, tax is deducted from your pay and your employer must make SG contributions on your behalf.

(continued)

(continued)

Establishing whether you're a contractor or an employee may be tricky because of the fine line between the two classifications. Here are some comparisons between the two to help you work out your employment status:

Contractors	Employees
Advertise for jobs	Don't advertise for jobs
Must supply their own tools and equipment	Use their employer's tools and equipment
Responsible for fixing defects	Don't necessarily need to fix defects
Can delegate tasks to other people	Can't bring in someone else to perform duties
Have flexibility relating to how tasks are completed	Don't necessarily have the flexibility relating to how tasks are completed
Paid to do specific tasks	Paid on an ongoing basis and performs many tasks as directed
Set their own hours and normally work at different locations	Works set hours and normally at a particular work location
Prepare a tax invoice setting out services rendered on completion of a task	Normally paid on an ongoing basis

You're considered to be running a personal services business if you satisfy a results test or an 80-per-cent-rule test. The first test checks whether more than 75 per cent of the income you derive is from using your own equipment to produce a result and whether you're required to fix any defects. The second test checks whether more than 80 per cent of your income is derived from at least two unrelated sources. Further, you satisfy this test if you have an unrelated employee (or apprentice) to help you perform at least 20 per cent of your work, or you operate from business premises that are separate from your main residence. If this test isn't satisfied, you need to get a PSB determination from the Tax Office.

You can access the Tax Office fact sheet 'Withholding for allowances' from the Tax Office website (www.ato.gov.au); this sheet outlines which allowances are tax deductible, such as allowances for qualifications (for example, a first-aid certificate), tools, clothing, laundry or transport.

Getting a living-away-from-home allowance

A living-away-from-home allowance (LAFHA) is an allowance employers pay their employees to compensate them for incurring additional expenses (such as accommodation, food and drink, or expense payments) while they're temporarily living away from their usual place of residence in order to perform their employment-related duties. For example, you ordinarily live in Brisbane and you're transferred by your employer to Alice Springs for three months to work on a project there. On completion of your employment-related duties, you return to your home in Brisbane.

The maximum period away is ordinarily limited to 12 months, but the good news is the limit won't apply if you're a 'fly-in fly-out' worker or if you receive travel and meal allowances. By the way, you'll need to keep a track of all your expenses while you're away.

If you maintain a home in Australia and you're living away from that home while performing your employment-related duties, the LAFHA is a fringe benefit and taxable under the fringe benefits tax (FBT) provisions. This means that the employer rather than the employee is liable to pay tax on this allowance. For more details see Chapter 16 and the Tax Office fact sheet 'Living-away-from-home allowance fringe benefits'. You can download a copy from the Tax Office website (www.ato.gov.au).

Adding to the nest egg via SG

Under the super guarantee (SG) legislation, in addition to paying you a salary or wage, your employer must make a super contribution to a complying super fund on your behalf. For the 2023–24 tax year, the SG amount is 11 per cent of your gross pay; this will increase by 0.5 per cent each year until it reaches 12 per cent in the 2025–26 tax year. This information is normally included in the salary package agreement you enter into at the time you're hired. (*Note:* From 1 July 2026, employers must pay the super guarantee amount at the same time employees are paid salary and wages.)

For example, if you earn $1,000 a week, your employer must contribute $110 (11 per cent of $1,000) into your designated super fund (see Chapter 13). This amount is then invested on your behalf. (*Note:* SG contributions can be made regardless of your age or how much you earn. But, if you're under 18 years of age, you need to work more than 30 hours in a week to qualify for SG contributions.)

The purpose of SG legislation is to help you accumulate funds during your working life that you can access when you finally hang up the pen, laptop or shovel, and retire. You can normally access your super benefits when you reach 60 years of age and retire, or satisfy a condition of release, such as physical or mental ill health or permanent incapacity. To add icing to the cake, super payments are normally tax free (see Chapter 18).

REMEMBER

Employers are required to make SG contributions to complying super funds of eligible employees regardless of their age or how much they earn. However, if you're under 18 years of age, you'll need to work more than 30 hours in a week to qualify for SG contributions.

TIP

If you want to know whether you've got any lost or unclaimed superannuation benefits, visit the Tax Office website (www.ato. gov.au) and check out fact sheet 'Searching for lost super'. When completing this search, you need to insert your name, TFN and date of birth.

WARNING

Maximum super contributions do apply. In the 2023–24 tax year, the maximum super contribution base is $62,270 income per quarter. This means if your income is over this amount, your employer is not obligated to pay super contributions on earnings that exceed the $62,270 per quarter limit.

Your employer's pay slip normally sets out the amount of the SG contribution that was forwarded to your super fund. If this information isn't supplied, you should check with your super fund to see whether an employer SG contribution was made on your behalf. If your employer fails to make a contribution, you should immediately report the matter to the Tax Office.

Adding to the nest egg via personal contributions

To help boost the nest egg, all individuals (employees, self-employed, retirees) who are under 75 years of age can claim a tax deduction for personal super contributions (referred to as *concessional contributions*) up to their concessional cap amount (at the time of writing, $27,500 per annum). Concessional contributions can include employer SG contributions and top up contributions you can make under a salary sacrifice arrangement. However, if you're between 67 and 74 years of age, you need to satisfy a work test. To satisfy this test, you need to work at least 40 hours over 30 consecutive days. (*Note:* Concessional contributions can't be accepted if you're aged 75 years or over.) For more info, see Chapter 18 and Tax Office fact sheet 'Contributions you can accept' on the Tax Office website — www.ato.gov.au.

TIP

Individual superannuation fund members can split concessional contributions made in the previous financial year with their (non-income or low-income earning) spouses or partners. The maximum permitted is 85 per cent of the concessional contributions cap. For more info, see Tax Office fact sheet 'Contributions splitting' on the Tax Office website.

WARNING

Concessional contributions you make to a complying super fund are treated as assessable income and liable to a 15 per cent contribution tax. If you earn more than $250,000 and you make a concessional contribution, the rate of tax payable increases from 15 per cent to 30 per cent. Either you or your super fund can pay the additional 15 per cent contribution tax. (For more details visit the Tax Office website and read the fact sheet 'Division 293 tax – information for individuals'.)

Easing the pain: Getting a termination payment

If you receive a polite tap on the shoulder from your employer and you're informed your valuable services are no longer required because your job has been terminated, you may be entitled to receive an employment termination payment (ETP) and/or a redundancy payment to help ease the pain.

SIGNING UP TO THE SUPER CO-CONTRIBUTION CLUB

If you want to make some free money, the following may interest you. If your total assessable income for the 2023–24 tax year is less than $43,445 and you make a $1,000 non-concessional contribution (a contribution you make from your personal savings that doesn't qualify for a tax deduction) to your super fund, under the superannuation co-contribution scheme, the federal government makes a $500 contribution to your super fund on your behalf (with no strings attached!). This amount reduces as you earn more money and ceases after you earn more than $58,445.

However, the one proviso is this: You can't get your hands on this money until you satisfy a condition of release, such as when you reach your preservation age and retire. (See Chapter 18 for more about conditions of release.)

If you qualify for this government freebie, after you lodge your tax return, the Tax Office calculates the amount you're entitled to receive and notifies you of the amount that was credited to your super fund account.

If you receive an ETP within 12 months of being terminated, the payment is concessionally taxed at a particular rate, as set out in Table 5-1. The following payments are examples of an ETP you're likely to receive:

>> Compensation for loss of job

>> Golden handshake

>> Unused rostered days off

>> Unused sick leave

An ETP doesn't include payments you receive in respect of unused annual leave and long-service leave.

TABLE 5-1 **Employment Termination Payments (ETP)**

Financial Year	Lower Cap Amount (LCA)
2023–24	$235,000
Under preservation age	*Preservation age and above*
Up to LCA: Tax rate 32%	Up to LCA: Tax rate 17%
Above LCA: Tax rate 47%	Above LCA: Tax rate 47%

When you receive an ETP, the amount of tax you're liable to pay depends on whether you're under or over your preservation age (the age you must reach before you can retire and access your superannuation fund benefits — see Chapter 18) and whether the payment is a tax-free component or taxable component. As a general rule, an ETP is a taxable component. The rate of tax you're liable to pay (plus the Medicare levy) is set out in Table 5-1. An ETP must be taken as a lump sum payment and you can't roll over (transfer) the amount into a complying superannuation fund.

WARNING

If you receive an ETP (particularly a golden handshake) and your taxable income increases to more than a non-indexed 'whole of-income' cap amount, $180,000 at the time of writing, the amount up to $180,000 is concessionally taxed (refer to Table 5-1), and the excess above $180,000 is liable to tax at the top marginal rate (plus the Medicare levy) (see the later section 'Working Out Your Income Tax Rate' for more info). But this isn't the case if you receive a fair dinkum redundancy payment, invalidity payment or compensation payment due to an employment-related dispute or as a consequence of an injury or death — phew, what a relief! (See Tax Office fact sheet 'Taxation of termination payments' and the following section for more info.)

Moving on: Getting a redundancy payment

If your employment is terminated, you may receive a redundancy payment. This is a gratuitous payment in recognition of your past services. The amount you receive normally depends on your length of service.

A payment received under these circumstances is concessionally taxed at a particular rate (as set out later in this section) if certain conditions are met. Two categories of redundancy payments may qualify for concessional tax treatment:

>> **Bona fide redundancy payment:** A bona fide redundancy payment is a payment you may receive as a result of being made redundant or retrenched. This situation normally arises if an employer makes a decision that your job as an employee is no longer necessary and ceases to exist, which can happen due to a change in work practices or because your employer has decided to do something different. But a bona fide redundancy can't occur if you're dismissed on reaching your normal retirement age or because of disciplinary reasons. (For more info, check out fact sheet 'Redundancy payments' on the Tax Office website — www.ato.gov.au.)

>> **Payment under an approved early retirement scheme:** You may receive a payment under an approved early retirement scheme if your employer offers incentives to encourage a certain group of people to retire early or resign. The Tax Office must first approve the scheme before the redundancy payment can be concessionally taxed at a particular rate as set out in this section. (For more info, check out Tax Office fact sheet 'Approved early retirement schemes'.)

Under both arrangements, redundancy payments that can qualify for concessional tax treatment include

>> A gratuity or golden handshake

>> Lump sum payments of unused long-service leave paid on termination of employment, but not under a formal arrangement

>> Payment in lieu of notice

>> Severance payment of a number of weeks' pay for each year of service

WARNING

The following aren't treated as part of a redundancy payment that qualifies for concessional tax treatment:

>> Lump sum payments of unused long-service leave paid on termination of employment under a formal arrangement

>> Salary and wages owed for work performed

>> Unused annual leave

Redundancy payments are concessionally taxed in the following way. The amount that falls below a statutory limit (adjusted annually) is exempt from tax. For the 2023–24 tax year, the limit means the first $11,985 (base limit) you receive is tax free — plus, $5,994 for each completed year of service is also tax free.

Any part of the payment above the statutory limit is treated as an ETP from an untaxed source.

TECHNICAL STUFF

If you want more info about how termination payments are taxed, visit the Tax Office website (www.ato.gov.au) and check out fact sheet 'Schedule 7 — Tax table for unused leave payments on termination of employment'.

Working Out Your Income Tax Rate

Income tax is set by marginal tax rates. Table 5-2 shows the marginal tax rates for resident individuals in the 2023–24 tax year. (See Appendix A for the rates for non-residents and also visit the Tax Office website, www.ato.gov.au, for more information.)

TABLE 5-2 Individual Income Tax Rate for Australian Residents, 2023–24

Taxable Income	Marginal Tax Rates
$0–$18,200	0%
$18,201–$45,000	19%
$45,001–$120,000	32.5%
$120,001–$180,000	37%
$180,001 and over	45%

REMEMBER

According to Table 5-2, the tax-free threshold for resident individuals in the 2023–24 tax year is $18,200. But the good news gets even better because when you take the $700 low income tax offset into account, the tax-free threshold effectively increases to $21,884 (refer to Chapter 3 for more details).

The marginal tax rates for Australian resident individuals in the 2024–25 tax year are set to change (referred as the *Stage 3 tax cuts*). Under these changes, taxable income between $45,001 and $200,000 will be liable to a 30 per cent marginal rate, while taxable income $200,001 and over will be liable to a 45 per cent marginal rate. Taxable income $45,000 and below will be liable to tax as set out in Table 5-2.

If you're an author, artist, inventor or sportsperson, you may be eligible for special professional income averaging in respect of the income you derive from your professional activities. For more info, read Tax Office publications 'Income averaging for special professionals' and 'Professional sportsperson – income and work-related deductions'. You can get a copy from the Tax Office website (www.ato.gov.au). Also check out Taxation Ruling 'TR 2005/1 Income tax: carrying on business as a professional artist' for more information.

If you're a professional sportsperson, receipts such as salary and match payments, appearance fees, media awards, cash prizes and grants, and sponsorship endorsements are ordinarily treated as assessable income. Also assessable is income derived from exploiting your public fame or image to advertise or promote products. (*Note:* Non-cash benefits — for instance, your club giving you a work car for private use — are ordinarily liable to FBT, with tax being payable by your employer.)

According to Tax Office Ruling TR 1999/17 'an award in medal or trophy form will not be assessable income as it is given and received on purely personal grounds, recognising and recording a particular achievement of a person'.

With respect to work-related deductions, expenses you can claim as a professional sportsperson include management fees, protective gear, gym fees to maintain fitness and, to help ease the pain, fines and penalties incurred for on-field misconduct (plus legal costs to defend incurring a fine or penalty). But you can't claim the cost of private health insurance and the cost of food and drink — even if it's a condition of employment that you reduce your weight — because they are considered to be private in nature. (See Appendix B for more info on leading tax cases relating to professional sportspersons.)

Claiming a Tax Deduction: What's On the Menu

You can claim as a tax deduction any loss or outgoing incurred in gaining or producing assessable income (refer to Chapter 2). If you derive personal exertion income (and property income), you must be able to show a direct connection between the expenditure you incur and what you do for a living before you can claim a deduction. If the expenditure doesn't meet these criteria, it's regarded as private or domestic in nature and not tax deductible. For example, you can't claim travel expenses from home to work (your train, bus or tram fares), nor can you claim childminding expenses to look after your children while you're at work.

TIP

If your expenditure is likely to be substantial, you can request the Tax Office to vary the rate of tax payable on your salary and wages. For example, this scenario can arise if you borrow money to buy a rental property and claim an interest expense (see Chapter 10).

CHECK
THE NET

To have the Tax Office vary your rate of tax payable, you need to complete the form 'PAYG withholding variation application (NAT 2036)'. You can get a copy of this form from the Tax Office website (www.ato.gov.au).

Proving what you did: Substantiation provisions

Salary and wage earners who incur work-related expenses are required to substantiate (prove or justify) their expenses. To do this successfully, you must satisfy these three important conditions:

>> A direct connection must exist between your work-related expenses and the derivation of your assessable income.

>> Your expenses must be incurred in the course of gaining or producing your assessable income.

>> You must keep written evidence to substantiate your claim for a work-related expense (for instance, receipts).

Common types of work-related deductions

The types of work-related expenses you need to substantiate to claim a tax deduction include business travel, car and work expenses. Each of these is looked at in the following sections. By the way, the Tax Office has issued a comprehensive list of work-related expenses that you can claim if you work in a specific industry. For more info, check out Tax Office fact sheet 'Occupation and industry specific guides'. You can download a copy from its website (www.ato.gov.au).

TIP

If you receive an overtime meal allowance under an industrial agreement, the allowance is assessable; however, you can claim the cost of food and drinks you incur as a tax deduction. The amount the Tax Office considers reasonable for the 2023–24 tax year is $35.65 per meal. You'll need to substantiate your deduction if you spend more than what the Tax Office considers reasonable.

CHECK THE NET

If you want to know the Tax Office view about substantiation, reasonable travel and overtime meal allowance expenses, visit the Tax Office website (www.ato.gov.au) and check out Tax Office fact sheet 'Travel allowances'. You may also find it useful to review 'Taxation Determination TD 2023/3' for the reasonable travel and meal allowance expense amounts for the 2023–24 tax year.

Claiming work-related travel expenses

If you're required to travel in the course of gaining or producing your assessable income (for instance, your employer asks you to travel overseas or interstate), you need to keep a travel record such as a diary to substantiate your deductions. You need to record the reason you travelled, the date and time it happened, how long it lasted and the places you visited. (For more information about claiming travel expenses, refer to Chapter 3.)

WARNING

Under the substantiation provisions (refer to the previous section), you need to supply written evidence to substantiate your claim for work-related expenses that exceed $300. If your total work-related expenses are $300 or less, you need only satisfy the direct connection test and that the expenses are incurred in the course of gaining or producing your assessable income (provided they're not capital, private or domestic in nature). The document you receive from the supplier of the goods and services to which the expense relates must include the following:

>> Amount of the expense

>> Date the document is made out

>> Date the expense was incurred

>> Name or business name of the supplier

>> Nature of the goods or services

TIP

If you receive an allowance from your employer, you don't have to substantiate your claim for a tax deduction if the Tax Office considers the amount is reasonable (that is, it isn't excessive and falls within Tax Office guidelines). But, if you claim a tax deduction greater than the allowance you receive, you need to substantiate the full amount.

Claiming work-related car expenses

Under the substantiation provisions, you can use two statutory methods to substantiate your work-related car expenses. The two methods are discussed in detail in Chapter 3.

Claiming work-related expenses

To claim work-related expenses, they must have a direct and relevant connection with your occupation, and can include expenditure such as

>> Work-related reference books and journals

>> Protective clothing and safety items (such as hard hats — for more info, check out Taxation Ruling 'TR 2003/16')

>> Uniforms (including the laundry and dry-cleaning of certain work-related clothing) and occupation-specific clothing (such as nurse and police officer uniforms — for more info, check out Tax Office fact sheet 'Clothing, laundry and dry-cleaning expenses')

- Subscriptions to trade unions or other professional memberships

- Costs of renewing an employment agreement with an existing employer (for more info, check out Taxation Ruling 'TR 2000/5')

- Tools of trade and home office expenses (see Chapter 6)

TIP

If you seek the services of a recognised tax adviser (registered tax agent or a legal practitioner) to help you manage your tax affairs (for example, prepare and lodge your tax return), the expenditure you incur is ordinarily tax deductible.

Increasing your skills and knowledge: Claiming work-related self-education expenses

If you incur self-education expenses to help you improve or maintain your skills and knowledge while performing your current employment duties, or to increase your chances of getting a promotion and/or earn more salary, the expenses are ordinarily tax deductible. For example, you're a junior accountant and you incur self-education expenses to become a certified practising accountant or chartered accountant. But you can't claim a tax deduction if you incur self-education expenses to gain a different qualification or skill that has no relevance to your current occupation or employment duties. For example, you're a nurse and you incur self-education expenses to become a school teacher.

You can claim expenses such as the following:

- Course or tuition fees to attend an educational institution or work-related conference or seminar

- Text books and stationery

- Travel from work to the educational institution

- Fares, accommodation and meal expenses on overseas study tours or work-related conferences or seminars

- Student services and amenities fees

TIP

Personal development courses (such as presentation skills and written communication skills) that have a relevant connection with an employee's current income-earning activities are ordinarily tax-deductible expenses.

WARNING

You can't claim a tax deduction for payments under the compulsory Higher Education Loan Program (HELP) or Higher Education Contribution Scheme (HECS). And you can't claim a tax deduction (for example, for self-education expenses) against all government-assisted payments.

TECHNICAL
STUFF

For a comprehensive discussion on self-education expenses, visit the Tax Office website (www.ato.gov.au) and check out fact sheets 'Self-education expenses' and 'Education, training and seminars'.

IN THIS CHAPTER

» **Examining what constitutes a main residence**

» **Understanding the tax concessions when purchasing your main residence**

» **Looking at exemption provisions and when you have to pay tax**

» **Finding out how home offices fit in**

» **Transferring property after a relationship breakdown**

Chapter **6**

Living in Your Castle: Main Residence

The great Australian dream is to own your home, especially your main residence. Owning the very roof you've got over your head is something most people would like to experience.

In this chapter, I explain the tax concessions that are available to home owners in some instances. I also look at the rules that you need to comply with to gain these valuable concessions.

Addressing the Issue: This is Where I Live

A *main residence* is a place where you and your family normally reside and use for private or domestic purposes. It can include a standalone house, an apartment or unit, a caravan or other mobile home, an underground house, or even a garage or storage room. Your main residence can also include up to 2 hectares of land that surrounds your house.

To qualify for a main residence exemption, you need to move in to your home as soon as practicable after you buy it, and live there for a reasonable period of time (for instance, three months). A mere intention to do so isn't enough. So it's important that you keep documentary evidence (such as gas and electricity bills) and that your name and address is on the electoral roll, to prove that you're actually residing in your home. On the other hand, if you buy a vacant block of land, you need to build your home within four years for the land to qualify for a main residence exemption.

WARNING

A company or trust structure can't own a main residence for CGT exemption purposes, even if the shareholders or beneficiaries reside in the property (check out Chapter 12 for more). And, you can't reside in a residential property that is owned by your self-managed superannuation fund (SMSF) — see Chapter 18 for more on SMSFs.

TIP

Ordinarily, if you sell your main residence and buy another one, you need to move into your new home within six months of selling your old home for both properties to qualify for a main residence exemption.

TECHNICAL
STUFF

The Tax Office (www.ato.gov.au) has issued two tax rulings to help you understand what constitutes a main residence. These are 'Taxation Determination TD 92/158' and 'Taxation Determination TD 1999/69'.

Buying Your Main Residence: Taxation Concessions

Unfortunately, housing affordability puts owning a main residence out of reach for many Australians. This scenario is because a major barrier to getting into property (and, more particularly, buying your dream home) is the need to get together a truckload of money to buy a house outright. Depending in which state or territory you reside, the price of a home can vary upwards from around $500,000 to well over a few million dollars. Getting the necessary finance to buy a property can prove a difficult exercise to manage. And even if you're successful, having a mortgage can adversely affect your lifestyle and standard of living while you endeavour to service the loan repayments.

To add tax salt to the cost wound, in addition to paying the purchase price you can be liable to pay a 10 per cent goods and services tax (GST) at the time you buy the home. You're liable for this additional cost if you buy new residential premises (such as a newly constructed house). But wait, there's more! You're also hit with stamp duty, which Australian states and territories levy on property transactions.

Fortunately, state and territory governments have a number of concessions to help you achieve the dream of owning your own home. Provided you satisfy certain conditions, you can access two concessions:

>> The first home owner grant

>> Stamp duty relief

The *first home owner grant* is to help first home buyers purchase a property. To qualify for this grant, you (and/or your spouse or partner) must not have previously owned a property. Under this scheme, if you're a resident of Australia you may be eligible to receive a one-off payment to help purchase or build a property you intend to use as your main residence. One condition is that you need to reside in the property within 12 months of the settlement date.

First home owner grants are administered by the various state and territory governments of Australia, so you need to check their respective eligibility tests to see whether you qualify for this grant and the amount you could receive. By the way, the grant is only available for properties valued up to a certain amount and is ordinarily limited to eligible buyers of new homes. See Table 6-1 for the first home owner grant limits, at the time of writing.

Stamp duty is a one-off payment levied on a progressive basis, which means the more you pay for your home, the greater the amount of stamp duty you're liable to pay. Stamp duty relief is available under certain circumstances in respect of the purchase of your main residence.

CHECK
THE NET

To find out more about the current first home owner grant and/or whether you're eligible for any stamp duty relief, you can check out the website of your local state and territory government revenue office.

TABLE 6-1 **First Home Owner Grant — Eligibility**

Jurisdiction	Limits on Value of Property
ACT	$750,000
NSW	$800,000
NT	$600,000
QLD	$750,000
SA	$650,000
TAS	No limit at time of writing
VIC	$750,000
WA	$750,000 ($1,000,000 if property is north of 26th parallel)

TIP

Under the federal government First Home Super Saver Scheme (FHSSS), super fund members can use their super fund to help save for a deposit to buy their first home. So when you're ready to buy, you can withdraw up to $50,000 of your FHSSS contributions (and deemed earnings) for a home deposit. But, as always, 'conditions apply'. For more details, check out fact sheet 'First home super saver scheme' on the Tax Office website (www.ato.gov.au).

WARNING

A major stumbling block to buying a home is that under Australian income tax law, interest on borrowings to finance the purchase isn't a tax-deductible expense. This is sadly because the purpose (or use) of the loan is to buy a non-income-producing property. On the other hand, if you buy an income-producing property (for example, a property you intend to lease), the interest is tax deductible (see Chapter 10). To help ease the pain, the trade-off here is your main residence is exempt from CGT. I suppose you can't have it both ways, because if the interest of the loan for the property is tax deductible you're liable to pay CGT when you sell that property (see Chapter 11).

Commencing in 2024 under the federal government's Help to Buy scheme, financial assistance will be provided to help low and middle income earners purchase a home. The amount potential buyers can apply for will be up to 30 per cent of the purchase price for an existing property, and up to 40 per cent of the purchase price for a new property. To be eligible, you can't earn more than \$90,000 as an individual, while a couple's combined earnings can't exceed \$120,000. A property price cap will also apply (with the level of this cap depending on which state or territory you reside in). Under this scheme, the government will make an 'equity contribution' — meaning it will own part of your property until you've repaid the contribution or you sell the property (and use the proceeds to repay the debt). For more info, check out the website of your state or territory government revenue office.

For a comprehensive discussion on the CGT issues associated with owning a main residence, the Tax Office provides the publication 'Guide to capital gains tax'. To get a copy of this guide, go to the Tax Office website (www.ato.gov.au).

Keeping What's Yours: Exempt from Tax

Ahh, now for some good news! Under the CGT provisions, owning a main residence is normally exempt from tax, which means any increase in its value during the period you own the property isn't going to be taxed. If you examine this issue from a tax planning point of view, buying your home in a location where property prices are continually rising may prove to be prudent. As a general rule, property in good locations tends to double in value every seven to ten years. The strategy then of buying a home may prove an excellent way of building up wealth that isn't liable to tax. The downside is if your property falls in value, any capital loss you make on disposal can't be offset against any current or future capital gains because your main residence is exempt from tax.

WARNING

Under the CGT provisions, *disposal* means a change in ownership. A disposal normally arises when you sell an asset such as property. A disposal can also arise if you donate an asset to someone (for example, your children) or it gets lost, destroyed or compulsorily acquired.

Here's something that may be of interest. Under the temporary absence rule, if you move out of your main residence and you lease out your property, it is still exempt from tax for up to six years while you're away — for example, if you move interstate or go overseas for an extended period. However, if you decide not to lease out your property, it is exempt from tax during the entire period you're away (rather than just six years if the property was leased).

If you buy another property and move into it, you need to make an election as to which one is your main residence, because under the CGT provisions, you can't own two main residences. It would be great if you could! From a tax planning point of view, you're best to keep the property more likely to appreciate in value at a faster rate as your main residence. If you choose the new property as your main residence, under these circumstances, your old home ceases to be exempt from CGT. This choice means that from this point onwards you're liable to pay CGT on any subsequent increase in value, from the date your old property stops being your main residence to the date you sell it.

But it's not all bad. If you buy land adjacent to your property and use it as a part of your main residence (for instance, you buy your neighbour's block of land), the additional land is also exempt from tax. However, this exemption is on the condition the total land surrounding your property doesn't exceed the 2-hectare limit. And, for a further condition, if you sell your main residence at a later date, you have to sell both holdings simultaneously to the new owner. If you don't do this, the land adjacent to your original property is liable to CGT.

TIP

If you're 55 years or over and planning on selling your main residence that you've held for at least 10 years, I've got some good news. Under the federal government Downsizer Contribution scheme, you can make up to a maximum $300,000 ($600,000 per couple) downsizer contribution to your super fund to help boost your retirement nest egg. But you'll need to do this within 90 days of transfer of ownership. By the way, no maximum age limit is in place, which means you can make a downsizer contribution if you're 75 years or over. (See Tax Office fact sheet 'Downsizer contributions for individuals' for more details.)

Sharing What's Yours: When You Have to Pay Tax

A major condition for your main residence to be exempt from tax is that the property must be used solely for private or domestic purposes; that is, you can't use it to earn assessable income. The moment you start to use your home to earn assessable income, the residence is no longer fully exempt from CGT and you may have to pay CGT when you sell or otherwise dispose of your home. For example, this liability can arise if you use part of your home for residential accommodation and you use part for running your business activities (for example, you own a shop and you reside in the back of the premises).

Further, if the land that surrounds your home covers more than two hectares (for example, you own a 10-hectare property), the amount in excess of the 2-hectare limit (8-hectares) is liable to CGT on disposal.

REMEMBER

If your main residence is situated on more than 2 hectares, you're allowed to choose the best two hectares for the purposes of qualifying for the CGT exemption.

If you subdivide your main residence and sell off part of your property, the part you sell is liable to CGT, because to gain a full exemption you need to sell your main residence in its entirety. Under these circumstances, you need to apportion the property's cost base at the time you do the subdivision, for the purposes of calculating whether you made a capital gain or capital loss on disposal.

CHECK
THE NET

If you want to know more about the taxation of a main residence, visit the Tax Office website (www.ato.gov.au) and check out 'Guide to capital gains tax' (particularly the bit that deals with 'Real estate and main residence' within 'Part A – About capital gains tax').

Maintaining a Home Office

If you need to do some employment-related work at your home (for instance, you're a school teacher and it's more convenient to check your students' homework at home or you work from home on some days as part of a hybrid workplace model), I have good news for you.

If you have a private study or home office, you could qualify for certain *running expenses* such as cleaning costs, depreciation and repairs of your computer and office furniture, heating/cooling, lighting, internet and telephone calls. Be sure to keep receipts and a record of the number of hours you work at home because you can claim a tax deduction based on the actual expenses you incur ('actual cost method'). Alternatively, you can use a fixed hourly rate of 67 cents per hour, at the time of writing ('fixed rate method').

The bad news is you can't claim a tax deduction for *occupancy expenses* such as mortgage interest, council rates, house insurance, rent and repairs, unless you work from home and your home is your place of business. For example, you're a self-employed script writer and you use one room to write your scripts and meet business clients.

REMEMBER

If you plan to run a home-based business and claim occupancy expenses, you run the risk that your home will no longer be fully exempt from CGT. If you reside in a location where property valuations are continually rising it's best to weigh up the benefits of running your business from home and claiming these expenses against the limitations of losing part of this valuable CGT exempt concession (that could be substantial), before you commit yourself to a home-based business.

TECHNICAL STUFF

The Tax Office has issued the publication 'Small business: Home-based business expenses (NAT 75196)', which explains the taxation issues you need to know if you're running a small business at or from your home. Also check out Taxation Ruling 'TR 93/30 Income tax: deductions for home office expenses'.

Transferring Property: Marriage or Relationship Breakdown

If you transfer (roll over) ownership of a property to a former spouse as a consequence of a marriage or relationship breakdown, no CGT issues will ordinarily arise at the time of transfer until the property is eventually sold (see Chapter 11). This area of the law is complex, so you're best to seek advice from a registered tax agent or solicitor. For more details, see Tax Office fact sheet 'Marriage or relationship breakdown and real estate transfers'. You can download it from the Tax Office website (www.ato.gov.au).

Chapter **7**

Taxing Issues Affecting Students and Your Children

It goes without saying that children can be an expensive mob to raise and maintain, particularly when it comes to schooling!

A number of anti-avoidance tax provisions stop you from distributing 'unearned' income to your children. You can also use a number of tax benefits to help reduce the cost of raising children. In this chapter, I examine these anti-avoidance provisions and identify the various tax benefits you can gain from supporting your children.

Raiding the Piggy Bank: Taxing Under 18s

Be careful if you want to give money to your children, because anti-avoidance provisions apply with respect to income earned by children under 18. The purpose of the provisions is to stop parents putting (or perhaps hiding) large sums of money in their children's accounts, in order to avoid or reduce the amount of tax payable on the investment income derived. The good news is these rules no longer apply after a child turns 18 years of age. (In Australia, a child becomes an adult when reaching 18 years of age.)

The major concern here is this: if a child derives investment income, whose money is it? Does it really belong to the child or to a parent? The answer to this question determines who's liable to pay the tax. Read on!

Taxing your children's investment accounts

Children's savings and investment accounts can be in the name of the child or in a trust account, with the trustee normally being the child's parent. The latter is generally the preferred option. This section examines the taxation issues associated with each.

If an account is held in trust for a child under 16 years of age (which is normally the case) and the account earns more than $120 a year, the trustee needs to provide a tax file number (TFN) to a bank, building society or credit union (check out Chapter 5 for how to apply for a TFN). The number can be either the trust's TFN or the trustee's personal TFN. If no TFN is quoted, tax is withheld from the payment at the rate of 45 per cent. This is because the account is deemed to belong to the trustee (for example, a parent).

On the other hand, if a child is under 16 years of age and holds an investment account in her own name, she doesn't have to provide a TFN to a financial institution if she receives less than $420 investment income each year. However, the $420 threshold doesn't apply where a child under 16 years of age receives dividends from a public company. No threshold applies for income received from these investments. (*Note:* A child isn't required to lodge a tax return if their only source of income is interest totalling less than $416, but they do need to lodge one to get a tax refund if tax has been withheld.)

The Tax Office website (www.ato.gov.au) offers some helpful fact sheets (such as 'Children's savings accounts' and 'Children's share investments'), and tax ruling 'TD 2017/11 Income tax: who should be assessed to interest on bank accounts?'

Taxing the paper round: Employment income

A low income earner (such as a child under 18 years in full-time education) who works part-time is unlikely to pay tax on the income derived. The reason is because low income earners can take advantage of the taxable income threshold for individuals combined with the low income tax offset (refer to Chapter 3 for information about this offset).

For the 2023–24 tax year, no tax is payable if your child's taxable income is below $18,200. The good news gets even better because low income earners also qualify for a $700 low income tax offset. When you take the $700 tax offset into account, no tax is payable if your child earns less than $21,884 (refer to Chapter 5 for more details).

TIP

For low income earners, 70 per cent of the low income tax offset is taken into account when working out how much tax is deducted from the week-to-week pay packet. This means the majority of the tax offset is refunded at regular intervals rather than at the end of the tax year.

TECHNICAL STUFF

To find out more about income derived by minors, check out the Tax Office fact sheet 'Your income if you are under 18 years old' from the Tax Office website (www.ato.gov.au).

CASE STUDY: CHILD IN PART-TIME EMPLOYMENT

Kim is 16 years of age and works part-time for a fast-food outlet. During the 2023–24 tax year, she earns $16,000 and pays $1,000 PAYG withholding tax. When she lodges her tax return, she's not liable to pay any tax because her taxable income is below the tax-free threshold. This means she pays no tax on the $16,000, and she receives a $1,000 tax refund in respect of the amount of PAYG withholding tax her employer deducted from her pay.

(**Note:** Kim doesn't also get the $700 low income tax offset on top of this refund. The benefit can only be used to offset a tax liability — it's not refundable.)

Getting a Distribution from a Trust

One popular way you can invest your money is to set up a trust, particularly a family discretionary trust. Under this arrangement, the trustee (the person in control) has discretion about how trust net income (such as interest, dividends, rent and capital gains) should be distributed to the beneficiaries (normally family members). (To explore in more detail how a trust operates, check out the nearby sidebar, 'Understanding trusts'.)

One great thing about setting up a trust is your ability to distribute trust income to specific beneficiaries to meet their particular needs. For example, if you have two adult children attending university, you're able to distribute $21,884 to each of them that isn't going to be taxed if that's their sole source of income (see the sidebar 'Case study: Distributing trust income' later in this chapter). But it becomes a bit of a minefield if you want to distribute money to children under 18 years of age.

It you intend to set up a family trust, you need to apply for a TFN (refer to Chapter 5) and lodge a trust tax return disclosing the trust net income or (loss) at the end of the financial year (refer to Chapter 3). However, the trust isn't liable to pay tax on the net income it derives. Instead, it becomes part of the assessable income of either the trustee or beneficiaries.

As soon as the trustee has calculated the trust net income, the trustee is required to ascertain

>> Who the beneficiaries are.

>> Whether any beneficiary is presently entitled to receive a distribution (meaning the beneficiary has a legal right to demand payment).

>> Whether any beneficiary is under a legal disability. This normally arises if a beneficiary is under the age of 18. (**Note:** This could also be the case if a beneficiary is bankrupt or deemed insane.)

TECHNICAL STUFF

A trustee who makes beneficiaries of a discretionary trust entitled to trust income by way of a trustee resolution must make that resolution no later than 30 June. For more info see 'Tax issues for trusts — tips and traps' and particularly the bit about 'Trustee resolutions' on the Tax Office website (www.ato.gov.au).

UNDERSTANDING TRUSTS

The Tax Act doesn't define the meaning of a trust. A *trust* is a legal obligation, binding a person (referred to as the *trustee*) who has control over certain business and/or investment assets (referred to as *trust property*), for the benefit of certain persons (referred to as *beneficiaries*).

Expressed simply, a trust is a combination of four key components:

- **Beneficiary:** The person who stands to benefit from the trust. Companies and other trusts can also be beneficiaries.

- **Trust deed:** A legal document that sets out all the rights and obligations of the trustee.

- **Trust property:** May be money, real estate, shares or a business being used to derive income for the benefit of the beneficiaries (see Chapter 12).

- **Trustee:** The person responsible for administering and managing the trust property over which the trustee has control for the benefit of the beneficiaries. A trustee holds legal title to the trust property, but the property isn't beneficially the trustee's. Further, a trustee must act in accordance with the terms of the trust deed. A trustee can be either a person or a company.

To put it simply, if a beneficiary is presently entitled to receive a distribution and has a legal right to demand payment, the distribution is part of the beneficiary's assessable income, and the beneficiary is liable to pay tax on that distribution. On the other hand, if a beneficiary is presently entitled but under a legal disability, the trustee has to pay the tax. The trustee is also liable to pay the tax if no beneficiaries are presently entitled or if the trustee decides not to make a distribution.

If a trustee makes a distribution to a minor beneficiary who is under a legal disability (that is, under 18 years of age), the trustee is liable to pay a penal rate of income tax, commonly known as Division 6AA tax (see Table 7-1). This part of the Tax Act is an anti-avoidance provision to discourage trustees from distributing unearned income to children under the age of 18 (for instance, interest, dividends and rent). Since 1 July 2011, a minor beneficiary cannot claim a low income tax offset in respect of distributions of unearned income. This means the most that they can receive that's not liable to tax is limited to $416 (see Table 7-1).

TABLE 7-1 ## Division 6AA — Penal Rate of Income Tax

Taxable Income	Rate of Tax
$0–$416	Nil tax payable
$417–$1,307	66% of excess over $416
Above $1,307	45% on entire amount of taxable income

WARNING

If you're running a family trust, the Tax Office tends to closely monitor reimbursement payments within the trust structure. This is to ensure all family trust distributions to family beneficiaries are properly made in accordance to Tax Office guidelines. For more info, check out Tax Office fact sheet 'Trust taxation – reimbursement agreement' on its website (www.ato.gov.au).

TIP

A beneficiary under 18 years of age who is disabled or orphaned can claim a low income tax offset. This is also the case if a minor beneficiary derives employment income and/or unearned income from compensation payments and inheritances. Under these circumstances, when you take the low income tax offset into account, you can distribute $21,884 in the 2023–24 tax year before you're liable to pay tax (because these receipts are ordinarily taxed at normal rates).

WARNING

Complications can arise if you find trust net income as calculated under trust law is different from the way you calculate it under income tax law. This is especially so when making certain trust distributions (such as capital gains and dividend franking credits) to your beneficiaries, because two different methods to do so are available. Because this can get a little tricky, you should seek professional advice.

A resident trustee is liable to pay tax on any trust distributions to non-resident beneficiaries. If the non-resident beneficiary is required to lodge a tax return, the non-resident beneficiary can claim a tax credit in respect of the tax paid. (For more, see Tax Office fact sheet 'Tax on trust distributions to non-resident beneficiaries'.)

CASE STUDY: DISTRIBUTING TRUST INCOME

The trustee of the Phoenix family discretionary trust calculates the trust net income to be $66,000. The trust has two beneficiaries: Maria and Charlie.

At the end of the financial year, the trustee distributes $22,000 to Maria (who is a 21-year-old university student), $22,000 to Charlie (who is aged 12 and is in full-time education), and decides to retain and re-invest the balance ($22,000).

The $66,000 trust net income is taxed as follows.

Because Maria is over 18 years of age, she's considered to be

- Presently entitled to the trust distribution. (*Note:* It must be a fair dinkum distribution in accordance to Tax Office guidelines — see Chapter 12.)
- Under no legal disability.
- Personally liable to pay tax on the $22,000 she receives at her marginal tax rates.

Although Charlie is presently entitled to the trust distribution, in this case:

- He's under a legal disability because he's younger than 18 years of age.
- The trustee is liable to pay tax on the $22,000 distributed to Charlie.
- The trustee is liable to pay a penal rate of income tax under Division 6AA (at the time of writing, 45 per cent plus 2 per cent Medicare levy).

The $22,000 that isn't distributed (that is, the portion retained and re-invested) is classified as income to which no beneficiary is presently entitled. Under these circumstances, the trustee is liable to pay a 45 per cent rate of tax (plus 2 per cent Medicare levy) on this amount.

WARNING

Beneficiaries of closely held trusts (such as family discretionary trusts) must supply their TFN to the trustee. If you don't follow this rule, the trustee must withhold amounts from trust distributions at the top marginal rate (refer to Chapter 5) plus the Medicare levy (refer to Chapter 1). Beneficiaries who have tax withheld from their distributions can claim a tax offset in their individual tax returns.

With respect to a distribution to a minor beneficiary, the Tax Act uses the following technical terms:

>> **Prescribed person:** A person under 18 years of age and liable to pay a penal rate of income tax under Division 6AA (at the time of writing, 45 per cent plus the 2 per cent Medicare levy). For example, this could be the case because the person is in full-time education.

>> **Excepted person:** A person who is under 18 years of age but not liable to pay a penal rate of income tax under Division 6AA. This could occur if a person is in full-time employment or suffers from some disability.

>> **Excepted assessable income:** The Division 6AA penal rate of income tax doesn't apply to employment income or business income that a minor beneficiary may earn — for example, if a minor beneficiary derives a salary for services rendered. Also, the provision doesn't apply to investment income arising as a result of a deceased estate or from investing the excepted assessable income.

Checking Out Special Disability Trusts

The federal government has introduced a number of tax and CGT concessions to assist family members who set up a special disability trust for the future care and accommodation needs of a person (such as a child) with a severe disability. For more info see the Department of Social Services fact sheet 'Special Disability Trusts' — you can download a copy from its website at www.dss.gov.au — and Tax Office fact sheets 'Reporting the income of a special disability trust' and 'People with disability'.

Getting Something Back: Family Tax Offsets

As every parent can testify, raising children isn't an easy or inexpensive exercise. The job seems to be getting more and more difficult every year. Besides having to continually feed and clothe children, you have to provide a roof over their head as well as educate them. If you have to go to work, you may have to pay childminding expenses while you're working to support your family. To add salt to the wound, if you're raising more than one child, the costs start to escalate. Fortunately, you can tap into a number of tax benefits to help ease the pain.

Family Tax Benefit (Part A)

Family Tax Benefit (Part A) is an annual tax benefit to help you raise your children. To qualify you must have a dependent child under 16. You also qualify if you have a dependent child 16 to 19 years who is in full-time study to complete their Year 12 certificate or equivalent qualification. This payment is subject to you satisfying an income test — see the Services Australia website (www.servicesaustralia.gov.au) for more details.

Family Tax Benefit (Part B)

If you're a single-income family or a sole parent, you may qualify for an extra payment under Family Tax Benefit (Part B) to help you raise your children. This payment is subject to you satisfying an income test — see the Services Australia website (www.services australia.gov.au) for more details.

Paid parental leave scheme

The federal government has introduced a government-funded, taxable, paid parental leave scheme. The payment is at the rate of the national minimum wage. Its purpose is to provide financial support for the parents of newborn children. To be eligible, you must satisfy a work test and you can't earn more than $168,865 (at time of writing). If you're a couple your combined income can't exceed $350,000.

THANKING THE GOVERNMENT FOR THEIR HELP

If you did a course at a higher education institution (for instance, university) and you received a student loan under the HECS or HELP scheme, once you earn more than $51,550 (for the 2023-24 tax year), you're obligated to start paying back your HELP debt. (HELP stands for Higher Education Loan Program; it's the new name for what used to be called HECS.) The compulsory repayment rate is between 1 and 10 per cent (ouch!). See the Study Assist website (www.studyassist. gov.au) for further details. All Australian graduates who reside overseas for more than six months will have a legal obligation to repay their student loan if they earn more than the threshold amount.

To help share the workload, working fathers can get taxable government-funded paid parental leave at the rate of the national minimum wage as well. From 1 July 2024, the total paid parental leave that single and two-parent households can take will increase from 20 weeks to 22 weeks; and this will increase by a further two weeks each year until it reaches 26 weeks from 1 July 2026. Eligible two-parent households can split this leave entitlement if they decide to do so. See the Services Australia website for more details (www.servicesaustralia.gov.au).

Child care subsidy

Under current legislation, a child care subsidy payment is provided by the federal government to help you to cover the costs associated with child care. This subsidy is subject to you satisfying a number of conditions — see the Services Australia website (www.servicesaustralia.gov.au) for more details.

3

Tax-Effective Investments

Investigate traditional investments such as interest-bearing securities, shares and property, and identify what tax deductions and tax offsets you can claim.

Examine the various taxation issues associated with investments, and the difference between deductible expenses and capital improvements.

Find out about taxing capital gains and, more particularly, how to calculate a capital gain or capital loss.

Chapter **8**

Interesting Stuff: Bank Deposits and Tax

When you invest in interest-bearing securities, you normally deposit your money with financial institutions such as banks, credit unions and building societies. In return for the use of your money, you receive interest on your deposit, which is ordinarily payable at regular intervals. When the loan matures, you get your initial capital back. Because this class of investment can't increase in value, no capital gains tax (CGT) issues arise. If you decide to stay with this investment, the purchasing power of your capital decreases if inflation increases, and the income you derive decreases if interest rates fall. Sure is interesting stuff, isn't it?

In this chapter, I discuss the taxation issues associated with interest-bearing securities and your investment options. I also examine tax deductions associated with earning interest, and look at interest and tax implications from investing in company and/or government bonds and life insurance bonds.

Banking the Return: Interest

When you invest in an interest-bearing security such as a term deposit, you earn interest in return for the use of your capital (the money that you invest). Generally, you're liable to pay tax when the interest is credited to your account. You need to quote your tax file number (TFN) to the financial institution at the time you open the account. If you don't, the financial institution may withhold tax at the top marginal rate (45 per cent) on the interest you earn (referred to as *TFN amounts withheld from gross interest*). This withholding tax is taken into account when calculating your tax liability and is refunded if you pay too much tax. No CGT issues are likely to arise, and no 10 per cent goods and services tax (GST) is levied on input taxed financial transactions (see Chapter 15 for more about GST). For more info, visit the Tax Office website (www.ato.gov.au) and check out fact sheets 'Investment income' (listing the various sources of interest you need to declare) and 'Investing in bank accounts and income bonds'.

WARNING

If you run a company deriving predominantly passive investment income (such as interest, dividends, rent, royalties and net capital gains), it could be liable to pay a 30 per cent rate of tax. This could arise if more than 80 per cent of its assessable income is passive investment income.

REMEMBER

If you're under 16 years of age, you don't have to quote your TFN to a financial institution if you earn less than $420 interest from your account each year (refer to Chapter 7).

Interest isn't taxed at the time it's paid to you, so under the pay-as-you-go (PAYG) withholding tax system, if you derive a significant amount of interest (generally $4,000 or more per annum), you may need to prepare an *instalment activity statement* disclosing the amount of interest you receive, and pay tax on an ongoing basis (usually quarterly). The Tax Office notifies you if you need to do this. If you take this route, you have to keep accurate records of the interest you receive or that's credited to your account and, more particularly, the date you receive the payments. The tax you pay in instalments is credited against your end of financial year assessment (or final tax bill).

If you want to learn more about preparing an instalment activity statement, visit the Tax Office website (www.ato.gov.au) and search for the fact sheet 'PAYG instalments – how to complete your activity statement'.

As part of an ongoing compliance program, the Tax Office regularly checks on people by matching interest paid by Australia's major financial institutions against individual tax returns. You need to disclose the interest you derive in your tax return, and penalties apply if you fail to disclose the correct amount.

The Tax Office pays you interest when you make an early payment of tax or an overpayment of tax. But you need to declare the amount of any such interest you receive on your tax return as part of your assessable income.

Interesting Claims

You can deduct from your assessable income any loss or outgoing to the extent the loss or outgoing is incurred in gaining or producing assessable income (refer to Chapter 2). So, to qualify for a tax deduction, a direct and relevant connection must exist between the expenditure you incur and earning your assessable income — more particularly, the interest you derive.

The types of expenditure generally associated with earning interest that you're likely to incur are

>> Interest on borrowings, provided the purpose (or use) of the funds was to gain assessable income and, more particularly, the interest you derive.

>> Account-keeping fees that a financial institution may charge you.

>> Certain taxes that a state or territory government may charge you.

For more info on interest expenses, check out Tax Office fact sheet 'Interest, dividend and other investment income deductions', which lists the various deductions associated with interest income expenses — go to www.ato.gov.au to access.

CASE STUDY: INTEREST VERSUS DIVIDENDS

Bianca is contemplating whether to invest $100,000 in a term deposit or in shares. For the purpose of this case study, let's say Bianca has found a term deposit paying a 5 per cent rate of interest ($5,000 per year). Her other option is to buy shares in a company that's listed on the ASX paying a 5 per cent fully franked dividend (also $5,000).

Although the interest and dividend payments are identical and both are liable to marginal tax rates, investing in shares will give Bianca a better return on her investment. Why? Because in addition to receiving a $5,000 dividend payment, she'll also receive a $2,142 franking credit ($5,000 × 30/70 = $2,142) to offset against any tax she's liable to pay (see Chapter 9 for more on franking credits and dividends). This isn't the case with interest payments.

If the franking credit tax offset Bianca receives exceeds the net tax payable, the Tax Office refunds the excess back to her, and the overall return on her investment in shares will increase. Receiving a franking credit significantly benefits investors who pay a minimal amount of tax or no tax at all; for instance, because their taxable income is below the $18,200 tax-free threshold or because they have a self-managed superannuation fund (SMSF) that's in the pension phase. (See Chapters 18 and 19 for more on SMSFs and retirement.)

Investing in Company or Government Bonds

Another interest–paying investment option is company and/or government bonds. These ordinarily pay regular interest (referred to as *coupon interest payments*) — which is liable to tax — and you'll ordinarily get your initial capital back ('face value') when the bond matures.

REMEMBER

If you sell a company or government bond before it matures, the amount you receive will ordinarily depend on current interest rates and the time left before your bond matures. For example, say the bond you hold matures in seven years' time and pays a

5 per cent coupon rate of interest. You decide to sell this bond and, at time of sale, the current rate of interest is 4 per cent. In this case, your bond will ordinarily increase in value and you may make a capital gain if you've an investor (or ordinary income if you're a trader). Why? Because your bond paying 5 per cent may appeal to potential investors who are willing to pay you a premium to lock in the higher rate (5 per cent for the next seven years). On the other hand, if interest rates were sitting at 6 per cent at time of sale, your bond may decrease in value and you may make a capital loss if you're an investor (or revenue loss if you're a trader). Why? Because your bond paying 5 per cent is less attractive to potential investors (who can get 6 per cent elsewhere). Thus, you may need to sell your bond at a discount to generate a potential sale.

For more details in this area, check out the fact sheet 'How to invest' on the australiangovernmentbonds.gov.au website and more particularly the bit that deals with 'Tax considerations'. As this type of investment can get rather complicated (and is risky), you're best to seek professional advice.

TECHNICAL STUFF

If you invest in government bonds, the Tax Office has issued a number of taxation rulings relating to the tax treatment of certain government bonds, which you may find helpful. Visit www.ato.gov.au and check out the following for more information:

>> 'TR 93/28 Income tax: basis of assessment of income derived from securities purchased and sold cum interest'

>> 'TR 96/14 Income tax: traditional securities'

Investing in Life Insurance Bonds

Life insurance bonds (also known as *investment bonds*) are long-term investments (minimum ten years) that are ordinarily offered by life insurance companies. With life insurance bonds, you usually get to choose the investment mix (such as interest-bearing securities and/or shares) to help grow your capital. (Chapter 9 delves into shares in more detail.) For more information on insurance bonds as an investment option, check out the fact sheet 'Insurance Bond' on the moneysmart.gov.au website.

REMEMBER

The life insurance company is liable to pay a 30 per cent rate of tax on the earnings derived, and the net balance is reinvested on your behalf. The good news here is that you can make additional contributions of up to 125 per cent of any investment you contributed in the previous tax year — and any withdrawals you make after ten years are ordinarily excluded from your assessable income (which is good to know if your initial capital grows substantially in value).

WARNING

The bad news is that if you withdraw funds within the first ten years, you can become personally liable to pay tax at your marginal tax rates.

The amount of tax payable depends on whether withdrawals are made within the first eight years, during the ninth year or during the tenth year. But, on a brighter note, you can then claim a 30 per cent tax offset to help ease the pain!

For more info, see Taxation Ruling 'IT 2346 Income tax: bonuses paid on certain life assurance policies – section 26AH – interpretation and operation'. You can download a copy from the Tax Office website at www.ato.gov.au.

Chapter **9**

Owning Part of the Company: Investing in Shares

When you invest in the share market, you're pinning your hopes for income and capital growth on the business operations of publicly listed companies such as CBA, Qantas and Woolworths. In this chapter, I explain the unique taxation issues associated with this category of investment.

Sharing the Profits: Dividends

When you buy shares in a company, you become a part owner — a shareholder — of the company. This status means you can vote at the annual general meeting and give your two bob's worth of advice to the company directors. One tangible benefit of being a shareholder is the right to receive a share of the profits, referred to as *dividends*. Companies ordinarily pay dividends to you twice a year, and dividends are normally liable to tax when they're paid.

When you buy shares, quote your tax file number (TFN — refer to Chapter 5) to the company. Otherwise, the company is liable to withhold tax at the top marginal rate (45 per cent) on your dividend payment (referred to as *TFN amounts withheld from dividends*). This situation may arise if the company pays you an unfranked dividend. Under these circumstances, you can claim a tax credit on the amount the company withholds when you lodge your tax return.

'Frankly, my dear'. . .

Franking is a very important concept that you need to be aware of. When a company pays you a dividend, it must tell you whether the payment is fully franked, partially franked or unfranked. *Franking credits* are tax offsets that you can apply against the net tax payable on dividends (and other income) you derive. The good news is that if your total franking credits exceed the net tax payable, the Tax Office refunds you the difference. *Note:* If you're not required to lodge a tax return, you need to complete and lodge an application to get a refund of your franking credits. Refer to the Tax Office publication 'Refund of franking credits instructions and application for individuals (NAT 4105)' at www.ato.gov.au.

Your dividend payment could be

>> **Fully franked:** A fully franked dividend means the company has paid 30 per cent tax on its profits. This benefit, referred to as a *franking credit*, can be passed on to you (and your dividend yield increases!). You can get a franked dividend only from a resident Australian company.

>> **Partially franked:** If the dividend is partially franked, you receive a franking credit to the extent the dividend is franked.

>> **Unfranked:** If you receive an unfranked dividend, the company may not have paid taxes on its profits. You receive no franking credits if the dividend is unfranked. If you receive an unfranked dividend, you pay more tax because no tax offset is available for you to deduct from the net tax payable (as is the case when the dividend is fully franked or partially franked).

CASE STUDY: RECEIVING A FULLY FRANKED DIVIDEND

At the end of the financial year, Paz Fisher derives a $25,000 salary from her employment activities and pays $1,600 PAYG withholding tax. She also receives a $4,000 fully franked dividend from XYZ Ltd. The franking credit is $1,714.

Fully franked dividend

XYZ Ltd

Holder identification number: X 000438791

Payment date: 5 March 20XX

Paz Fisher

14 Roberts Street

Robertsville

Shareholder dividend statement

Fully franked final dividend for year ended 31 December 20XX

Class of shares	Dividend rate per share	Number of shares held	Franked amount	Franking credit (30% tax rate)
Ordinary shares	80 cents	5,000	$4,000	$1,714
Dividend amount			$4,000	

When Paz lodges her tax return, she needs to include the $4,000 dividend plus the $1,714 franking credit as part of her assessable income. She also incurs $1,000 interest on borrowings to finance the purchase of her share portfolio. Paz is taxed as shown in the following table.

(continued)

(continued)

Tax return for individuals

Income

Salary or wages		$25,000
Dividends: Franked amount		$4,000
Franking credit		$1,714
TOTAL INCOME OR LOSS		$30,714
Less Interest deductions		$1,000
TAXABLE INCOME		$29,714

Calculation of tax payable/refund

Tax payable on $29,714		$2,187
Plus		
2% Medicare levy		$594
Tax payable		$2,781
Less		
PAYG withholding tax	$1,600	
Low income tax offset*	$700	
Franking credits	$1,714	$4,014
REFUND OF TAX		**$1,233**

In this case study, Paz is also entitled to a $700 low income tax offset. For further details, refer to Chapter 3.

When you lodge your tax return, you need to include both the dividend and franking credit as part of your assessable income. This process is called *grossing-up*. You're taxed on the total amount and the franking credit is applied against the tax payable.

When you prepare your tax return, you find the following items in the section of the return form that deals with income:

>> Unfranked amount

>> Franked amount

>> Franking credit

You may find helpful the following fact sheets from the Tax Office (visit their website at www.ato.gov.au):

>> 'You and your shares (NAT 2632)'

>> 'Capital gains tax' (the section on 'Shares and similar investments')

>> 'ATO is here to help first-time share and ETF investors'

>> 'Investing in shares'

The following example shows you how to include both the dividend and franking credit as part of your assessable income:

If a company pays you a $1,000 fully franked dividend and tells you the franking credit is $428, you need to include $1,428 as part of your assessable income ($1,000 + $428) in your tax return (refer to the sidebar 'Case study: Receiving a fully franked dividend'). You're liable to pay tax on the gross amount ($1,428). The good news is you can offset (deduct) the franking credit ($428) against the net tax payable. If your total franking credits exceed the net tax payable, the Tax Office refunds you the difference. This offset can significantly benefit investors who pay no tax or a 19 per cent marginal rate of tax, because the refund increases the overall return on your investment (cash dividend received + refund of tax). However, if your marginal tax rate is above 30 per cent, you're liable to pay tax on the difference between the higher marginal rate (for instance, 32.5 per cent) and 30 per cent.

The formula used to calculate the franking credit on a dividend payment is:

$$\text{Cash dividend} \times \frac{\text{Company tax rate } (0.30)}{1 - \text{Company tax rate } (0.70)}$$

Using the earlier example, the $428 franking credit was calculated as follows:

$$\$1,000 \times 30/70 = \$428$$

If the company pays a 50 per cent partially franked dividend, the franking credit is reduced to the extent it's franked (for example, $428 × 50% = $214). If the dividend is unfranked, you receive no franking credits.

REMEMBER

Large companies (such as those listed on the ASX) pay a 30 per cent flat rate of tax on taxable net income derived, and the franking credit rate is 30 per cent.

WARNING

The Tax Office may deny you a franking credit if you buy and sell ordinary shares within 45 days of acquiring them (or 90 days if they're preference shares) and you become entitled to receive a franked dividend. During this qualifying period the shares must be held 'at risk', meaning there's a possibility that they could fall in value (as is ordinarily the case with shares listed on the ASX). However, under the *small shareholder exemption* provisions, this ruling isn't applicable if the total franking credits you receive from all your share holdings is less than $5,000. This means that you can receive up to $11,666 franked dividends before the 45-day holding period starts to apply ($11,666 × (30/70) = $5,000). *Note:* The $5,000 small shareholder exemption rule is only available to individual shareholders. Because the application of these taxation provisions can be complex, you're best to seek advice from a qualified accountant or tax agent. For more details visit the Tax Office website (www.ato.gov.au) and read the fact sheets 'Allocating franking credits' and 'When you are not entitled to claim a franking tax offset'.

REMEMBER

If your SMSF buys and sells ordinary shares within 45 days of acquiring them (or 90 days if they're preference shares), and becomes entitled to receive a franked dividend, your fund can't take advantage of the $5,000 small shareholder exemption provisions. This concession is only available to natural individual shareholders.

Under the PAYG withholding tax system, if you receive $4,000 or more investment income per annum (such as from dividend payments), you may need to prepare an instalment activity statement disclosing dividends (but not the franking credits) paid or reinvested on your behalf, and pay tax on an ongoing basis (usually quarterly). The Tax Office notifies you if you need to follow this procedure. You're required to keep all the dividend statements you receive and note the date you receive the payment. The tax you pay in instalments is credited against your end of financial year assessment.

For details about preparing an instalment activity statement, you can visit the Tax Office website (www.ato.gov.au) and go to 'PAYG instalments'.

If you participate in a dividend reinvestment plan (where you receive additional shares instead of a dividend payment), you still need to declare the dividend as part of your assessable income.

WHY COMPANIES MAY NOT PAY FULLY FRANKED DIVIDENDS

A company may not pay you a fully franked dividend for a number of reasons. The main ones are

- A company may not have sufficient tax credits in its franking account to pass on to its shareholders (see Chapter 12).

- A company may have prior year losses that they can offset against current year profits, which affects the amount of tax payable on net profits derived.

- Net profit calculated under tax law may not be the same as that calculated for accounting purposes — you're able to make a loss under income tax law and a profit under commercial law. (**Note:** Tax is payable only on profits calculated under tax law.)

- A company may derive much of its profits from overseas sources, which may affect the rate of Australian tax payable on the profits that a company derives.

- A company policy may include not fully franking its dividends.

- Under tax law, a company may be prohibited from paying a franked dividend. This could arise if your company offers to buy back your shares under a capital raising off-market buyback arrangement, and a dividend component is included in the sale price.

RUNNING A SHARE TRADING BUSINESS

You can apply a number of tests to check whether you're running a share trading business, as follows:

- Do you intend to make a profit?
- Are you running your activities in a business-like manner?
- How much capital are you planning to invest?
- Do you plan to trade on a regular basis (for example, 10 trades per week)?
- What volume of trades do you plan to make each year (for instance, 500 trades per year)?
- Are you keeping proper records (for example, stockbroker buy and sell contract notes)?

Generally, passing these tests isn't difficult. The stumbling block to being accepted as running a share trading business is normally the volume of trades you make each year. As a general rule, the more trades you make, the greater the chance of being accepted as a share trader. A significant advantage of being accepted as a share trader is any trading losses you incur can be offset against other assessable income you derive.

On the other hand, if you're an investor, any capital loss you incur can be offset only against a capital gain. The downside is a share trader can't take advantage of the 50 per cent discount on gains made on shares held for more than 12 months. However, this rule is unlikely to be a major concern because a share trader is unlikely to hold shares for more than 12 months.

Reducing dividend payments: What can I claim?

In Chapter 2, I explain the rules of claiming a tax deduction under the general deduction provisions. With respect to dividend payments, to qualify for a tax deduction, a direct and relevant connection must exist between the expenditure you incur and the dividends you receive. Examples of the types of expenditure that meet this key test include

» Bookkeeping and postage to manage your share portfolio.

» Costs of subscriptions to share market information services, investment journals and newspapers, provided they're for the purpose of deriving dividends.

» Interest on money you borrow to buy shares in companies that normally declare dividends.

» Depreciation of share trading software, internet and data access costs incurred for share trading activities and mobile phone call costs for a share trader to access live market information.

» Travel expenses to consult a stockbroker or attend company annual general meetings.

For more info on dividends and share income expenses, check out Tax Office fact sheet 'Interest, dividend and other investment income deductions', which lists the various deductions associated with investing in shares at www.ato.gov.au.

TIP

If you donate shares to a deductible gift recipient (such as an approved hospital, school building fund or library) valued at $5,000 or less, and the companies in question are listed on an approved stock exchange (for example, the ASX), the amount you contribute could qualify for a tax deduction. For more info, check out the Tax Office fact sheet 'Shares valued at $5,000 or less' at www.ato.gov.au.

TECHNICAL
STUFF

The Tax Office has issued the fact sheet 'Share investing versus share trading', which deals with share trading activities. Check it out at www.ato.gov.au.

Borrowing to build your wealth: Interest payments

When you borrow money, one major expense you're likely to incur is interest. Provided the purpose (or use) of the loan is to derive assessable income, especially dividends, you can normally claim the interest as a tax-deductible expense. Before you borrow to buy shares though, you need to check the company's dividend payment history. If you find that a company has never declared a dividend, a looming and strong possibility is that the interest expense may not be tax deductible. This possibility presents because the purpose or use and direct and relevant connection tests are not being satisfied: You're not going to be earning assessable income, because the company doesn't pay dividends.

This scenario can arise if you buy shares in mining companies that don't declare dividends.

If you borrow to buy shares and then find that the companies don't pay dividends and you're not sure what to do, your best bet is to seek professional advice. However, all is not lost! Under the capital gains tax (CGT) provisions, the interest you incur (referred to as *non-deductible holding costs*) can be added to the share's cost base. However, this provision applies only to investments and, more particularly, shares you bought after 20 August 1991, and can be taken into account only if you make a capital gain. Unfortunately, the provisions can't be used to create or increase a capital loss. The nearby sidebar 'Case study: Non-deductible holding costs — shares' illustrates these points.

CASE STUDY: NON-DEDUCTIBLE HOLDING COSTS — SHARES

Eleven months ago, Angela borrowed $30,000 to buy a parcel of shares in a mining company that hasn't ever declared a dividend. She paid $30,000 for the shares and sells the parcel of shares today for $40,000. During the time Angela owned the shares, she paid $3,000 interest. The Tax Office advises her that the interest isn't tax-deductible because her mining shares don't pay dividends. Under these circumstances, the interest can be added to the cost base. The net capital gain Angela makes on disposal is calculated as follows.

Capital proceeds (sale price)		$40,000
Less		
Cost base		
Purchase price	$30,000	
Non-deductible holding costs	$3,000	$33,000
NET CAPITAL GAIN		**$7,000**

If the sale price is $20,000, Angela can't take the $3,000 non-deductible holding costs (interest) into account, because she can't use it to create or increase a capital loss. On the other hand, if the sale price is $32,000, she can take $2,000 of her non-deductible holding costs (interest) into account.

WARNING

If you enter into a capital protection loan agreement to buy shares, the amount of interest you can claim is restricted to the Reserve Bank of Australia's indicator rate for standard variable housing loans (plus a further 1 per cent). Under a capital protection loan arrangement, you can protect yourself from incurring losses (if your shares fall in value) by paying for a risk premium in your interest charge (so you don't have to repay the loan if the investment arrangement is unsuccessful). For more details see Tax Office publication 'Capital protected products and borrowings' and 'Taxation Determination TD 2016/10'.

Taxing Your Gains and Losses

When you buy shares from a stockbroker you receive a *buy contract note*, which sets out the price (plus costs) you pay and the date of purchase. If you sell the shares at a later date, you receive a *sell contract note*, which sets out the sale price (minus costs) and the date of sale. You use these two documents to quickly calculate whether you make a capital gain or capital loss on sale. The documents also tell you how long you owned the shares. You need to know this to check out whether you made a discount capital gain or a non-discount capital gain and how much tax you're liable to pay on the gain. Check out more details in Chapter 11.

Your capital gains can be taxed in two ways:

>> **Discount capital gain:** Only 50 per cent of the gain is taxed at your marginal tax rate if you hold the shares for more than 12 months (refer to the sidebar 'Case study: Making a capital gain').

>> **Non-discount capital gain:** If you hold the shares for fewer than 12 months, the entire gain is taxed at your marginal tax rate.

If you sell shares and make a capital loss, and you buy them back immediately (referred to as a *wash sale*), you take a risk that the Tax Office may disallow the capital loss you make. This interpretation may apply because the Tax Office may take the view that you only sold the shares in order to gain a tax benefit that arises when the capital loss is deducted from a capital gain.

CASE STUDY: MAKING A CAPITAL GAIN

Three years ago, Fabien purchased 1,000 CBX Ltd shares. The buy contract note shows he paid $20,100 for them (including $100 brokerage and GST). Fabien sells the shares today. According to the sell contract note, the sale price is $29,000 and he pays $100 brokerage and GST to sell them.

The net capital gain Fabien makes on disposal is calculated as follows.

Capital proceeds (sale price)			$29,000
Less			
Cost base			
Purchase price		$20,000	
Brokerage & GST (buy)	$100		
Brokerage & GST (sell)	$100	$200	$20,200
NET CAPITAL GAIN			**$8,800**

Because Fabien held the shares for more than 12 months, he's taken to have made a discount capital gain. Just 50 per cent of the gain ($4,400) is liable to be taxed at his marginal tax rate.

TECHNICAL STUFF

The Tax Office has issued Taxpayer Alert 'TA 2008/7', which deals with wash sales arrangements and sets out the Tax Office policy on these types of transactions.

REMEMBER

If you're a member of a complying superannuation fund and you're in the pension phase, all investment earnings (such as dividends) and capital gains on sale of investment assets (such as shares) that your super fund derives to help fund your pension payments are exempt from tax. If the dividends are franked, all franking credits are refunded back to your super fund, and the return on your investment will increase. (For more details, see Chapters 18 and 19.)

CASE STUDY: MAKING A CAPITAL LOSS

Julianne purchases a parcel of shares for $20,000. Her brokerage fees and GST are $100. She sells them for $9,000 (again, her brokerage fees and GST are $100), making a capital loss on disposal. Under these circumstances, the net capital loss she makes on disposal is calculated as follows.

Capital proceeds (sale price)			$9,000
Less			
Reduced cost base			
Purchase price		$20,000	
Brokerage and GST (buy)	$100		
Brokerage and GST (sell)	$100	$200	$20,200
NET CAPITAL LOSS			**$11,200**

Note: If you make a capital loss, the cost base becomes the reduced cost base.

Because Julianne makes an $11,200 capital loss, she can offset this loss only against any capital gains she may make. If she makes no capital gains during the financial year, she can carry forward the capital loss for an indefinite period and apply it against future capital gains that she may make. She can offset the capital loss against capital gains she may make on disposal of other categories of assets, such as property. The only exception is Julianne can't offset a capital loss against a capital gain on a collectable.

TIP

If you own worthless shares in a company that's been placed in liquidation, and the liquidator declares in writing that it's unlikely you'll get a distribution in the course of winding up the company, you can realise (claim) a capital loss as at the time of the declaration. For more details visit the Tax Office website (www.ato.gov.au) and read the fact sheet 'Disposing of shares' and go to the 'shares are worthless' link.

Investing in Overseas Share Markets

If you derive dividends from shares listed on an overseas stock exchange, you're ordinarily liable to pay withholding tax on the dividends you receive. The rate of tax payable depends on whether an international tax treaty exists between Australia and the country where the shares are listed.

The rate of tax withheld is ordinarily 15 per cent if Australia has a tax treaty or 30 per cent if no tax treaty exists.

You need to include both the dividend that you receive and any tax withheld as part of your assessable income; you may also be entitled to claim a *foreign income tax offset* in respect of the amount of tax you pay overseas.

If you sell shares listed on an overseas stock exchange and you make a capital gain on this sale, you must disclose the capital gain (or loss) that you make on disposal in your Australian tax return. You can also claim a 50 per cent CGT discount if you have owned the shares for more than 12 months.

If you're liable to pay foreign tax on the capital gain you make overseas, you may be entitled to claim a foreign income tax offset in respect of the amount of foreign tax you paid overseas. Chapter 11 explores CGT in more detail. See also the Tax Office website (www.ato.gov.au) and check out fact sheet 'Foreign and worldwide income'.

Chapter **10**

Building Your Dreams: Investing in Bricks and Mortar

I nvesting in real estate can range from buying residential property or land, to buying commercial property such as office space, shops and factories. If you plan to invest in bricks and mortar, you buy land and buildings for income and capital growth.

You can gain significant tax benefits from investing in real estate. In this chapter, I identify these tax benefits and explain what you need to do to qualify for them.

Collecting the Rent

One of the great pleasures of leasing a property is the regular rental payments you receive from your tenant.

You're normally liable to pay tax on rental income in the financial year you receive the payment. If you own an income-producing property, you may be liable to pay tax on the following types of transaction:

>> **Bond money:** If you receive bond money from a tenant, you normally pay tax on it at the time you're legally able to keep it. (This situation may arise, for example, when a tenant refuses to pay you rent or damages your property.)

>> **Insurance policy payments:** You may have to pay tax on payments you get from an insurance policy that compensates you for loss of rent.

>> **Prepaid rent:** You normally pay tax on this transaction in the financial year you receive the payment.

Rent isn't taxed at the time you receive the payment, and so under the PAYG withholding tax system (refer to Chapter 3), if your gross rent is $4,000 or more per annum, you may need to prepare an instalment activity statement disclosing the gross rent you receive and pay tax on an ongoing basis (usually quarterly). The Tax Office notifies you if you need to do this. This situation means that you need to keep an accurate record of the gross rent you receive and the date you receive it. The Tax Office credits the tax you pay in instalments against your end of financial year assessment (or tax bill).

For details about preparing an instalment activity statement, visit the Tax Office website (www.ato.gov.au) and go to 'PAYG instalments'.

If you lease residential property used predominantly for residential accommodation, you don't need to apply for an Australian Business Number (ABN) and quote it to your tenant. (An ABN is a number you have to quote when you enter into certain business transactions; otherwise, 45 per cent tax is withheld from your payments.)

If you run a business and you receive a cash incentive from a landlord to enter into a long-term lease or to remain on the premises, the receipt is normally treated as assessable income. (For more details, see Taxation Ruling 'IT 2631 Income tax: lease incentives'.)

Reducing the Costs: What You Can Claim

A major bugbear with rental investments is dealing with the constant stream of expenses — there's always a bill in the in-tray waiting to be paid! For an expense to be deductible, you must show a relevant and necessary connection between the expenditure you incur and the rental income you earn. If you own a rental property, you must charge a commercial rate of rent. Otherwise, your expenses may be disallowed or reduced to an amount the Tax Office considers reasonable. For example, if you charge a relative $10 a week rent and your annual rental expenses are $20,000, you risk a strong possibility that your deductions are going to be denied or substantially reduced because you're not charging a genuine rent. Further, you can claim rental property deductions only for the period that you rent out the property or, if the property is vacant, for when it's genuinely available for rent (for example, the property is with a real estate agent). For more info, check out Taxation Ruling 'IT 2167 Income tax: rental properties – non-economic rental, holiday home, share of residence, etc. cases, family trust cases'.

Expenditure associated with rental property normally consists of the following types of outlay:

>> Advertising to find a tenant

>> Agent's commission to manage your property and collect the rent on your behalf

>> Body corporate fees if you own an apartment

>> Capital works deductions (see the section 'Understanding capital works deductions', later in this chapter)

>> Council rates, land taxes, water and sewerage charges

>> Depreciation for items such as furniture (see the section 'Depreciating your assets', later in this chapter)

>> Insurance premiums for building and loss of rent and security costs

>> Interest to finance the purchase of an income-producing property (see the section 'Going in reverse: Negative gearing', later in this chapter)

>> Legal expenses associated with the preparation of a lease

>> Quantity surveyor fees relating to depreciation valuations and capital works deductions

>> Repairs and maintenance (see the section 'Repairing what's yours', later in this chapter)

>> Stationery, postage and telephone calls

WARNING

Travel costs to inspect a residential rental property, collect the rent and perform general maintenance are no longer a tax-deductible expense. This is not the case if you're in the business of letting rental properties. For more info, check out Tax Office fact sheet 'Rental properties and travel expenses' at www.ato.gov.au.

TECHNICAL STUFF

You may find the following information from the Tax Office website (www.ato.gov.au) helpful:

>> 'Rental expenses to claim'

>> 'Rental expenses you can claim now'

>> Taxation Ruling 'TR 2015/3 Income tax: matters relating to strata title bodies constituted under strata title legislation'

Apportioning Expenditure: The Bits You Can't Claim

If you use only part of your property to derive rental income, you have to apportion the expenses you incur. This rule applies because the Tax Office considers part of the expenditure to be private or domestic in nature and not tax deductible (refer to Chapter 2). Working out the percentage of deductible expenses is normally done on a floor or area basis; for example, if your property consists of 12 rooms and you use 4 rooms for income-producing purposes by leasing them or running a business from them, one-third of your total outlays are deductible expenses. The balance is considered to be private or domestic in nature and, therefore, not deductible.

TIP

The Tax Office has issued two booklets — 'Rental properties (NAT 1729)' and 'Guide to depreciating assets (NAT 1996)' — that provide guidelines on taxation of rental properties and expenses you can claim. Visit www.ato.gov.au for more.

Claiming Specific Deductions: What's on the List

To claim certain deductions, you need to follow specific rules, as the following sections describe.

Depreciating your assets

Nothing lasts forever, especially household items that seem to be always breaking down. You can claim *depreciation* (wear and tear) on certain assets or articles you own and use to derive rental income. (*Note:* The Tax Office prefers to use the term 'decline in value' rather than depreciation.)

You can depreciate items such as clothes dryers, curtains and blinds, dishwashers, floor coverings, furniture, refrigerators, stoves, television sets and washing machines. To fulfil the depreciation rules, though, you need to keep a depreciation schedule that lists all the items you can depreciate plus the date you buy them and the purchase price. When working out how much depreciation you can claim each year, you have the option to use a rate of depreciation based on the item's estimated effective life, or the Tax Office recommended depreciation rates as set out in its tax rulings (for more details check out Tax Office fact sheet 'Guide to depreciating assets NAT 1996'). If you buy a depreciable item costing $300 or less, you can claim an outright deduction in the financial year you incur the expense. You can make this claim only if you earn non-business income, such as rent you receive from a residential property.

And now for the bad news! You can't depreciate everything you own in a rental property. For example, you can't depreciate items such as built-in kitchen cupboards, carports, in-ground swimming pools, saunas and spas. Why? Because the Tax Office considers these types of items to form part of the building structure and, therefore, to be capital in nature (refer to Chapter 2). However, all is not lost. Although they're not depreciable, you may be able to claim a tax deduction under a different section of the Tax Act referred to as the 'capital works provisions' (see the following section).

You have a choice of two methods to work out how much depreciation (or decline in value) you can claim each year:

>> Using the prime cost method (PCM), you can claim a fixed amount each financial year.

>> Using the diminishing value method (DVM), you can claim a greater amount in the earlier years and a lesser amount in later years.

The method of depreciation that you select depends on the amount of depreciation you want to claim each year and how quickly you want to claim it.

REMEMBER

When weighing up which method to use, the rate of depreciation under DVM is always twice the rate under PCM. (When working out how much depreciation you can claim, you can use a rate of depreciation based on the item's estimated effective life, or the Tax Office recommended depreciation rates as set out in its tax rulings.) For example, if the rate of depreciation under PCM is 10 per cent, the rate under DVM is automatically 20 per cent. This difference means that if you choose DVM instead of PCM, you can recoup your initial outlay at a faster rate. (See the sidebar 'Case study: Claiming a depreciation deduction' for more info.)

When you sell a depreciable item, the Tax Office calls this a *balancing adjustment event*. If the sale price (or termination value) is less than the adjusted value, the amount not yet written off is a tax-deductible expense. For example, if the adjusted value is $10,500 at the time the balancing adjustment event occurs (that is, when you sell the asset), and you receive $5,000 for the asset, the $5,500 loss you incur is tax deductible.

On the other hand, if the termination value (sale price) is more than the adjusted value, the excess is assessable. For example, if you receive $12,000 when you sell the depreciable item and the adjusted value is $10,500, the $1,500 profit you make is assessable income that you must declare on your tax return and, therefore, is liable to tax.

CASE STUDY: CLAIMING A DEPRECIATION DEDUCTION

On 1 July 2023 Anton paid $15,000 for a new deluxe oven for his rental property. He chooses to use the PCM of depreciation (a rate of 10 per cent). (If Anton had chosen DVM, the rate would have been 20 per cent — twice 10 per cent.)

The amount Anton can claim each year under both methods is as follows.

	PCM (10%)	DVM (20%)
Deluxe oven	$15,000	$15,000
Decline in value (2024)	$1,500	$3,000
Adjusted value	$13,500	$12,000
Decline in value (2025)	$1,500	$2,400
Adjusted value	$12,000	$9,600
Decline in value (2026)	$1,500	$1,920
Adjusted value	$10,500	$7,680

TIP

Another method of depreciation, called *low value pools*, is where you can pool (accumulate) all items that cost less than $1,000. For example, if you buy five depreciable items that cost $600 each, the accumulated value under the low value pools method is $3,000 ($600 × 5). Under this method, the DVM is used and the rate of depreciation is 37.5 per cent a year. If you acquire a particular item part way through the financial year, the rate is 18.75 per cent in the financial year you acquire it. If you want to know more about low value pools, see the Tax Office publication 'Guide to depreciating assets (NAT 1996)'. You can get a copy from the Tax Office website (www.ato.gov.au).

Understanding capital works deductions

Ordinarily, you can't claim a tax deduction in respect of the purchase of a building. This rule applies because the outlay is considered to be capital in nature and not tax deductible under the general deduction provisions (refer to Chapter 2). However, you may be able to claim a tax deduction under the capital works provisions, which allow you to write off certain construction costs of a building over a period of time.

Under these capital works provisions, you can claim a 2.5 per cent deduction over a 40-year period. This rule applies to certain construction costs of new, income-producing property (for example, rental properties, business premises and factories) constructed after 15 September 1987. (The annual rate for property constructed between 22 August 1984 and 15 September 1987 is 4 per cent rather than 2.5 per cent.) The formula to apportion your annual tax deductions for a capital works deduction is:

Construction costs × the applicable rate (which can be either 2.5 per cent or 4 per cent)

This special capital works deduction also applies to any capital improvements or extensions you make to an income-producing property — for example, if you improve your property or add an extra room(s).

REMEMBER

Construction costs you can write off can include expenses such as architect fees, engineering fees, foundation excavation expenses and costs of building permits; however, you can't write off the cost of the land, clearing, demolition and landscaping expenses (for more info, see Tax Office fact sheet 'Capital works deductions').

TIP

In the Tax Office publication 'Rental properties (NAT 1729)', the Tax Office provides a number of examples of expenditure that qualify for a special deduction, and of expenditure types that don't qualify. You can get a copy from the Tax Office website (www.ato. gov.au).

Whenever you buy or build a rental property (or business premises), you need to know the building's construction cost for the purposes of working out the amount of capital works deductions that you can claim each year (see the sidebar 'Case study: Capital works deduction and capital gains tax'). On the other hand, if you sell an income-producing property that qualifies for a capital works deduction, the annual deduction not yet claimed can be transferred to the new owner.

CASE STUDY: CAPITAL WORKS DEDUCTION AND CAPITAL GAINS TAX

Seven years ago, Samuel paid $600,000 for a new residential property that he leases. He is advised the construction cost of the building for the purposes of claiming a 2.5 per cent capital works deduction is $400,000. Samuel sells the property today and receives $1,000,000. During the period of time Samuel leased the property, he claimed a $10,000 capital works deduction each year ($400,000 × 2.5%). Because Samuel has now sold the property, he needs to reduce the property's cost base by $70,000 ($10,000 × 7), for the purposes of working out the amount of net capital gain that's liable to tax.

Capital proceeds (sale price)		$1,000,000
Less Cost base (purchase price)	$600,000	
Less Capital works deduction	$70,000	$530,000
NET CAPITAL GAIN		**$470,000**

WARNING

If you sell an investment property (or business premises) you purchased after 13 May 1997, the accumulated amount of capital works deductions you claim each year must be deducted from the property's cost base (see Chapter 11). You need to do this in order to work out the correct amount of capital gain or capital loss you make if you sell it. The federal government is effectively giving you a tax deduction with one hand and taking it away from you with the other!

Repairing what's yours

When you own a property, over time you're likely to incur repairs. You may be able to claim a tax deduction on repair work, such as general property maintenance, painting, repairing the floor or roof, and replacing broken windows. But certain repairs you make to your property may not qualify as a tax deduction. This rule applies because if you make an improvement rather than a repair, the Tax Office considers the expenditure to be capital in nature and not tax deductible. The difficult part for the rental property owner is figuring out the difference between an improvement and a repair for income tax purposes. Because this area of tax law can be a bit tricky, you need to get your understanding of this difference right.

A *repair* is basically replacing or renewing worn-out parts of the item you're repairing with new parts. If you plan to repair an item, the important point is that you merely restore the item to its previous condition, and you don't *improve or change* the function or character of the item you're repairing. For example, if you repair a crack that appears in a wall made of timber with some appropriate filler, the expenditure you incur is clearly a repair. However, if you decide to pull the entire wall down and build a better and stronger brick wall in its place, the expenditure is going to be disallowed because you're considered to have improved and changed the character of the wall (rather than merely repairing a crack in the existing timber wall). Under these circumstances, the expenditure is considered to be capital in nature. However, you may qualify for a deduction under the capital works provisions (refer to the preceding section).

It's also important to know that you can't claim a deduction for initial repairs. These are repairs you make to a newly acquired income-producing property. For example, if you decide to paint the building before you lease it or you decide to repair existing defects, the Tax Office considers these expenses to be capital in nature and to form part of the cost base of the property. This rule applies because these repairs didn't arise during your period of ownership. Rather, they arose as a consequence of the previous owner's period of ownership. However, these costs can be deducted under the capital works provisions discussed in the preceding section.

TIP

If you undertake repairs to a rental property that has become vacant, the expenditure you incur may qualify as a tax-deductible expense. Further, repairing a property after it's no longer used to derive income may also qualify as a tax-deductible expense.

TECHNICAL
STUFF

The Tax Office has issued two important taxation rulings relating to repairs, 'TR 97/23 Income tax: deductions for repairs' and 'TD 98/19 Income tax: capital gains: may initial repair expenditure incurred after the acquisition of a CGT asset be included in the relevant cost base of the asset?' Visit www.ato.gov.au for more details.

Going in reverse: Negative gearing

A substantial outlay normally associated with investing in real estate is interest on borrowings. Provided the purpose (or use) of the loan is to finance the purchase of an income-producing property or to derive assessable income (for example, rental income), your interest payments are normally a tax-deductible expense. If the interest (plus other deductible expenses you incur) is more than the rent you receive, you can deduct the loss from your other assessable income — such as salary and wages, investment income and business profits (see the sidebar 'Case study: Negative gearing a property'). When you do this, you reduce the amount of tax you're liable to pay on your other assessable income. This tax approach to property investment is called *negative gearing*. If you negative gear, you effectively use the tax system to help you finance the purchase and service the debt — which isn't all bad!

If you have a split loan facility — where part of your loan is private in nature (such as a home mortgage) and part is investment-related (such as a rental property) — you need to comply with strict rules in order to claim interest deductions. For more details, see Taxation Ruling 'TR 98/22 Income tax: the taxation consequences for taxpayers entering into certain linked or split loan facilities', which you can find on the Tax Office website (www.ato.gov.au).

REMEMBER

The security or collateral you may need to offer (for example, your home) to secure an investment loan has no relevance to whether you can claim a tax deduction. It's the purpose (or use) of the loan that's important.

TIP

If you borrow to finance the purchase of an investment property that's currently under construction, the interest you incur during the construction period is ordinarily a tax-deductible expense. For more info, check out Taxation Ruling 'TR 2004/4 Income tax: deductions for interest incurred prior to the commencement of, or following the cessation of, relevant income earning activities'.

TIP

If your rental expenditure (for example, interest, land tax, rates, insurance and repairs) on a negatively geared property is likely to be substantial, you can request the Tax Office to vary the rate of tax payable on your salary and wages. To take this route, you need to complete the form 'PAYG withholding variation application (NAT 2036)'. Go to the Tax Office website (www.ato.gov.au) to get a copy of this form.

TIP

You can borrow money through a self-managed superannuation fund (SMSF) under a limited recourse borrowing arrangement to buy an investment property, or to do repairs and maintenance to a property that your super fund owns. But you can't borrow money to make improvements to a property that your super fund owns, such as renovations or adding an extension. Visit the Tax Office website (www.ato.gov.au) and check out the Taxation Ruling 'SMSFR 2012/1 SMSF: limited recourse borrowing arrangements – application of key concepts' for more information.

CASE STUDY: NEGATIVE GEARING A PROPERTY

Lance borrows $300,000 to buy an income-producing property that he intends to lease. At the end of the financial year, he calculates that he paid $25,000 interest on his loan and he received $16,000 rent. His other deductible expenses amount to $5,000. In the same year, Lance also derives a $60,000 salary, and his marginal tax rate plus the Medicare levy is 34.5 per cent.

Lance's taxable income is calculated as follows.

Rental income		$16,000
Less		
Interest on loan	$25,000	
Other deductible expenses	$5,000	$30,000
Net loss from rent		$14,000

Because Lance has incurred a $14,000 net loss on his rental property, he can deduct this amount from the salary he earned:

Salary and wages	$60,000
Less Net loss from rent	$14,000
TAXABLE INCOME	**$46,000**

Because his marginal tax rate plus the Medicare levy is 34.5 per cent, the tax payable on his salary is reduced by $4,830 ($14,000 × 34.5%).

Calculating non-deductible expenditure

You can't claim expenditure such as interest, rates and land taxes, insurance and repairs in respect of non-income-producing property (such as a holiday house that you use for your personal use and enjoyment). However, under the CGT provisions, you can use these costs to reduce a capital gain.

If you borrow money and the purpose of the loan isn't to derive assessable income, you can't claim a tax deduction for interest and other expenses you incur. This situation may be the case if you buy a block of land or a holiday house that you don't ever rent out. Under the CGT provisions, if you acquire a non-income-producing property after 20 August 1991, you can add non-deductible expenditure — such as interest, rates and land taxes, insurance and repairs — to the property's cost base.

These costs are referred to as *non-deductible holding costs* and form part of the third element of the cost base. (For more details, see Chapter 11.) So, you can take these expenses into account if you make a capital gain on disposal. To ensure you follow this rule correctly, you need to keep proper records of all the expenditure you incur. The bad news is you can't take these types of expenses into account if you happen to make a capital loss. The sidebar 'Case study: Non-deductible holding costs — real estate' explains how this principle works. (For more info, check out Tax Office fact sheet 'Cost base of assets'.)

CASE STUDY: NON-DEDUCTIBLE HOLDING COSTS — REAL ESTATE

Ten years ago, Roger paid $250,000 for a house that he uses for his personal use and enjoyment, but isn't his main residence for tax purposes. During the time he owns the house, he pays $35,000 interest on a loan he took out to buy the property, and $25,000 for rates and land taxes, insurance and repairs. Because these expenses aren't tax deductible, he can add them to the cost base. Roger sells the property today for $450,000.

(continued)

(continued)

The net capital gain Roger makes on disposal is calculated as follows.

Capital proceeds (sale price)		$450,000
Less		
Cost base		
Purchase price	$250,000	
Non-deductible holding costs		
Interest	$35,000	
Other expenses	$25,000	$310,000
NET CAPITAL GAIN		**$140,000**

If the sale price was less than his purchase price of $250,000, Roger couldn't take the $60,000 non-deductible holding costs into account, because you can't use them to create or increase a capital loss. On the other hand, if the sale price was $300,000, Roger could take $50,000 of his non-deductible holding costs into account.

Paying 10 per cent: Goods and services tax

The goods and services tax (GST) is a broad-based tax of 10 per cent on most goods and services that are sold or consumed in Australia. (See Chapter 15 for more about GST.) Generally, you're liable to pay GST if you buy new residential property from a registered entity such as a property developer (or a property that has been substantially renovated).

TIP

You're considered to have substantially renovated an existing property when all or substantially all of the building is removed or replaced. If you're a GST-registered entity (see Chapter 15) — for instance, a builder — the property is treated as a 'new residential premises' and is ordinarily liable to GST if you subsequently sell it. For more info, refer to Taxation Ruling 'GSTR 2003/3 Goods and services tax: when is a sale of real property a sale of new residential premises?' on the Tax Office website (www.ato.gov.au).

Under the GST provisions, if you lease a residential property used mainly for residential accommodation, the transaction is classified as an input taxed supply. This term means you can't charge GST on the rent you collect from your tenant. You also can't claim a GST credit on GST you incur on your rental expenditure (see Chapter 15 for more).

The following are liable to GST:

>> Advertising, repairs, agent commission and insurance

>> Alterations and renovations you make to your property

>> New property where the vendor is a registered entity

>> Property that's been substantially renovated

>> Rent on commercial property

>> Rent on short-term accommodation

>> Sale of commercial rental premises such as a motel

The following aren't liable to GST:

>> Rent from residential property used predominantly for residential accommodation

>> Water, sewerage and drainage

REMEMBER

If you lease a residential property used predominantly for residential accommodation, you don't need to get an ABN and quote it to your tenant.

TECHNICAL STUFF

You may find the following information from the Tax Office website (www.ato.gov.au) helpful:

>> GST Ruling 'GSTR 2012/6', which deals with commercial residential premises

>> 'GST and residential property'

>> 'GST and the disposal of capital assets'

TIP

Explore the benefits of setting up a SMSF and buying an invest-ment property in your fund. When you reach your preservation age and retire, all investment income and capital gains on the sale of investment assets that your fund derives during the pension phase to fund your pension payments are exempt from tax.

RENOVATING PROPERTIES AS A BUSINESS

If you enter into a profit-making activity of renovating property and selling it at a later date, the Tax Office may treat your activities as a business. If you're running these activities as a business, you may need to register for GST and charge GST on your sales (see Chapter 15). Further, you may be liable to pay tax on the entire profit you make on each sale. On the other hand, if you're not running a business, the Tax Office taxes the profit under the CGT provisions. Under these provisions — and if the property wasn't your main residence — 50 per cent of the capital gain is liable to tax if you sell the property after 12 months (see Chapter 11).

Here are the tests to check whether you're running a business of renovating properties:

- Are you running your activities in a business-like manner?
- Are you undertaking these activities for the purposes of making a profit?
- Are your activities similar to people who run a business of renovating properties?
- How much money are you outlaying?
- How often do you undertake these activities?
- Is the size and scale of your activities significant?

Because these issues are very complex, you may wish to seek profes-sional advice from a tax consultant. The Tax Office has issued the fact sheet 'Are you in the business of renovating properties?' that deals with this matter too so jump online and visit www.ato.gov.au for more info.

WARNING

The Tax Office has issued Taxpayer Alert 'TA 2012/7', which warns SMSF trustees who plan to acquire an investment property not to contravene the strict superannuation rules associated with acquiring a property. You can get a copy from the Tax Office website (www.ato.gov.au).

Deriving rent from overseas

If you derive rent from an investment property that you own overseas, you must disclose the rent in your Australian tax return. Any foreign expenses you incur (such as repairs and mortgage interest) may qualify as a tax deduction. If your foreign deductible expenses exceed your foreign rental income, the foreign loss you incur can be deducted from other Australian-sourced income you derive.

If you're liable to pay foreign tax on the rent you derive overseas, you may be entitled to claim a foreign income tax offset in respect of the amount of foreign tax you paid overseas. For more details see Tax Office fact sheets 'Foreign and worldwide income' and 'Guide to foreign income tax offset rules'. You can download them from the Tax Office website (www.ato.gov.au). *Note:* See Chapter 11 for CGT issues in respect to selling a property you own overseas.

TIP

For a list of tax mistakes to avoid where real estate and owning property in SMSFs are concerned, check out Chapter 22.

CASE STUDY: PROPERTY AND SMSFs — HOW TO AVOID PAYING CGT

Ten years ago Rafael and Caitlin's SMSF paid $500,000 for an investment property in a good location where real estate valuations — excuse the pun — subsequently began going through the roof. The property is valued at around $1.5 million, ten years later.

Rafael and Caitlin, who are both 60 years of age, have decided to retire and want to sell the property to help fund their retirement.

(continued)

(continued)

If the property is sold during the SMSF's accumulation phase, two-thirds of the capital gain is liable to capital gains tax (CGT) at the rate of 15 per cent (see Chapter 18). This means that if the super fund makes $1 million capital gain during the accumulation phase, it will be liable to pay $100,000 in tax ($1,000,000 × 2/3 × 15% = $100,000).

Because Rafael and Caitlin have reached their preservation age (60 years) and have satisfied a condition of release (retirement), it's best that they convert their SMSF from the accumulation phase to the pension phase before they sell the property. This is because all investment earnings and capital gains on the sale of investment assets (such as real estate) derived during the pension phase to fund pension payments are exempt from tax. This means if the super fund sells the property and makes a $1 million capital gain during the pension phase, no CGT is payable! To add icing to the retirement cake, all pension payments and lump sum withdrawals are tax free and excluded from Rafael and Caitlin's assessable income (see Chapters 18 and 19). (**Note:** The maximum amount of funds an individual can transfer from an accumulation account to a pension account (where earnings are exempt from tax) is capped at $1.9 million — see Chapter 19 for more details.)

Incidentally, if Rafael and Caitlin had originally purchased the investment property outside the superannuation system, and made a $1 million capital gain on sale, under these circumstances 50 per cent of the capital gain ($500,000) would be liable to CGT at their marginal tax rates plus a 2 per cent Medicare levy — ouch! (See Chapter 11 for more information.)

Chapter **11**

Catching Up on Capital Gains Tax

Y ou've just found out that the 'worthless' old painting you inherited from a distant relative is really a Renoir — and you can't call Christie's or Sotheby's soon enough. As soon as the auction gavel falls, you're going to be set for life. Right?

Well, probably, but unless you want to spend some time in the tax court, you're best to make sure the Tax Office gets its share. Why? Because if you sell things such as shares, real estate, works of art or other assets that you acquired after 19 September 1985, you may be liable to pay capital gains tax (CGT) on any capital gains you make on the sale. (This date is when the CGT provisions started.) Just to complicate things, the federal government tweaked the rules again in 1999. But don't worry, in this chapter I explain how to calculate a capital gain or capital loss, and how capital gains are taxed under the old rules (which are now basically redundant) and new rules. I also cover CGT requirements when selling the new kid in town — cryptocurrency.

Looking at the Rules: CGT Assets

The CGT provisions are all about taxing gains you make on disposal of CGT assets, and the rules to work out how much tax you have to pay. Perhaps the worst part about making a capital gain is giving some of it to the Tax Office.

I'm going to stick out my neck here and say of all the taxes you have to deal with, CGT is probably the easiest to understand. Why? Because you need to examine just three conditions to check whether you have to pay tax. When you do this exercise, keep in mind that if any of these conditions aren't present, generally, you don't have a CGT issue to worry about. The three conditions are

>> A CGT asset must exist (a question of fact).

>> The CGT asset must have been acquired after 19 September 1985. To fulfil this requirement you need to keep records to verify the date you acquired the asset. According to this condition, if you own assets that were acquired before this date, no CGT liability arises. This rule means that if you sell them today, you don't have to pay CGT on any gain you make.

>> A CGT event and, more particularly, a disposal of a CGT asset must have occurred. A disposal normally occurs when a change in ownership occurs, such as when you sell the asset. The Tax Act provides a comprehensive list of CGT events that can lead to a disposal of a CGT asset, such as selling a CGT asset, loss or destruction of a CGT asset and granting a lease.

REMEMBER

A *CGT event* normally arises at the time of the making of the contract to sell the asset rather than when you receive the money for the sale. This rule means that if the contract is signed during one financial year (for example, in June) and you receive the money two months later in the following financial year (in August), you're liable to pay tax in the financial year that you signed the contract.

A *CGT asset* is 'any kind of property or a legal or equitable right that is not property'. The definition is so broad it can range from your most-prized valuables such as real estate and shares, right down to your undies and shoelaces. (For more details check out Tax Office fact sheet 'List of CGT assets and exemptions'.)

Three categories of CGT assets are liable to tax: collectables, personal use assets and other assets. The good news is that some of these CGT assets are exempt from tax.

Figure 11-1 illustrates the various components that make up the CGT provisions and how they interact with each other.

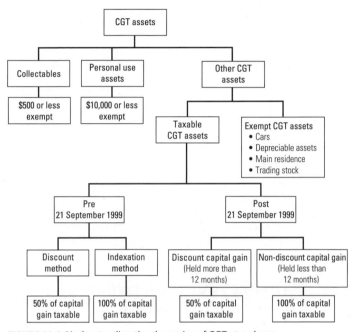

FIGURE 11-1: Understanding the dynamics of CGT at a glance.

If you have important CGT assets (for instance, prized collectables, a share portfolio and/or real estate) you can set up and record the details in a *CGT asset register*. To do this by the book, the relevant info you need to enter (such as date of purchase, purchase price and costs you incur) must be certified by a registered tax agent or a person approved by the Tax Office. For more info visit the Tax Office website (www.ato.gov.au) and check out Tax Office publication 'Personal investors guide to capital gains tax (NAT 4152)' and read the bit about 'Keep your records'. See also the Taxation Ruling 'TR 2002/10 Income tax: capital gains tax: asset register'.

Taxing your stamp collection: Collectables

The Tax Act defines collectables as '(a) artwork, jewellery, an antique, or a coin or medallion; (b) a rare folio, a manuscript or book; or (c) a postage stamp or first day cover; that is used or kept mainly for your or your associate's personal use and enjoyment'. A capital gain or loss you make on a collectable is exempt from tax if you originally acquire it for $500 or less. So, if you like collecting postage stamps that cost more than $500 you may be liable to pay tax on any gain you make on their disposal.

WARNING

As a general rule, if you sell individual items that are normally sold as part of a set, the individual items are exempt from tax only if the set was acquired originally for $500 or less (excluding any GST paid on acquisition).

TECHNICAL STUFF

You can offset a capital loss on disposal of a collectable only against a capital gain you make on disposal of another collectable. Further, you can't include the third element of the cost base (that is, non-deductible holding costs that don't qualify for a tax deduction) of a collectable in the collectable's cost base. See the section 'Adding up the costs: Cost base', later in this chapter for more.

Taxing your underwear: Personal use assets

Personal use assets are assets such as household items, furniture, electrical goods, boats and the clothes you wear, which you use for your personal use and enjoyment. So, basically, all your personal belongings, ranging from your cooking utensils and every button on your shirt, right down to your bras and underwear, are potentially liable to tax under the CGT provisions.

To avoid the absurdity of having to account for every item you own, the Tax Act conveniently deems items that fall under the definition of personal use assets to have a cost base of $10,000. For example, if you pay $80 for a dress, under the CGT provisions the cost base is $10,000 rather than $80. If you make a capital gain or loss on a personal use asset acquired for $10,000 or less, you're not liable to tax on it. This approach eliminates the need for you to account for these items and effectively takes them out of the CGT provisions. And, it becomes an issue only if you sell your personal use assets and receive more than $10,000 for each item. In the unlikely event of you actually getting this amount, you're liable to pay CGT only on any excess over $10,000. So, every time you put your clothes on, you should feel like a multi-millionaire, given that each item is worth $10,000 under the CGT provisions. Who says tax is boring!

Taxing all your treasures: Your other assets

Assets that don't fall within the definition of collectables and personal use assets are liable to CGT. These assets can include leases, goodwill, rights and options shares and real estate. You need to keep proper records of these types of CGT assets because they may be liable to CGT. Fortunately, a number of CGT assets are exempt from CGT. The most notable are

» Cars and motorcycles

» Compensation or damages for personal injury

» Depreciable business assets and trading stock

» Gambling wins, or proceeds from a game or a competition with prizes

» Marriage or relationship breakdown settlements

» Valour decorations (bravery medal awarded to holder)

One major CGT asset also on the exemption list is your main residence (the place where you reside). From a tax planning point of view, you're best to live in good locations where property values are continually rising, because you pay no tax on any gain you make upon disposal (refer to Chapter 6).

Cars are also on the list of exempt assets. If you happen to own a vintage car or a Ferrari and you make a $1,000,000 capital gain on disposal, no tax is payable on the gain (see Tax Determination 'TD 2000/35'). So why is the federal government so generous when it comes to cars, you may ask? The answer is quite clear. As a general rule, cars depreciate in value, which means everyone who owns a car could potentially claim a capital loss! If the odd car is sold at a profit, the Tax Office isn't going to be overly concerned.

TIP

Under the CGT small business concessions provisions, certain gains you make on disposal of active assets (such as business premises) that you use in running your business are exempt from tax. I discuss this issue in detail in Chapter 17. (*Note:* No CGT liability issues arise if you run a small business and decide to change the legal structure of your business — for example, from sole trader to a trust structure.)

TIP

If you invest in a new eligible start-up business (such as an early stage innovation company) and satisfy certain conditions, your investment may qualify for a CGT exemption. For more info, check out fact sheet 'Tax incentives for early stage investors' on the Tax Office website (www.ato.gov.au).

WARNING

If you gift or transfer a property (for example, a residential property or block of land) to a relative (for instance, your children) for nil consideration, under the CGT provisions you're deemed to have sold the property at its market value. Under these circumstances you may be liable to pay CGT if you make a capital gain on disposal. To add salt to the wound, the person who you gift or transfer the property to may be liable to pay state stamp duty for the property they receive. For info on what is 'market value' check out Tax Office publication 'Market valuation for tax purposes'.

TIP

If you own land that you acquired before 20 September 1985, and you construct a dwelling after this date, under the CGT provisions you're considered to own two separate assets. The land is treated as a pre-CGT asset and exempt from CGT, while the dwelling is a post-CGT asset and liable to CGT on disposal. This rule applies too if you make certain capital improvements to a pre-CGT property, and is triggered if the cost of the improvement in a particular year exceeds a threshold — for the 2023–24 tax year, this threshold is $174,465. Under these circumstances, the capital improvements you make after 19 September 1985 are treated as post-CGT assets. (For more info, check out the Tax Office fact sheet 'Property improvements and additions'.)

CHECK THE NET

For a discussion on capital improvements to a dwelling, visit the Tax Office website (www.ato.gov.au) and read the fact sheet 'Does capital gains tax apply to you?', particularly the section about 'What is a CGT asset?'

LEAVING THE LAND DOWN UNDER

If you decide you no longer want to live in Australia, a major issue to consider before you leave is how the Tax Office is likely to tax your CGT assets under the CGT provisions. This issue is important to consider because after you pack your bags and go, you're deemed to have disposed of your CGT asset(s) at their market value. This rule means you can be liable to pay CGT on any subsequent capital gain you make (thanks for the memories!).

If you find yourself in this predicament, I've got some good news: You can delay paying CGT by electing CGT assets you own to be taxable Australian property (see Appendix A). If you approach labelling your assets in this way, you can delay paying tax until they're eventually sold (at non-resident rates) or, if unsold, until you decide to become an Australian resident again. (**Note:** A non-resident is ineligible to claim a 50 per cent CGT discount on disposal of taxable Australian property, such as real estate.) For more info, visit the Tax Office website (www.ato.gov.au) and read fact sheet 'How changing residency affects CGT'.

WARNING

If a foreign resident disposes of certain taxable Australian property (such as a residential or commercial property), the purchaser may be required to withhold 12.5 per cent of the purchase price and forward the amount to the Tax Office. This is to cover any potential CGT obligations the foreign resident may incur. For more details visit the Tax Office website (www.ato.gov.au) and check out fact sheet 'Foreign resident capital gains withholding'.

Calculating a Capital Gain

Under the CGT provisions, you're considered to have made a capital gain if the capital proceeds (sale price) from the disposal of a CGT asset are more than the CGT asset's cost base (purchase price plus costs you incur). The way you calculate a capital gain depends on whether you acquired the CGT asset before or after 21 September 1999, and whether you held the CGT asset for more or fewer than 12 months. Here's how to determine the tax implications for a capital gain:

1. **Figure out how much you made on the deal.**

   Think these proceeds can only be cash? Think again, and then check out the following section.

2. **Calculate the cost base of the CGT asset you sold.**

   This calculation involves the purchase price and certain expenses you incur. (See the section 'Adding up the costs: Cost base', later in this chapter.)

   Subtracting the cost base (the number from Step 2) from how much you made on the deal (Step 1) gives you something called the notional capital gain.

3. **Subtract any losses on other CGT assets.**

   You can use the losses on one CGT asset to offset a gain on disposal of another CGT asset, or a cluster of assets. (The section 'Crying over spilt milk: Capital losses', later in this chapter, gives you more details.)

4. **Subtract any discounts you may be due — because it makes a difference when you purchased the CGT asset.**

   This situation normally arises if you owned a CGT asset for more than 12 months.

5. **Subtract any small business concessions for which you're eligible.**

   See Chapter 17 for more on small business concessions.

The sum of this grand exercise is called the net capital gain. The sidebar 'How to calculate a net capital gain' shows an example of how this all works, and the following sections drill down into some of the specifics about each of the categories.

Rolling in dough: Capital proceeds

Capital proceeds is a term associated with the disposal of a CGT asset. Capital proceeds can include money you receive, or are entitled to receive, from a CGT event and the market value of any property you receive, or are entitled to receive, from a CGT event. For example, when you sell a CGT asset, the capital proceeds can be a cash payment (which is normally the case), a cash payment plus property (such as a car or yacht) or property.

HOW TO CALCULATE A NET CAPITAL GAIN

You use five steps to calculate whether a net capital gain is liable to tax. The following example (with values I've inserted) explains how to do this calculation.

Total capital gains you made during financial year (Step 1)	$50,000
Less	
Total capital losses you made during financial year (Step 2)	$15,000
Equals	
Notional capital gain	$35,000
Less	
Prior year capital losses you may have made (Step 3)	$5,000
	$30,000
Less	
50% discount, if applicable (Step 4)	$15,000
	$15,000
Less	
Small business concession, if applicable (Step 5)	Nil
NET CAPITAL GAIN	**$15,000**

A CGT event is considered to have arisen when you make the contract, not when you receive the capital proceeds.

Adding up the costs: Cost base

The cost base of a CGT asset is made up of a combination of costs associated with buying, holding and selling a CGT asset. Under the CGT provisions, the cost base of a CGT asset is made up of five key elements:

>> **First element:** The money you pay to buy a CGT asset.

>> **Second element:** Incidental costs associated with acquiring (buying) a CGT asset plus costs associated with the disposal (selling) of a CGT asset. Incidental costs you're likely to incur when acquiring a CGT asset include stamp duty, brokerage, and legal and accounting costs. Incidental costs you're likely to incur when disposing of a CGT asset include agent commissions, brokerage and advertising costs, and legal and accounting costs.

>> **Third element:** Non-deductible holding costs are costs associated with owning a CGT asset such as interest, rates, insurance and repairs that don't qualify for a tax deduction.

The *non-deductible holding costs* associated with ownership — often called the 'third element of the cost base' because they're listed third in the tax codes — can't be included in a collectable's cost base for tax purposes.

>> **Fourth element:** Capital costs may be associated with increasing the value of a CGT asset. For example, this situation may arise if you add an extra room or rooms to an existing property.

>> **Fifth element:** Capital costs to preserve or defend title or right to a CGT asset may arise. This situation may happen if someone illegally builds a dwelling on land you own and you take legal action to stop this from happening.

You need to keep an accurate record to calculate the various elements that make up the cost base. If you don't retain any records, trying to work out the capital gain or capital loss you may have made on disposal can prove costly.

When you sell an income-producing property, any tax-deductible expenses you incur can't be added to the cost base.

Going modern: After 21 September 1999

If you're fortunate enough to make a capital gain on CGT assets you acquired after 21 September 1999, the good news is you pay tax only on 50 per cent of the gain if you owned the asset for more than 12 months. This gain is called a *discount capital gain*. The other 50 per cent is totally exempt.

However, the rules are different if you buy and sell a CGT asset within 12 months. Under these circumstances, the entire gain — called a *non-discount capital gain* — is liable to tax. So, if you're holding an asset that continues to increase in value, you're best to keep the asset for at least 12 months.

You can discount a capital gain by 50 per cent only after you deduct from your capital gains any current year losses and prior year losses that you may incur.

CASE STUDY: CALCULATING A NET CAPITAL GAIN

Six years ago, Hans paid $500,000 for a property he used to derive rental income. The incidental costs associated with acquiring the property were $8,000 stamp duty and $500 legal costs. Hans sells the property today for $800,000. The incidental costs associated with selling it are $10,000 agent's commission and $500 legal costs. Three years prior to selling the property Hans added an extra room at a cost of $25,000. Hans also incurs the following expenses, which are tax deductible.

Interest $15,000	Insurance $6,000
Rates and land taxes $10,000	Repairs $4,000

Two years ago, Hans made a $10,000 capital loss on the sale of shares that he hasn't yet claimed. The net capital gain Hans makes on disposal is calculated as follows.

Capital proceeds (sale price)		$800,000
Less		
Cost base		
First element		
Purchase price	$500,000	

(continued)

(continued)

Second element		
Stamp duty	$8,000	
Legal costs (buying)	$500	
Agent's commission	$10,000	
Legal costs (selling)	$500	
Third element		
Can't be used (see Note)	Nil	
Fourth element		
Extension	$25,000	$544,000
Notional capital gain		$256,000
Less		
Prior year capital losses	$10,000	
		$246,000
Less		
50 per cent discount		$123,000
NET CAPITAL GAIN		**$123,000**

Note: Because Hans is selling an income-producing property, the tax-deductible expenses he incurs can't be added to the cost base. Furthermore, because Hans holds the property for more than 12 months, just 50 per cent of the gain is liable to tax ($123,000). The balance is specifically exempt.

Getting a history lesson: Before 21 September 1999

Before 21 September 1999, the rules of calculating a capital gain were different from the way you do this calculation today. If you own assets you purchased before this date, you can choose between two ways to calculate the capital gain: the discount capital gain method and the indexed cost base method. You have the option to select the method that results in you paying the least amount of tax.

Discount capital gain method

The discount capital gain method, normally the preferred option of calculating a capital gain, is identical to the way you calculate a capital gain for a CGT asset purchased after 21 September 1999. Because you held the CGT asset for more than 12 months, just 50 per cent of the net capital gain you make on disposal (after you recoup capital losses) is liable to tax.

Indexed cost base method

Before the federal government changed the rules in September 1999, you were allowed to adjust the cost base of a CGT asset for inflation so that you didn't have to pay tax on gains that arose simply because of inflation. However, you had to be a mathematical genius to work it out. The rules were changed on 21 September 1999, so the indexed cost base method is practically obsolete and has limited application, because you can only adjust for inflation between the date you acquired the asset and 30 September 1999 — phew, what a relief!

Crying over spilt milk: Capital losses

No-one likes losing money, especially yours truly. Unfortunately, when you own CGT assets such as shares, real estate and collectables, you run the risk of incurring a loss if they fall in value. Under the CGT provisions, you can't deduct a capital loss from assessable income that you derive from other sources such as salary and wages, investment income and business income. You can deduct a capital loss only from a capital gain. If you don't make a capital gain in the financial year you make a capital loss, under these circumstances you can deduct it from capital gains you make in the future. If you find yourself in this position, make sure you keep an accurate record of all your capital losses.

By the way, you can deduct a capital loss that you make on one class of investment (for example, real estate) from a capital gain you make on disposal of another class of investment (such as shares). One exception applies to this rule. You can deduct a capital loss on a collectable only from a capital gain that you make on another collectable. (Refer to the section 'Taxing your stamp collection: Collectables', earlier in the chapter, for more information.)

CASE STUDY: CALCULATING A CAPITAL LOSS

Six years ago, Yelena bought a residential property. She paid $650,000 plus $12,000 stamp duty and legal fees to acquire it. Yelena sells the property today and receives $630,000. She pays $10,000 sale costs to sell the property. The capital loss she makes on disposal is calculated as follows.

Capital proceeds (sale price)		$630,000
Less		
Reduced cost base		
Purchase price	$650,000	
Purchase costs	$12,000	
Sale costs	$10,000	$672,000
CAPITAL LOSS		**$42,000**

Because the capital proceeds ($630,000) are below the reduced cost base ($672,000), Yelena makes a $42,000 capital loss. She can deduct this capital loss from a current capital gain, or future capital gain if she has no current capital gains.

TECHNICAL STUFF

When you sell a CGT asset and you make a capital loss, you need to use the reduced cost base rather than the cost base. Apart from a minor technical adjustment, the two are identical.

REMEMBER

If you sell a CGT asset that you own overseas (for instance, a property), you must disclose any capital gain you make on disposal in your Australian tax return. If you're liable to pay foreign tax on the capital gain you make overseas, you may be entitled to claim a foreign income tax offset in respect of the amount of foreign tax you paid overseas. For more info, read the Tax Office fact sheet 'Guide to foreign income tax offset rules'.

Selling or Transferring Your Business Premises to Your SMSF and CGT

If you run a small business and you sell or transfer your business premises (for instance, your office or factory) to your SMSF, you may be liable to pay CGT if you make a capital gain on the sale. This is because selling or transferring your business premises to your SMSF is classified as a CGT event — a change in ownership. If you do this 12 months after you bought the premises, only 50 per cent of the capital gain is liable to tax. But I can offer some good news. If you satisfy certain conditions, you may qualify for CGT relief under the CGT concessions for small business (see Chapter 17 for more information).

Investing in Cryptocurrency and CGT

Today, all the buzz is around getting into cryptocurrency. When you buy crypto (such as Bitcoin, Ethereum and Monero), you're investing in a digital asset that can only exist in an electronic format. You need computers and digital wallets to store your crypto, verify their existence and keep track of all your transactions. To keep the Tax Office folk happy, understanding the taxation issues relating to all your cryptocurrency transactions is important. How you're taxed will depend on whether you're an investor or trader. If you're not sure of your status or how you'll be taxed, you can seek a private ruling from the Tax Office. (See Chapter 4 for more details.)

If you're an investor who intends to merely keep crypto as a long-term investment, any capital gain or loss you make on disposal will ordinarily be liable to tax under the CGT-provisions (covered through this chapter). So you need to keep accurate records to calculate the cost base of all the cryptocurrency you intend to hold for investment purposes. On the other hand, if you merely intend to keep some crypto on hand (for instance, Bitcoin) to buy some personal use goods and/or services online from organisations that accept crypto (for instance, the latest computer game you're keen to get), your crypto will ordinarily be treated as personal use assets and excluded from the CGT provisions.

If you're a trader who frequently trades in crypto in the hope of making a quick profit on sale, your gains or losses will ordinarily be treated as assessable income or an allowable deduction. Keeping track of all your daily electronic transactions can be a bit of a minefield, so it's best to seek advice from a professional (such as a tax agent) regarding setting up a good record keeping system. By the way, if you receive rewards (for instance, staking rewards), they will ordinarily be treated as assessable income. For more info, check out Tax Office fact sheets 'Crypto asset investments' and 'How to work out and report CGT on crypto' on its website (www.ato.gov.au).

4

Running a Business

Start structuring a business and claiming tax deductions properly.

Weigh up the risks, legal obligations and responsibilities that come with running a business.

Consider tax issues you need to comply with according to the Tax Act.

Deal with goods and services tax (GST), fringe benefits tax (FBT) and capital gains tax (CGT).

Chapter **12**

Structuring Your Business for Maximum Gain

Before you hang up your 'Open' sign in the window, you need to be aware of a number of commercial and taxation issues that are associated with setting up a business in Australia.

In this chapter, I cover the major taxation issues that come into play when you set up a business, particularly the administration concerns that you need to get right in order to comply with Australian income tax law. I guide you through the various steps that are associated with setting up your business and advise where you can get additional help to fulfil all your legal obligations.

Choosing a Business Entity

Before you can start up a business, you need to give serious consideration to how you structure your business affairs. You can legally structure your business in one of four ways: sole trader, company, partnership or trust. The business structure you select depends on your personal circumstances and/or preferences.

You need to comply with many legal issues when setting up a business. Keep in mind when weighing up your options that you can set up a structure involving a mix of business entities (for example, a partnership of discretionary trusts). However, you need to consider the benefits and costs of developing such a structure.

WARNING

Setting up a business is a complex issue and you're best to seek advice from a qualified accountant, tax agent and/or solicitor before you sign on the dotted line. For a quick overview of business structures you can set up, check out fact sheet 'Setting up a business structure' on the Australian Securities & Investment Commission website (www.asic.gov.au).

TIP

Professional expenses (such as legal and accounting fees) associated with setting up a new business are tax deductible in the financial year in which you incur the expense. And even more good news —no capital gains tax (CGT) liability issues arise if you run a small business and decide to restructure your business (for example, changing your business structure from sole trader to a trust structure). (For more details check out Tax Office fact sheet 'Small business restructure roll-over'.)

The key issues you need to consider when assessing an appropriate business structure are

>> The extent to which you want to maintain legal control in respect of your business and financial affairs

>> The likely risks associated with operating under a particular business structure

>> The cost associated with setting up and running a business structure, and the capital you need to contribute

>> Income tax (and CGT on capital gains) that you're liable to pay under the different business structures

>> Your capacity to maximise deductible expenses you incur

>> Your capacity to distribute/split income and losses you derive between family members

>> The likely division of wealth from a marriage or relationship breakdown

>> Estate planning considerations

>> Protection of your capital from potential creditors if you're sued or if your business venture fails

The following sections set out the key issues you need to examine to determine which of the four legal business structures suits you. You need to look at the various benefits each structure can offer you, along with the potential limitations of each.

CHECK THE NET

If you want to know more about choosing a business entity, check out Tax Office fact sheet 'Business structures – key tax obligations'. You can download a copy from the Tax Office website (www.ato.gov.au). Also check out the fact sheet 'Business structures' on the business.gov.au website.

Becoming a Sole Trader: Going It Alone

If you decide to carry on a business as a *sole trader*, you're in total control of all your assets and business decisions. This level of control can be good and bad. The good bit is you stand to retain all the income you derive and any capital gain you make on the sale of your assets. The bad bit is that you're on your own, which means that every time you need help, you have to open your wallet or purse and pay for it solo.

REMEMBER

Being a sole trader means you're personally liable for any debts that your business incurs, and your personal assets can be used to cover these debts. So you need to know what you're doing from the outset — that you have the appropriate skills and experience to run a successful business. For more info, check out the fact sheet 'Sole trader' on the business.gov.au website.

As a sole trader, you're required to use your individual TFN and lodge an annual income tax return disclosing the taxable income you derive.

Inhaling the good news

You may find that operating as a sole trader has a number of significant and appealing benefits. These include

>> The business is easy to establish and operate.

>> Fewer legal restraints exist.

>> You can calculate your income using the cash or receipts basis if you run a small personal services business.

>> Your financial affairs aren't available for public scrutiny, as is the case with a company structure.

>> You can nominate beneficiaries in your will.

Some of the tax issues involved in operating as a sole trader are as follows:

>> You don't have to register for goods and services tax (GST) if your GST turnover is less than $75,000 a year.

>> You can own a main residence that's exempt from CGT (which isn't the case in a company or trust structure).

>> You benefit from the 50 per cent discount on disposal of CGT assets owned for more than 12 months. (This discount isn't available in a company structure.)

>> You benefit under the CGT small business concessions (see Chapter 17 for more details).

>> You can gain immediate access to all the losses that the business may incur to be offset against other assessable income you may derive. (Not so in a company or trust structure.)

>> You can claim a tax deduction when you make a concessional contribution to a complying super fund.

>> The tax-free threshold is $18,200, which means sole traders aren't liable to pay tax on the first $18,200 they earn (refer to Chapter 5).

>> If your annual aggregated turnover (sales) is less than $5 million, you can claim a 16 per cent small business income tax offset (capped at $1,000) on tax payable on your business's income (see Chapter 13).

Exhaling the bad news

Although the benefits from operating as a sole trader are attractive, you also need to take into account the various limitations and risks that you're taking.

On a commercial basis, operating as a sole trader may not appeal to you because

>> You risk being sued and, if you get into financial difficulty, your creditors may have a legal claim over all your personal assets.

>> Your ability to grow the business is limited to the capital you can raise and your capacity to service the debt.

Some of the scary taxation issues involved in operating as a sole trader are as follows:

>> You can't split business profits (or losses) and capital gains (or losses) with family members.

>> You're personally liable to pay tax on all the income and capital gains derived.

>> You're generally required to pay tax on an instalment basis (usually quarterly) if your gross sales or fees are $4,000 or more per annum, which may affect your cash flow (see Chapter 13).

TIP

Check out fact sheet 'Taxation' on the business.gov.au website for a quick overview of the tax issues associated with running a small business, particularly the article 'Tax differences between a sole trader and a company'.

Forming a Partnership: Sharing the Workload

Remember the old saying 'two heads are better than one'? No truer words have been spoken when it comes to running a business. One of the great things about running a *partnership* is that you can spread the workload between the business partners.

You can have no partnership existing under commercial law but one existing under Australian income tax law. Here's why:

>> Under commercial law, a partnership is a business with two or more people running that business, each aiming to make a profit. For more info, check out the fact sheet 'Partnership' on the business.gov.au website.

>> Under Australian income tax law, you need only to be 'in receipt of ordinary or statutory income jointly' for a partnership to exist (commonly referred to as a *tax law partnership*). Further, a profit motive isn't essential, and no limits exist restricting the number of people who can be partners for income tax purposes.

A partnership isn't treated as a separate legal entity, as is the case with a company, but you need to apply for a partnership TFN (refer to Chapter 5) and lodge a partnership tax return (refer to Chapter 3). A partnership isn't liable to pay tax on any net partnership income it derives. The partnership net income (or loss) must be distributed in accordance with the partnership agreement to the individual partners and each partner is liable to pay tax on the amount distributed. (Refer to Chapter 3, and in particular the 'Case study: Preparing your tax return' sidebar.)

If you derive investment income jointly — such as interest, dividends or rent — you don't have to lodge a partnership tax return. However, you're required to disclose your share of the investment income (and expenses) in your individual tax return. For more info, check out Tax Office fact sheet 'Partnerships' on its website (www.ato.gov.au).

Each partner is personally responsible for any (and potentially all) debts that the partnership incurs.

If you plan to set up a partnership, you need to consult a solicitor to help you enter into a formal partnership agreement.

Key partnership taxation principles

Keep the following tax principles in mind if you're thinking of setting up a partnership:

>> If a new partner is introduced or an existing partner retires, the old partnership ceases and a new partnership comes into existence. This may affect certain partnership assets such as real estate, trading stock, depreciating assets and work-in-progress.

>> Because a partnership isn't a separate legal entity for tax purposes, a partner can't be an employee of the partnership. The tax implication is that a partnership can't claim a tax deduction in respect of any super contributions the partnership makes on behalf of the partners.

>> Partners aren't paid a salary, but are entitled to a distribution of the partnership net income (or loss). The tax implication of this is that a partnership can't claim a tax deduction in respect of payments of salaries to partners.

>> Interest payable on a partner's capital or current account by the partnership is regarded as a distribution of partnership net income and isn't a tax-deductible expense.

>> Partnership assets are proportionally owned by each partner in accordance with respective partnership interests. Any capital gains or losses made on the disposal of these assets are proportionally derived by each partner for disclosure in individual tax returns.

TECHNICAL STUFF

Visit www.ato.gov.au and check out the following Tax Office Taxation Rulings for more details about business partnerships:

>> 'GSTR 2004/6 Goods and services tax: tax law partnerships and co-owners of property'

>> 'IT 2316 Income tax: distribution of partnership profits and losses'

>> 'TR 93/32 Income tax: rental property – division of net income or loss between co-owners'

>> 'TR 94/8 Income tax: whether business is carried on in partnership (including "husband and wife" partnerships)'

>> 'IT 2540 Income tax: capital gains: application to disposals of partnership assets and partnership interests'

>> 'TR 2005/7 Income tax: the taxation implications of "partnership salary" agreements'

>> 'TD 2015/19 Income tax: if a retiring partner is entitled to an amount representing their individual interest in the net income of the partnership for an income year, will section 92 of the *Income Tax Assessment Act 1936* apply?'

Sharing the good stuff

Running a business in partnership has many unique features that may appeal to you. The main benefits are summarised in this section.

On a commercial basis, operating as a partnership may suit you because

>> A partnership is easy to set up, operate and dissolve.

>> Partnership details and accounts aren't available for public scrutiny, as is the case with a company.

Some of the taxation issues involved in operating as a partnership are

>> A partnership allows you to split income and expenses among family members in proportion to their legal entitlement. (This option isn't the case for sole traders.)

>> You can distribute net partnership losses to individual partners to be offset against other derived income, such as investment income. (This option isn't the case in a company or trust structure.)

>> A partnership allows you to access capital gains tax exemptions. (Not necessarily so in a company structure.)

>> If your annual aggregated turnover (sales) is less than $5 million, a partner can claim a 16 per cent small business income tax offset (capped at $1,000) on tax payable on the partnership's income (see Chapter 13).

Taking on board the bad stuff

You may find certain features associated with running a business as partners not so appealing, because

>> Individual partners may need to give personal guarantees where partnership loans are concerned.

>> Each partner is responsible for the actions and decisions of the other partner(s). Conducting your commercial activities in a businesslike manner is really important.

Some of the potentially less-than-appealing taxation issues involved in operating as a partnership are

>> A partnership can't elect how partnership net income or losses should be distributed to partners. For example, you can't distribute income only to partners who pay no tax or

distribute partnership losses to those partners who stand to gain the most from such a distribution.

>> A partnership can't retain profits within the partnership structure, as is the case with a company. Partnership net profits must be distributed to the partners.

>> A partnership can't carry forward partnership losses; partnership losses must be distributed to the partners.

>> Superannuation contributions made on behalf of the partners can't be taken into account when calculating allowable deductions.

WARNING

Anti-tax-avoidance provisions are in place to prevent you distributing partnership income to certain partners in a partnership (for instance, children under 18) who have no real and effective control and disposal of their share of partnership income. The 'uncontrolled partnership income' may be liable to a special rate of tax.

Creating a Company: The More the Merrier

A company can be classified as a *public company* (such as those companies listed on the Australian Securities Exchange) or a *private company*. If you plan to set up a company, you're most likely to set up a private company. (You're a private company if 20 or fewer persons control at least 75 per cent of the company; known as the '20/75 test'.) When a business is set up as a company, shares are issued in this company. These shareholders are the owners of the company. For more info, check out fact sheet 'Company' on the business.gov.au website.

A company is a separate legal entity, and so needs to have a TFN (refer to Chapter 5), an Australian Business Number (ABN, see Chapter 13) and a public officer. A company can carry on a business in its own right, own assets, sue someone and can also be sued. At the end of the financial year, a company must lodge a company tax return disclosing the taxable net income (or loss), and self-assess the amount of tax payable (refer to Chapter 3).

If you want to be a company director, you need to apply for a Director Identification Number. (See the Australian Business Registry Services website — abrs.gov.au — for more details.)

Companies with an annual aggregated turnover (sales) of more than $50 million are liable to pay a 30 per cent flat rate of tax on taxable net income (derived). The rate reduces to 25 per cent for small or medium size business companies with an annual aggregated turnover of up to $50 million. For more info, check out Tax Office fact sheet 'Company tax rates'.

The Tax Office has issued the fact sheet 'Incorporating your business – tax implications' to help small businesses decide whether to incorporate and to explain the tax implications of that decision. You can get a copy from the Tax Office website (www.ato.gov.au). See also Tax Office Interpretative Decision 'ID 2004/760' regarding the 20/75 test.

Certain tax concessions are available to you (for instance, CGT rollover relief) if you transfer assets to a company structure. For example, you're a sole trader, partnership or trust and you transfer certain business assets to a wholly owned company. For more details see Tax Office publication 'Concessions for your small business' and ATO Interpretative Decision 'ID 2005/218'.

Understanding the good bits

A company structure has specific advantages that may appeal to you. The main advantages are

>> A company can benefit from limited liability, which means shareholders' liability is limited to the value of their shares in the company, even if company losses were to exceed that value.

>> A company has a continuous life.

>> A company can own assets in its own right.

>> A company can be operated by one person.

Some of the taxation issues involved in operating as a company are

>> A company doesn't have to distribute net profits it derives to shareholders. Company profits can be retained within the company structure.

>> Shareholders may receive dividend franking credits in respect to the dividends they're paid (refer to Chapter 9).

>> Company losses can be carried forward for an indefinite period and offset against future company profits (subject to meeting certain tests discussed in the next section).

>> Company superannuation contributions made on behalf of company directors and employees are tax deductible.

>> A company can act as trustee for a self-managed superannuation fund (SMSF; see Chapter 18).

>> A company can claim a research and development (R&D) tax concession in respect of eligible expenditure incurred on R&D activities. For more details check out fact sheet 'Check if you're eligible for the R&D Tax Incentive' on the business. gov.au website.

Dealing with the bad bits

Here are the main disadvantages to assess when considering a company business structure:

>> A company is an expensive business structure to set up, operate and dissolve.

>> Company directors and/or shareholders may need to give personal guarantees in respect to company loans.

>> A company must comply with complex legal rules as set out under the Corporations Act and Income Tax Act.

>> Company details and accounts must be made available for public inspection.

>> Shareholders aren't the legal owners of assets that belong to a company.

Some of the taxation issues involved in operating as a company are

>> Company profits derived from various sources are ordinarily taxed as dividends when distributed to the shareholders (for more info, check out Taxation Ruling 'TR 2012/5' at www.ato. gov.au).

>> A return of capital to shareholders is not ordinarily treated as a dividend and isn't liable to tax, but you need to adjust

the cost base of your shares under the CGT provisions by the amount you receive. (For more info, check out Tax Office publication 'Personal investors guide to capital gains tax (NAT 4152)' and also refer to Chapter 11.)

>> A company can't stream profits to specific shareholders. Dividend distributions are made in proportion to the shares held by the shareholders.

>> A company can't distribute losses to its shareholders. Company losses are retained within the company structure. This means shareholders can't deduct these losses from other assessable income that they derive.

>> Under the CGT provisions, a company can't own a main residence that's normally exempt from tax. This rule applies even if a shareholder resides in the property.

>> A company can't gain a 50 per cent discount on capital gains that it may make on disposal of assets owned for more than 12 months (which is available to individuals). Refer to Chapter 11 for more.

>> A company must keep franking accounts to distribute franking credits to shareholders. For more info, check out the Tax Office fact sheet 'Franking account tax return and instructions' and also refer to Chapter 9.

>> A private company must satisfy a 50 per cent continuity ownership test to access a carry forward loss. To satisfy this test, more than 50 per cent of the shareholders must be present in the loss year through to the year the loss is recouped. If you fail this test, you get another opportunity to access the loss if you can satisfy an alternative test, called the 'predominantly similar business test', which checks whether the new owners are predominantly running a similar business to the one the previous owners were running. If this is the case, you can claim the carry forward loss. (For more info, see Tax Office fact sheet 'How to claim a tax loss' and check out the Companies section.)

>> Payments and loans (and forgiveness of debts) made by a private company to shareholders (or their associates) are deemed unfranked dividends unless the company enters into a commercial loan agreement before the company's tax return is lodged. For more details see Tax Office fact sheet 'Private company benefits – Division 7A dividends'. (***Note:***

The benchmark interest rate relevant to private company loan agreements for the 2023–24 tax year is 8.27 per cent.)

>> A private company that owns assets such as cars, boats and real estate must charge a commercial rate of rent if they're made available to their shareholders or associates. Otherwise, the Tax Office treats the benefit as a deemed dividend and, therefore, liable to tax.

>> A private company may be liable to pay fringe benefits tax if a shareholder/employee (for example, a company director) receives a benefit as a consequence of being an employee of that company — for instance, the use of a company car for private use. (See Chapter 16 for more information.)

>> Shares and/or options issued to employees under a company's employee share scheme may be concessionally taxed if certain conditions are satisfied. (See Chapter 13 for more information.)

>> Company directors may become personally liable for unpaid company tax debts such as unpaid PAYG withholding and employee super guarantee payments. (For more info, check out the Tax Office fact sheet 'Director penalties'.)

>> A company must reconcile net profit as calculated under commercial law with its taxable income as calculated under income tax law.

WARNING

The payment of director fees is ordinarily a tax-deductible expense. But if you're not definitely committed to paying them within a reasonable time period, there's a risk the Tax Office may disallow the deduction. For more info, see Taxpayer Alert 'TA 2011/4 Deductibility of unpaid directors fees'.

Trusting in Trusts

Running a business through a *trust* structure is similar to operating as a sole trader or partnership, with the notable differences being

>> The way you're taxed on income that the trust derives

>> The trustee's capacity to distribute trust net income to those beneficiaries who stand to benefit from the trust

As the *trustee* (the person in control), you're required to apply for a TFN (refer to Chapter 5) and lodge an annual trust return disclosing the net income of the trust (refer to Chapter 3). The trust isn't liable to pay tax on income derived. Tax is assessed to the trustee or beneficiaries if they're entitled to receive the trust net income.

The most popular types of trusts are family discretionary trusts where the trustee has discretion as to how trust net income is to be distributed to the beneficiaries, who are normally family members (refer to Chapter 7). For more info, check out fact sheet 'Trust' on business.gov.au.

Examining what's good about trusts

You may benefit from the advantages associated with running a business through a trust structure. The main ones are

» A trustee's assets may potentially be protected from creditors if correctly structured.

» As the trustee, you can have beneficial use and control of the trust property without actually owning it.

Some of the taxation issues involved in operating as a trust are

» The trustee can stream trust net income between family beneficiaries, which isn't the case with a sole trader or company.

» Distributions that flow through a discretionary trust retain their identity when distributed to beneficiaries. For example, if the trust pays you a capital gain or dividend, this payment is a capital gain or dividend in your hands. This situation isn't the case in a company structure because a company can only distribute dividends to shareholders.

» If your annual aggregated turnover (sales) is less than $5 million, a beneficiary can claim a 16 per cent small business income tax offset (capped at $1,000) on tax payable on a trust-structured business's income (see Chapter 13).

WARNING

If you're running a family trust, the Tax Office tends to closely monitor reimbursement payments within the trust structure — for example, scrutinising family trust distributions (payments) to low income (child) beneficiaries who then gift the amount back to the parent. This is to ensure all family trust distributions to family beneficiaries are properly made in accordance to Tax Office guidelines. For more info, check out Tax Office fact sheet 'Trust taxation – reimbursement agreement' on its website (www.ato.gov.au).

TECHNICAL
STUFF

If you want more info about trust income, see the Taxation Ruling 'TR 2012/D1 Income tax: meaning of income of the trust estate' and the Tax Office fact sheets 'Trusts' and 'Trust income'. See also Taxpayer Alert 'TA 2013/1 Arrangements to exploit mismatches between trust and taxable income'. You can find these resources online at the Tax Office website (www.ato.gov.au).

Checking out the evils of trusts

The main limitations associated with running a business through a trust structure are

>> Net trust distributions paid to minor beneficiaries (under 18 years) are liable to pay tax at the top marginal rate plus the Medicare levy (47 per cent). Refer to Chapters 5 and 7 for more.

>> The trustee can't distribute trust losses to beneficiaries as is the case with partnerships. Like companies, trust losses are retained within the trust structure and can be applied only against future trust income.

>> Trusts must undertake complex tests set out in the Tax Act in order to claim a trust loss (such as a '50% stake test', 'Business continuity test', 'pattern of distributions test', 'control test' and/or 'income injection test'. . .Ouch!).

CHECK
THE NET

To find out more about claiming a trust loss, visit the Tax Office website (www.ato.gov.au) and read the fact sheet 'How to apply the trust loss tests'.

>> If a trustee doesn't distribute trust net income, the trustee is liable to pay tax at the top marginal rate plus the Medicare levy (47 per cent) on the undistributed amount — refer to Chapter 7 for more. (This rule doesn't apply in a company structure.)

>> A trust can't own a main residence for CGT exemption purposes, even if the beneficiaries reside in the property.

>> A discretionary trust with a nil net income or a net loss isn't entitled to a refund of excess dividend franking credits (refer to Chapter 9).

>> Complications can arise if trust net income as calculated under trust law is different to the way you calculate it under income tax law.

>> Making certain trust distributions (such as capital gains and dividend franking credits) to your beneficiaries can get a little tricky because two different ways are available; namely, the 'Quantum view' and 'Proportionate view'.

TECHNICAL STUFF

If you run a small business, complications can arise if a trust doesn't distribute trust net income that a related private company beneficiary is entitled to receive. For more details, see Taxation Determination 'TD 2015/20' and Tax Office publication 'Unit trust arrangements and unpaid present entitlements' at www.ato.gov.au.

Chapter **13**

Starting a Business: On Your Mark! Get Set! Go!

After you set up your business structure, you need to familiarise yourself with all the legal obligations and responsibilities that come with running a business. Keep in mind that pulling out at a later date can prove very costly, especially if you plan to borrow a substantial amount of money and employ people to help run the business. In this chapter, I emphasise the legal requirements associated with running a business, and what you need to do to comply.

Getting the Show on the Road

As soon as you decide on your business entity (refer to Chapter 12), you need to attend to the admin involved in setting it up.

In the following sections, I cover just the basics. See *Small Business For Dummies*, 6th Australian Edition, by Veechi Curtis (Wiley) for more detailed information on setting up and running a business.

CHECK THE NET If you want to know more about setting up a business, also check out www.business.gov.au and their AusIndustry program (www.business.gov.au/grants-and-programs/ausindustry).

Obtaining a tax file number

Individuals, partnerships, companies, trusts and superannuation funds that derive assessable income must contact the Tax Office and apply for a tax file number (TFN). This number is required under the Income Tax Assessment Act and must be quoted to the Tax Office when lodging your annual income tax returns.

Applying for an Australian Business Number

You need to quote an Australian Business Number (ABN) whenever you conduct a business transaction. If you don't have an ABN or quote this number on your invoices, an amount of tax equivalent to 45 per cent may be withheld from payments made to you. The amount withheld is remitted to the Tax Office.

CHECK THE NET To apply for an ABN, visit Australian Business Register (www.abr.gov.au) and go to Apply for an ABN. See also Miscellaneous Taxation Ruling 'MT 2006/1' regarding entitlement to an ABN at www.ato.gov.au.

Registering for GST

You must register for GST and collect tax if your GST turnover is likely to be $75,000 or more (or $150,000 or more for non-profit entities). You can still register for GST if you're below the threshold and you intend to claim back GST credits. Claiming back your GST credits is the amount of GST that you were charged on your own purchases. For more details see Chapter 15.

CHECK THE NET To register for GST, check out Tax Office fact sheet 'Registering for GST' from the Tax Office website (www.ato.gov.au).

Getting to Grips with Record Keeping

The Tax Office requires you to keep proper records of your financial transactions, and more particularly your assessable income and allowable deductions. You may find it helpful to do a basic bookkeeping course so that you know how to balance the books and minimise headaches. Also check out *Bookkeeping For Dummies*, 3rd Australian Edition, by Veechi Curtis (Wiley).

WARNING

You may find yourself paying a truckload of money at the end of each month if you use an accountant to do all your record-keeping paperwork. Take the time to do it yourself — practice makes perfect!

TECHNICAL STUFF

The Tax Office fact sheet 'Record keeping for small business' provides information on business records that you need to keep (such as those mentioned in this section) and outlines a basic record-keeping system. Also check out fact sheet 'Tax reporting requirements' on the Western Australian Small Business Development Corporation website (smallbusiness.wa.gov.au) for a quick summary of what you need to do.

If you're registered for GST, you're obligated to prepare a business activity statement (BAS — normally on a quarterly basis) and disclose the amount of GST you collect from your customers, and to remit the net GST payable (online or by mail) to the Tax Office. To complete this step correctly, you need to keep a record of all your sales and purchases, especially your tax invoices. (For more details, see Chapter 15.) You also need to keep records to support the annual tax return that you lodge with the Tax Office.

The following are the types of records that you need to keep to make the Tax Office folk happy:

>> A record of all your sales (assessable income), such as bank deposit books and statements (including credit cards), cash register tapes and sales invoices (particularly tax invoices). *Note:* Under the PAYG withholding tax system, if your gross sales or fees are $4,000 or more per annum, you may need to pay tax on an ongoing basis — usually in quarterly instalments. The Tax Office notifies you if you need to follow this procedure.

>> A record of all your expenses (allowable deductions), such as cheque butts and bank statements, purchases and expenditure, particularly your tax invoices (see Chapter 15), motor vehicle expenses and records to do with how you calculate any expenditure that is private or domestic in nature.

>> Other records such as depreciation schedules, details of fringe benefits provided (see Chapter 16), lists of all your debtors and creditors, a register of your capital gains and capital losses, stocktakes (especially the valuation method you used) and superannuation records.

TIP

One of the great things about receiving regular bank statements is that they provide details of all your business transactions. Your accountant can use them when preparing your annual tax return to identify and summarise the revenue you receive and the expenditure you incur.

WARNING

For the purposes of the Tax Act, you're required to keep all business records (in the English language) for five years. Penalties may apply if you fail to comply with this legal requirement.

Taking on Employees

So, business is booming and you intend to employ people in your business on a full-time, part-time or casual basis. You need to comply with the following taxation and superannuation obligations when you start employing.

Under the PAYG withholding tax system, you're required to register and withhold the prescribed amount of tax from your employees' pay and forward the amounts withheld to the Tax Office at regular intervals. A new employee needs to complete a TFN 'Withholding declaration (NAT 3093)' form and this must be forwarded to the Tax Office within 14 days of commencing employment. This declaration covers payments in respect of work and services performed and payments of superannuation benefits. For more details, see the Tax Office fact sheet 'PAYG withholding'.

CHECK THE NET

To calculate the amount of tax you need to withhold from your employees' pay, visit the Tax Office website (www.ato.gov.au) and check out the fact sheet 'Tax withheld calculator'.

If you provide a fringe benefit to an employee (for example, you make a car that you own or lease available for the private use of an employee), you're liable to pay fringe benefits tax on the taxable value of the benefit provided. (See Chapter 16 for more on this tax.)

You must make super guarantee contributions (SG) on behalf of eligible employees to a complying superannuation fund or retirement savings account. (At the time of writing, these contributions are 11 per cent of the employee's gross pay.) Payments are made on a quarterly basis (namely, by 28 October, 28 January, 28 April and 28 July) and you're liable to pay a superannuation guarantee charge if you fail to meet your statutory obligations. (*Note:* From 1 July 2026 the SG amount must be paid at the same time employees are paid salary and wages.)

You need to give new employees a 'Superannuation standard choice form (NAT 13080)' to complete within 28 days of commencing employment, which you can get from the Tax Office. If an employee has no particular preference, you can choose a default superannuation fund — commonly known as 'MySuper'.

The super contributions that you make on behalf of eligible employees are tax-deductible expenses. For info about choosing a super fund, check out the fact sheet 'Choosing a super fund' on the moneysmart.gov.au website. See also fact sheet 'Superannuation' on the business.gov.au website.

REMEMBER

Eligible employees can nominate a super fund to accept employer super guarantee contributions. If you run a small business and have fewer than 20 employees, you can make a payment electronically to one single location (commonly known as the 'SuperStream'). This is a free small business superannuation clearing house service administered by the Australian Taxation Office. For more details see Tax Office fact sheet 'Small Business Superannuation Clearing House'.

TIP

You need to set up a super fund (commonly known as a *default fund*) to make super guarantee contributions on behalf of your employees. You can also contribute on your own behalf. Employer-nominated super funds must offer a minimum level of life insurance cover for members.

If you intend to employ an associated person (for example, a relative such as your spouse or child), make sure you pay this person a commercially acceptable salary for work provided. The Tax Office has the authority to reduce your claim for a tax deduction (if excessive) to an amount that it considers to be reasonable. (See Tax Office fact sheet '44 Payments to associated persons'.)

If your business entity utilises a company structure, any shares and/or options that you issue to employees under an employee share scheme are concessionally taxed if you satisfy certain conditions. This is a great way to reward loyal employees and attract new employees to your company, because it effectively makes them part-owners of the business. For more information on this, see the Tax Office fact sheet 'Employee share schemes'.

TIP

Recreational and child-minding facilities, and the provision of amenities such as tea-making or coffee-making facilities that are located on your business premises for the benefit of your employees are exempt from fringe benefits tax (FBT). For more details see Chapter 16. Also check out the Tax Office publication 'Fringe benefits tax: a guide for employers', and particularly Chapter 20 in this guide.

TIP

Check out fact sheet 'Hiring employees checklist' on the business.gov.au website for a quick summary of what you need to do when hiring employees, particularly your tax and super obligations.

Examining Tax Concessions for Small Business

Surprise! Your business may be entitled to freebies that the federal government hands out. You usually find them popping up around election time or the last May Budget before the next federal election.

If you operate a small or medium business, you may be eligible to pick and choose from a number of tax concessions. The tax concessions that you can access will depend on your annual turnover (sales).

The tax concessions you may be able to access include

>> **Accounting for GST on a cash basis:** This concession means you need only to account for GST when you receive a cash payment from your customers. Who's eligible? Small businesses with annual turnover (sales) of less than $10 million. (For more details, see Chapter 15 and more particularly 'Case Study: Preparing a BAS'.)

>> **Annual apportionment of GST input tax credits:** This concession applies when you purchase something partly for business and partly for private use. Under this concession, you can make an annual private apportionment election. This election means you don't need to estimate the private portion when making a GST claim. You need only make one single adjustment at the end of the financial year. Small businesses with annual turnover less than $10 million are eligible.

>> **Digital technology expenditure:** You can claim an extra 20 per cent (or 120 per cent in total) on certain expenditure you incur on improving your business's digital technology (such as portable payment devices, cyber security systems and cloud-based services — capped at $100,000). This also applies to external training courses for your employees, and relates to expenditure you incur between 29 March 2022 and 30 June 2024. Businesses with annual turnover (sales) less than $50 million are eligible.

>> **Immediate deductions for certain prepaid business expenses:** You can immediately claim certain prepaid expenses, instead of having to apportion them over the period to which they relate; for example, if you make a prepayment of rent or interest during the financial year that isn't due until the next financial year. For more info, check out Tax Office fact sheet 'Deductions for prepaid expenses'. Businesses with annual turnover (sales) less than $50 million are eligible.

>> **Instant asset write-off:** Small businesses with annual turnover (sales) less than $10 million can claim an instant asset write off for each depreciable asset that cost less than $20,000. The asset will need to be first used or installed ready for use between 1 July 2023 and 30 June 2024.

>> **Paying GST by instalments:** This concession gives you the option to pay or claim GST on an instalment basis (for example, every three months rather than monthly). Small businesses with annual turnover (sales) of less than $10 million are eligible.

>> **Simplified trading stock rules:** The Tax Act stipulates that you can use cost price, market selling value or replacement value to value your trading stock. However, under the simplified trading stock rules, you can use a different way to value your trading stock. Under this rule, you don't need to do a stocktake or make any adjustments if your stock valuations are unlikely to vary by more than $5,000 each year, which means your closing stock valuations are deemed to be the same as your opening stock valuations. Small businesses with annual turnover (sales) less than $50 million are eligible.

>> **Small business CGT concessions:** You can consider four concessions: CGT 15-year asset exemption, CGT 50 per cent active asset reduction, CGT retirement exemption and CGT rollover concession. These concessions allow you to reduce or exempt capital gains you may make on disposal of your active business assets. I discuss this in more detail in Chapter 17. Small businesses with an annual turnover (sales) less than $2 million are eligible.

>> **Small Business Energy Incentive:** Small businesses with annual turnover (sales) of less than $50 million are eligible to claim an additional 20 per cent 'bonus' tax deduction that supports electrification and more efficient use of energy. It applies to eligible assets such as electrifying heating and cooling systems, to energy saving white good upgrades and installing batteries and heat pumps. The asset will need to be first used or installed ready for use between 1 July 2023 and 30 June 2024. You can claim up to $100,000 for this type of expenditure plus the additional bonus tax deduction capped at a maximum $20,000 ($100,000 × 20 per cent = $20,000).

>> **Small business income tax offset:** If you run a small unincorporated business (sole trader, partnership or trust), you can claim a 16 per cent tax offset (capped at $1,000 per annum) off your tax bill. For example, if your business tax bill is $12,000, you can claim a $1,000 tax offset. ($12,000 × 16 per cent = $1,920; however, the tax offset is up

to a maximum of $1,000.) Small businesses with annual turnover (sales) less than $5 million are eligible.

>> **Small business simplified depreciation pool:** Under this concession, you can pool assets that cost $20,000 or more and depreciate them at the rate of 15 per cent in the first year and 30 per cent each year after the first year. Small businesses with annual turnover (sales) less than $10 million are eligible.

If you're contemplating using the small business concessions, discuss the matter with your accountant and/or tax agent before you commence business and before deciding whether to adopt some or all of the concessions.

REMEMBER

To qualify for these small business concessions, you need to prove that you're running a fair dinkum business (for instance, that you have an ABN and lodge ongoing business activity statements).

CHECK
THE NET

For a discussion on tax concessions for small business, visit the Tax Office website (www.ato.gov.au) and check out fact sheet 'Concessions for eligible businesses'. See also Chapters 15, 16 and 17.

To help you to comply with the taxation and superannuation obligations associated with running a small business, see the fact sheets 'GST', 'Fringe benefits tax' and 'Tax basics for small business video series' from the Tax Office website (www.ato.gov.au).

Choosing How You Recognise Your Income

I once saw a sign in a shop in outback Australia that read: 'In God we trust. Everyone else pays cash'. When you operate a business, you need to be assured that your customers are going to pay you for the goods you sell them and/or services you perform. Otherwise, you can quickly find yourself in financial difficulty. You also need to know how you recognise income from your business transactions.

When you run a business, you need to decide at what point in time you recognise the profits you make for income tax purposes and, more particularly, how those profits need to be calculated.

Under Australian income tax law, you can run your business accounts in one of two ways:

>> **Cash or receipts basis:** Under the cash or receipts basis, income is recognised only when a payment is actually received. Put simply: No dough, no show!

>> **Accruals or earnings basis:** The accruals or earnings basis takes into account money due but not yet paid to you. You have a legal right to demand payment, such as when you invoice a customer for the services you have rendered. If you run a business and sell trading stock, income is ordinarily recognised when you invoice your customers and not when the money is received. This means you need to keep an account of all your debtors and creditors and do a lot of bookkeeping.

The way you calculate and recognise income for tax purposes, therefore, varies in accordance with the accounting basis you use. Both methods aren't alternatives that you can choose whenever you feel like it, and you can't vary the basis you select from year to year. The correct basis of accounting for income ultimately depends on its actual appropriateness and whether in the circumstances of the case it is calculated to give a true indication of your income.

Generally, the cash or receipts basis is considered the appropriate method to use if you run a small business, and more particularly a personal services business, where you're responsible for the work you do and employ a few people (for example, you run a small legal, accounting or medical practice).

On the other hand, the accruals or earnings basis would be the appropriate method to use if you run a business on a large scale and you employ many people to service your customers. If you're not sure which method to choose, you can seek professional advice from a tax accountant. (See also Taxation Rulings 'TR 98/1 Income tax: determination of income; receipts versus earnings' and 'TR 93/11 Income tax: assessability of income on an accruals basis: when professional fees are derived'. See also Tax Office fact sheet 'Accounting methods for business income'.)

Here are some legal principles that you need to know about before you make your decision:

>> Fees paid in advance for work not yet commenced aren't assessable income in the year of receipt and aren't derived until they're earned (for example, until you have a legal right to demand payment for the work you performed) where such advance payments are potentially refundable. (See *Arthur Murray (NSW) Pty Ltd v FC of T (1965)* 114 CLR 314 online in Appendix B — www.dummies.com/go/taxforaustraliansfd.)

>> Under the accruals or earnings basis of accounting for income, the Tax Office points out in Taxation Ruling 'TR 93/11' that professional fees are normally derived 'when a recoverable debt is created such that the taxpayer is not obliged to take any further steps before becoming entitled to payment'.

Taking Stock of Things

When you're running a business, you need to hold sufficient trading stock in your warehouse, store or garage to sell to your prospective customers. Unfortunately, at the end of the financial year, you need to count all the stock you have on hand and put a value on each item to verify the accuracy of your accounting records and to check the closing value of stock on hand for taxation purposes.

FINDING OUT WHETHER YOUR HOBBY IS A BUSINESS

Any proceeds from a hobby or pastime are normally exempt from tax. However, if your output increases significantly you may, in fact, be running a business. If you contact the Tax Office for some friendly advice, the types of questions staff ask are

• Do you have a business plan?

• Do you use specialised knowledge or skills?

(continued)

(continued)

- How much capital have you invested in the activity?
- How much time do you spend on the activity?
- Do you give quotes and supply invoices?
- Do you advertise?

Although you may be considered to be running a business under commercial law, this may not be the case under tax law. A number of technical tests are used to establish whether you're running a fair dinkum business.

Some of the key tests you need to satisfy are as follows:

- Do your activities have a significant commercial purpose?
- Do you have a genuine intention to carry on a business?
- Do you have the intention to make a profit (or is it likely to be profitable)?
- Do you keep proper records?
- Are you doing this on a regular basis?
- Are your activities similar to what other people do in your industry?
- Are your activities planned and carried out in a businesslike manner with a view to making a profit?

The greater the time you devote to the job and the more money you make, the greater the chance that you're running a business. If you're not sure, seek advice from a qualified accountant or registered tax agent, because you may quickly find yourself with one big headache if things go wrong.

See also the Tax Office fact sheet 'Business or hobby?' at www.ato. gov.au and fact sheet 'Difference between a business and a hobby' at business.gov.au.

By the way, if you have trading stock that's currently in-transit, you can't count it as trading stock 'on hand' unless you have a legal right to sell the stock to someone else before it arrives in your warehouse, store or garage. Further, if you make prepayments for trading stock in one financial year and they're not delivered until the next financial year, you can't claim a tax deduction until the stock is 'on hand'.

Section 70–10 of the *Income Tax Assessment Act 1997* defines trading stock as:

> '(a) anything produced, manufactured or acquired that is held for the purposes of manufacture, sale or exchange in the ordinary course of running a business; and (b) live stock.'

The following are things you need to do to complete your stocktake:

>> List all the items of trading stock that you have on hand.

>> Put a value on each item that you have on hand.

>> Record the name of the person who's doing the stocktake.

>> Record the date the stocktake takes place.

>> Record the method you used to value your trading stock.

One of the concessions for small businesses is that if the value of your trading stock hasn't changed by more than $5,000 over the year, you don't have to do a stocktake. This concession may be worth considering — it can save you a lot of time and money.

Valuing your trading stock

At the end of each financial year, you need to count your trading stock when you calculate your taxable income. You must keep accurate records, such as invoices of your purchases. A stocktake is done to verify the accuracy of your record-keeping obligations.

The Tax Act sets out three methods that you can use to value your trading stock:

>> **Cost price:** This valuation method is used most in practice. The cost of an item of stock is normally the price you paid to acquire it plus any costs you incur to bring the stock to your place of business.

>> **Market selling value:** This valuation method is the current market value of stock that you sell to your customers.

>> **Replacement value:** This method is the cost to replace (buy) an item of stock on the last day of trading at the end of the financial year.

Understanding the nitty gritty of trading stock

Each financial year, you can change the way you value your trading stock. However, one important rule that you must follow is that the closing value of your trading stock on hand at the end of the financial year must be the same as the opening value of your trading stock on hand at the beginning of the next financial year. For example, if the closing value on 30 June was $25,000, the opening value on 1 July must also be $25,000.

If the value of your closing trading stock (for example, $30,000) is greater than the value of your opening trading stock (for instance, $27,000), the excess ($3,000) is included as part of your assessable income. On the other hand, if the opening value of your trading stock is greater than the closing value of your trading stock, the difference is allowed as a tax deduction. The increase or decrease in the value of trading stock must be based on the records you keep.

If you're running a business, the following items are trading stock for the purposes of the Tax Act, and must be taken into account when you calculate your taxable income:

>> Land if you're a land dealer

>> Live stock (for instance, milking cows) if you're a farmer running a primary production business (see Chapter 14)

>> Packaging items (such as containers and labels) if you're running a packaging business

>> Shares if you're a share trader (refer to Chapter 9)

>> Work in progress if you're a manufacturer

But the following items aren't trading stock for tax purposes:

>> Animals used as working beasts if you're not running a primary production business

>> Consumables (such as cleaning agents) used in manufacturing trading stock

>> Hire or rental of certain goods (for instance, you run a DVD-lending business), because they're not held for manufacture, sale or exchange

>> Spare parts held by a manufacturer for repairs or maintenance to plant and equipment

>> Standing or growing crops, timber or fruit — until they're harvested, felled or picked

>> Work in progress if you're running an accounting practice

TECHNICAL
STUFF

For further help, check out Tax Office fact sheets 'Accounting for business trading stock' and 'General trading stock rules' on the Tax Office website (www.ato.gov.au).

TIP

If you find you've got trading stock on hand that you consider obsolete (such as due to a change in fashion) or that any other special circumstances apply (for example, you no longer sell it), you can elect to value your trading stock below the cost price, market selling value or replacement value. The Tax Office has released Taxation Ruling 'TR 93/23', which deals with the valuation of trading stock subject to obsolescence or other special circumstances.

WARNING

If goods are taken from trading stock for personal use (for instance, you run a restaurant and use some of the food for personal use rather than buy the food at the supermarket), the value must be taken into account when calculating your assessable income. If you don't keep records, the Tax Office has issued guidelines of acceptable estimates of trading stock taken for private use by sole traders and partners in a partnership (for more details, see Tax Office fact sheet 'Using trading stock for private purposes').

TIP

The cost of moving trading stock from one business location to another business location is ordinarily a tax-deductible expense.

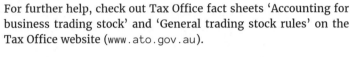

TAXING MATTERS FOR MANUFACTURERS

If you're running a manufacturing business, you're required to use the absorption cost method to value your goods and work in progress. Because this method is a very complex issue (and the entire process can turn into a messy affair if you don't understand what you're doing), your best option is to consult your accountant or tax agent.

(continued)

(continued)

How messy? According to the Tax Office, the cost price of manufactured trading stock on hand at the end of the year includes not just the material and direct labour costs that went into producing the product, but also an appropriate proportion of production overhead costs. And you have to weigh the same factors when adding up how much your work in progress is worth too. What? Don't have that all handy? That's why you should call in the experts to get things right and keep things tidy.

Planning Ahead: Business Succession Planning

When you run a small business, you need to plan ahead. A good business succession plan involves choosing an appropriate structure to run your business (refer to Chapter 12), reducing the impact of CGT if you sell the business, and utilising the CGT small business concessions, particularly the 15-year asset exemption provisions (see Chapter 17).

Business succession planning can be a complex issue, so you're best to seek advice from a qualified tax accountant or solicitor.

CHECK THE NET

If you want to know more about developing a business succession plan, visit the Business Victoria website (www.business.vic.gov.au) and search for 'Find a buyer or successor for your business'. See also Tax Office fact sheet 'Prepare an exit strategy' (at www.ato.gov.au).

Chapter **14**

Reducing Your Small Business Tax Bill

When you run a business, logic dictates that if more money is coming in than is going out, then you're ahead. However, if more of the hard-earned stuff is going out than coming in, you could quickly find yourself with one big headache. Under these circumstances, two options are available to you: You can either seek professional advice, or simply shut up shop for good and go fishing!

Expenditure that you incur in earning business income may qualify for a tax deduction. In this chapter, I guide you through the legal ways you can claim a tax deduction and the different types of expenditure you can claim — all of which is going to help keep your business in the black.

Understanding the Rules and What You Can Claim

You can use two methods to find out what is a tax-deductible expense: Get the Tax Office to compile a comprehensive list of every conceivable item you're likely to incur, or use a general deduction formula (referred to as the *general deduction provisions*). If you choose the former option, you need to constantly thumb through a pile of books equivalent in size to your local telephone book — remember those? So, reason concludes that the alternative method has more merit.

Under the general deduction provisions, you can deduct from your assessable income any loss or outgoing that is necessarily incurred in carrying on a business for the purpose of gaining or producing your assessable income. A direct connection must exist between the expenditure and earning your assessable income, and you must incur the expenditure in the course of deriving your assessable income. I discuss the general deduction provisions in Chapter 2.

The following business expenses are examples of the types of loss and outgoing that qualify for a tax deduction:

>> Advertising expenses and costs from recruiting employees

>> Car expenses

>> Cost of providing fringe benefits to employees

>> Depreciation and trading stock

>> Entertainment expenses to help promote or advertise your business, goods or services to the public (for instance, at a public exhibition)

>> Insurance premiums rates and land taxes

>> Interest on borrowings and borrowing expenses, and bad debts

>> Internet and telephone costs

>> Legal expenses and tax-related expenses

>> Operating a commercial website

>> Rent or lease of your business premises

>> Repairs and maintenance to your business premises

>> Salary or wages and super contributions

WARNING

You can't ordinarily claim entertainment expenses (such as entertaining business clients at 'business lunches' and the cost of recreational club memberships), and you can't claim a deduction if you incur a penalty (such as a car parking fine or speeding fine) imposed under an Australian law, foreign law or by a court.

You can't ordinarily claim an immediate deduction for prepaid expenses (for instance, lease payments) that's not less than $1,000 and covers an eligible service period that exceeds 12 months. You need to apportion the prepaid expense over the relevant period or over 10 years (whichever is less). See Tax Office fact sheet 'Deductions for prepaid expenses' and Taxation Determination 'TD 93/118' for more details at www.ato.gov.au. (*Note:* Different rules will apply if you use the small business provisions — refer to Chapter 13.)

You may also find the three following Tax Office publications helpful: 'Tax and small business', 'Deductions for small business' and 'Super for employers'. Also check out the fact sheet 'Income tax for business' on the business.gov.au website for a quick overview of the tax issues associated with running a small business.

Ordinarily, cash discounts given to customers for prompt payments (for example, within 30 days) can be deducted in determining the gross profit of a retailer.

Every time you open your wallet or purse to pay a bill, ask yourself why you're paying this amount. If the payment is part of the cost of running your business operations and is similar in nature to the expenses mentioned earlier, your bill is likely to be an allowable deduction. If no direct link exists (for example, you purchase tickets to the footy or you pay your dentist bill), the bills are most likely private or domestic in nature and, therefore, not tax deductible.

If you purchase a car for business use, a car depreciation limit cuts in, in respect of the amount of depreciation you can claim. For the 2023–24 tax year, the car depreciation cost price limit is $68,108. This rule means that you can't claim depreciation for amounts that exceed this limit. For example, if you pay $80,000 for a car, the cost price limit for depreciation purposes is $68,108.

If you buy a car and the cost is above a luxury car tax (LCT) threshold, less GST, you could be liable to pay 33 per cent tax in respect of the amount that exceeds the threshold. For the 2023–24 tax year, the LCT threshold is $89,332 for fuel-efficient cars and $76,950 for other cars.

The federal and state governments have introduced incentives (such as rebates, stamp duty and registration discounts, and FBT exemptions) to encourage you to buy eco-friendly electric vehicles below a certain price. With respect to FBT, for example, if the price is below the $89,332 luxury car threshold for fuel-efficient vehicles, it'll be exempt from FBT. *Note:* You'll need to include the value of this exempt benefit in the calculation of an employee's reportable fringe benefits amount. See Tax Office fact sheet 'Electric cars exemption' from the Tax Office website (www.ato.gov.au), and visit business.gov.au for more details.

You can't claim a tax deduction if the expenditure is capital in nature. Unfortunately, this is a very difficult part of the law to come to terms with. While a library full of books that have examined this matter in much detail may interest (or bore) you, a general rule to remember is this: Expenditure associated with establishing, replacing, enlarging, protecting or improving the business structure is considered to be capital in nature, and distinct from the day-to-day operating expenses of running your business. (Refer to Chapter 2 for more information.) This rule also applies to expenses associated with selling your business.

Some capital expenses may be deductible over a period of time (for example, capital improvements you make to an income-producing property), while some may be deductible outright under a specific provision (for example, under the small business concessions 'instant asset write-off' — refer to Chapter 13 for more info). Because this capital concept is a complex issue, you're best to seek professional advice if you're not sure what to do.

Getting Specific with Problematic Deductions

You can claim certain specific deductions. When you examine these deductions, you find that they contain their own rules that you need to satisfy before you can claim a tax deduction.

Writing off your depreciating assets

You can claim a depreciation deduction if you hold depreciating assets that have a relevant connection with running your business that you use to derive your assessable income; simpler depreciation rules apply if you run a small business (refer to Chapter 13).

A *depreciating asset* (such as plant and equipment, furnishings, motor vehicles and electrical tools) is an asset that has a limited effective life and can reasonably be expected to decline in value (due to constant use) over the time you use it to derive your assessable income. To work out an item's effective life, you can use your own estimate or an estimate as determined by the Tax Office. (The start time of a depreciating asset is when you first use it, or have it installed ready for use — it's unpacked, set up and ready to rock'n'roll — for any purpose.)

The cost of a depreciating asset can include the purchase price plus transport costs to bring the depreciating asset to your business premises, as well as installation costs.

Computer software costing more than $300 is depreciable over a period of 2.5 years at the rate of 40 per cent per annum. But if the cost is $300 or less, you can claim the amount outright.

WARNING

The cost of relocating your depreciating assets from one business location to another business location is considered to be capital in nature and not deductible. But the expense can be included as part of the cost of a depreciating asset.

TIP

Certain items aren't able to be depreciated. The main ones are land, an item of trading stock, certain intangible assets (for example, goodwill) and buildings (unless they form an integral part of the manufacturing process). *Note:* Buildings may qualify for a tax deduction under the capital works provisions (refer to Chapter 10).

How you claim a depreciation deduction is discussed in detail in Chapter 10. (For more info, also check out Tax Office fact sheet 'Depreciation and capital expenses and allowances'.)

Dealing with bad debts

Unfortunately, when you run a business you're going to come across the odd occasion where customers don't pay you for the services you provide. Under these circumstances, you can either call in a 'heavy' (a debt collector) to get the money or you can take legal action. If your chance of getting the money is really grim, you can write off the debt as bad and claim a tax deduction.

However, getting to that point isn't as simple as it may seem at first glance, because you have to satisfy a number of technical conditions.

Under Australian income tax law, four key tests (conditions) must be present for you to claim a deduction for bad debts:

>> A debt must be in existence.

>> The debt must be bad rather than merely doubtful.

>> The debt must've been included in your assessable income for the income year or for an earlier income year (which means that if you use the cash or receipts basis — refer to Chapter 13 — you can't claim a bad debt).

>> You must write off that debt as bad in the income year.

To claim a deduction for bad debts, you must physically write off the debt as bad (for example, in your accounting records you write a note as to why you consider the debt is bad). For more info see Taxation Ruling 'TR 92/18 Income tax: bad debts' and Tax Office fact sheet 'Deductions for unrecoverable income (bad debts)'.

TIP

You can claim a tax deduction only for bad debts that are still in existence at the time you write them off. The reason being that a debt can't be written off as bad after it ceases to exist (for example, because the debt has been settled, compromised, extinguished or assigned).

WARNING

The way you account for bad debts depends on whether you elected to use the cash or receipts basis or the accruals or earnings basis to recognise your revenue. For more details on this, refer to Chapter 13.

Paying interest on borrowings

A major business expense you're likely to incur is interest on borrowings — you need money to make money! Borrowing money is normally required to fund the acquisition of income-producing assets and your ongoing business operations. Interest payable on business borrowings is a tax-deductible expense. However, you have to obey certain rules before you can claim a tax deduction.

Examining the purpose (or use) of the loan

Interest payable on borrowings is a tax-deductible expense if the purpose (or use) of the loan is to earn assessable income (for example, business profits) or to acquire an income-producing asset (such as your business premises, trading stock, and plant and equipment). To qualify for a tax deduction, a direct connection must exist between the expenditure and earning your assessable income.

On the other hand, if the purpose (or use) of the loan is to buy an asset that doesn't generate revenue (for example, you purchase your main residence), the interest isn't tax deductible. Further, if just part of the loan is for the purpose of deriving assessable income, under these circumstances you're entitled to just a part deduction. For example, if you purchase a computer for your business and you use it only 50 per cent of the time for business purposes, you can claim only 50 per cent of the interest you incur as a tax deduction.

REMEMBER

If you use an asset partly for business purposes and partly for private use, you need to keep a record of how the use was calculated.

A point to keep in mind if you intend to borrow money is that the security or collateral you offer to secure a business loan has no relevance to whether you can claim a tax deduction. For example, whether or not you offer as security a non-income-producing property such as your main residence to obtain a business loan is irrelevant.

Interesting deductions: When interest is and isn't deductible

You're also entitled to a deduction on interest payable on loans used to finance the purchase of shares that pay dividends.

Interest isn't tax deductible in the following circumstances:

>> Partners aren't entitled to a deduction for interest on borrowings to pay personal income tax (see Taxation Determination 'TD 2000/24').

>> Interest on money borrowed to make non-concessional superannuation contributions.

>> Interest incurred on a loan taken out after the cessation of a business (see ATO Interpretative Decision 'ID 2002/1092').

>> Interest incurred by an individual taxpayer on a loan taken out in order to pay a tax debt (see ATO Interpretative Decision 'ID 2002/607').

Borrowing expenses

When you borrow money from a financial institution, you may incur borrowing expenses such as loan establishment fees, mortgage insurance and legal fees. If the purpose (or use) of the loan is to earn assessable income, the costs associated with borrowing are tax deductible. In most cases, you need to spread the expenditure you incur over the period of the loan. If your borrowing costs are $100 or less, you can claim the amount outright. Borrowing costs that exceed $100 need to be spread over the period of the loan or over five years if the period is more than five years.

The following formula is used to apportion your annual tax deductions for a borrowing expense:

$$\text{Borrowing costs} \times \frac{\text{Period in year}}{\text{Total period of loan (maximum 5 years)}}$$

If you take out a loan part way through the financial year, you're entitled to just a partial deduction in the first year.

WARNING

CASE STUDY: CLAIMING A BORROWING EXPENSE

On 1 September 2023, Masato, who is a sole trader running a retail business, incurred $5,000 borrowing costs in respect of a loan he took out to finance the purchase of his business premises. The period of the loan is ten years. Because the purpose (or use) of the loan is to buy an income-producing asset, Masato can spread the $5,000 borrowing costs over the shortest of either the period of the loan (ten years) or five years. Because the loan he takes out exceeds five years, Masato needs to apportion the $5,000 borrowing expenses over a five-year period (1,826 days), as shown here.

Year	
2024	$830 (303 days ÷ 1,826 days × $5,000)
2025	$1,000
2026	$1,000
2027	$1,000
2028	$1,000
2029	$170 (being the balance of deduction)

Losing money by theft

When you run a business, you may have money stolen from you in various ways. However, you may be able to qualify for some tax relief to help offset your loss.

To qualify for a tax deduction under the Tax Act, a loss caused by theft, stealing, embezzlement, larceny, defalcation (misappropriation by a trustee) or misappropriation by your employee or agent is deductible only if the money was previously included in your assessable income for the income year or for an earlier income year. For example, if your auditor finds that one of your employees stole business takings that are included as part of your assessable income in a previous tax year, the loss is a tax-deductible expense.

TIP

If you can't claim a tax deduction under the provision that allows you to claim a deduction for loss by theft, you can have another go under the general deduction provisions (refer to the section 'Understanding the Rules: What Can I Claim?' earlier in this chapter). You need to demonstrate that a direct or necessary connection exists between your business activities and the loss you incur. You may need to talk this matter over with a tax agent because this issue can be a rather tricky one to deal with.

Getting a legal opinion: Legal costs

When you run a business, you may need to consult a lawyer about various legal issues associated with running your business. This need for referral can arise when dealing with complex tax law matters and having to comply with all the red tape that goes with running a business.

Legal expenses associated with running your business are tax deductible, provided they're not capital, private or domestic in nature. You can also claim specific types of deductible legal expenses, such as those relating to tax, lease documents, borrowing (refer to the section 'Borrowing expenses', earlier in the chapter), or discharging a mortgage.

Unfortunately, a major dilemma is whether your legal costs are revenue in nature and deductible, or whether they're capital, private or domestic in nature and not deductible. The answer depends on why you had to seek legal advice.

REMEMBER

If the nature or character of the legal expenses is part of your day-to-day activities associated with running your business, they're most likely tax deductible. On the other hand, if they relate to the business structure (such as protecting the business entity), they're capital in nature and, therefore, not tax deductible. At the time you seek legal advice, checking with the person giving you advice whether the bill you receive is tax deductible always pays.

Getting tax help: Tax-related expenses

Unfortunately, trying to understand and comply with Australian income tax law can be mind-boggling. The good news is if you seek the services of a recognised tax adviser (registered tax agent or a legal practitioner) to help you manage your tax affairs, the expenditure you incur is normally tax deductible. When you seek the advice of professionals, they generally tell you whether you can claim a tax deduction for the advice they give you.

The types of tax-related expenses you can claim are

>> Assistance with a tax audit (refer to Chapter 4)

>> Costs incurred to prepare your individual tax return

>> General tax advice for the purposes of complying with the Tax Act

>> Help you received to complete your business activity statement (see Chapter 15)

>> Lodgement of an objection and appeal against an assessment notice (refer to Chapter 4)

Stamping a lease: Lease document expenses

You can claim a tax deduction for expenditure you incur for preparing, registering or stamping a property lease, or an assignment or surrender of a property lease, provided you use the property for earning assessable income.

Discharging the mortgage

You can deduct expenditure you incur to discharge a mortgage that you give as security for the repayment of money you borrow, provided the money you borrow is used to derive assessable income. For example, if you use your property as collateral to secure a business loan that you no longer need and you incur a fee to discharge the mortgage, you can deduct the expenditure.

Claiming a superannuation deduction

All individuals (employees, self-employed and retirees) up to age 74 can claim a tax deduction for personal super contributions up to their concessional cap amount (at the time of writing, $27,500). Concessional contributions can include employer contributions and contributions you make under a salary sacrifice arrangement. But you'll need to satisfy a work test if you are aged between 67 and 74 years of age. To satisfy this test you'll need to work at least 40 hours over 30 consecutive days. (*Note:* Concessional contributions can't be accepted if you're aged 75 years or over.)

REMEMBER

If you want to claim a tax deduction for your super contributions, you must notify the trustee of your super fund and the trustee must acknowledge your request and the amount you're claiming. For more details see Tax Office fact sheet 'Personal super contributions' particularly the section 'Claiming deductions for personal super contributions'.

WARNING

If you earn more than $250,000 and you make a concessional contribution to a complying super fund, the superannuation contribution rate of tax payable increases from 15 per cent to 30 per cent. Either you or your super fund can pay the additional 15 per cent contributions tax. For more details visit the Tax Office website (www.ato.gov.au) and check out fact sheet 'Division 293 tax on concessional contributions by high-income earners'.

Using a service entity: Claiming for service fees

If you set up a service entity to provide certain services (such as equipment, administrative services, staff and office premises) to an associated professional practice or other business entity, make sure that the service fees you charge are commercially realistic and reasonable. If they're grossly excessive, the Tax Office folk may disallow a tax deduction to the associated professional practice or business entity utilising the services provided.

The Tax Office has issued guidelines for determining whether certain charge rates are reasonable. For more details see the Tax Office fact sheet 'Your service entity arrangements'. You can find it online on the Tax Office website: www.ato.gov.au.

Running a primary production business

If you're a primary producer (for instance, you're a farmer or catch fish for a living), you may be eligible to claim certain tax concessions specifically relating to running a primary production business (such as valuing livestock, water facility expenditure, accelerated depreciation, landcare operations expenditure, taxing abnormal receipts, and tax averaging your income and tax payable). For more details see Tax Office fact sheets 'Information for primary producers', 'Primary production depreciating assets', 'Farm management deposits scheme' and 'Primary production activities'. You can find them online at the Tax Office website (www.ato.gov.au).

Losing money: Business losses

When you run a business, you run the risk of incurring business losses. This scenario can arise while you build up your business or if you run it on a small scale. Ordinarily, you can offset business losses against other assessable income you earn, such as employment income, interest, dividends or rent. If you don't have any other income, you can carry forward your business losses for an indefinite period and offset them against your future income. *Note:* Prior year business losses are ordinarily deductible against your future income in the order you incur them.

Special rules apply for claiming business losses incurred by a sole trader or partnership. Under the non-commercial losses provisions, you may be denied from offsetting your business losses against other assessable income you earn. This rule is an anti-avoidance provision to stop people who don't operate a commercial business (for example, running a hobby type business) from accessing those losses.

In order to claim a business tax loss, you need to pass at least one of the following four technical tests:

>> **Assessable income test:** Under this test, you need to be earning at least $20,000 assessable income (such as gross earnings and capital gains) from your business activities.

>> **Other assets test:** Under this test, you need to use other assets (other than motor vehicles) in excess of $100,000 on a continuing basis.

>> **Profits test:** Under this test, your activity must have resulted in taxable income in at least three out of the last five years (including the current financial year).

>> **Real property test:** Under this test, you need to have property (such as land and buildings) worth at least $500,000.

The good news is you can carry forward and utilise these losses when you finally satisfy one of these tests. If you find yourself in this position, you're best to seek advice from a qualified accountant or tax agent.

WARNING

An income test applies to restrict high-income earners from claiming a tax deduction for business losses. If your adjusted taxable income is more than $250,000 and you incur losses from non-commercial business activities, you can't offset those losses from your salary and wages and other income you derive. These losses are quarantined and you can only deduct them from the business activities you're running. The good news is the rules still apply if your adjusted taxable income is less than $250,000.

TIP

The Tax Office has discretion to allow you to claim a business loss under certain circumstances. For example, such a situation may arise if special circumstances beyond your control affect your business activities (for example, due to weather conditions) or because you may need to wait for a period of time before your business is likely to become a commercially viable operation.

You may find the Tax Office fact sheets 'Business losses', 'Non-commercial losses' and '16 Deferred non-commercial business losses 2023' helpful.

Appendix B sets out a number of leading tax cases in respect of claiming certain business-related expenses. This useful online tool (available at www.dummies.com/go/taxforaustraliansfd) is a handy reference if you want to know whether a specific expense is tax deductible or you're studying tax law.

Chapter **15**

Collecting Tax for the Government: Goods and Services Tax

A goods and services tax (GST) was introduced in Australia on 1 July 2000. This broad-based tax of 10 per cent is added on to the cost of most goods and services sold or consumed in Australia. The *A New Tax System (Goods and Services Tax) Act 1999* requires entities, particularly business entities registered for GST, to collect 10 per cent tax from their customers and remit the amount to the Tax Office on either a monthly, quarterly or annual basis.

In this chapter, I discuss the three different types of GST sales (or supplies) and how GST is collected only on taxable sales. Further, if you register for GST (refer to Chapter 13), you can claim a GST credit in respect of any GST you're charged on your own acquisitions that are made in the course of making supplies (other than input taxed supplies).

Collecting 10 Per Cent

Under the GST provisions, you're likely to enter into three types of GST sales (or supplies — see Figure 15-1):

>> Taxable sales (or supplies)

>> Input taxed sales (or supplies)

>> GST-free sales (or supplies)

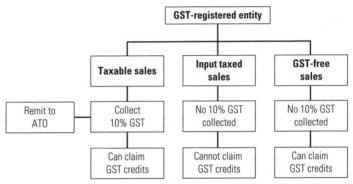

FIGURE 15-1: Understanding the three types of GST sales.

Every time you conduct a financial transaction, you need to know whether the transaction is a taxable sale, an input taxed sale or a GST-free sale.

Ordinarily, the issue is relatively straightforward. If in doubt, your best action is to immediately contact the Tax Office or seek professional advice because you're personally liable to collect the tax. This is a tax imposed on the end consumer, so GST-registered entities can claim a GST credit in respect to GST they're charged on their own acquisitions (other than in respect of input taxed supplies).

Taxing your sales: What are taxable sales (supplies)?

Taxable sales (supplies) are transactions of most goods and services sold within Australia by registered entities.

They can include

>> Sale of goods such as your trading stock

>> Sale of specific services such as repairs and tax advice

>> Buying and leasing property

If you're not registered for GST, no GST is charged on your supply of goods and services. However, you need to apply for an Australian Business Number (ABN, refer to Chapter 13) and quote this number when you enter into a supply of goods and services. Otherwise, your customers are required to withhold tax on the payments they make to you.

TECHNICAL
STUFF

The GST Act points out four conditions that must be present for an entity to make a taxable supply and collect GST on behalf of the federal government:

>> You make a supply for consideration.

>> The supply is made in the course or furtherance of an enterprise that you carry on.

>> The supply is connected with Australia.

>> The entity is registered or required to be registered. This condition applies if your GST turnover (or sales) is or is likely to be $75,000 or more a year (or $150,000 a year if you operate a non-profit organisation).

TIP

If you purchase goods with a value of less than $1000 (referred to as 'low value imports') from an overseas supplier — for instance, you buy the goods via the internet through a site such as eBay — you may be liable to pay GST on the goods you purchase. This will be the case if the non-resident business is registered for GST. For more info, check out Tax Office fact sheet 'GST on low value imported goods' on its website (www.ato.gov.au).

If you're a registered entity (which is most likely to be the case if you run a business), you become a mini tax collector with respect to the taxable sales you make to your customers. As if you don't already have enough on your plate, under this system the Tax Office makes you do all the hard work. This is because when you make a taxable sale, you're obligated to collect GST (being one-eleventh of your invoice price) and forward the amount to the Tax Office. For example, if you charge a customer $880 (including GST) you need to collect $80, which is one-eleventh of $880.

You need to issue a tax invoice for taxable sales of more than $82.50 (including GST) if a customer requests one within 28 days of the sale. If you issue a tax invoice to your customers, the information you need to disclose depends on whether the amount is more or less than $1,000.

For amounts less than $1,000, you must disclose the following on your invoice:

>> The words 'tax invoice'

>> Your ABN (that is, the supplier's ABN)

>> Your name (that is, the supplier's name)

>> Date of issue

>> A description of the goods and/or services supplied

>> The total price (including GST)

>> A statement that the price includes GST (alternatively, the GST can be shown separately)

For amounts over $1,000, in addition to the above details, you also need to disclose the purchaser's name, the purchaser's ABN or address, and the quantity supplied (see Figure 15-2).

Tax invoice		R. G. Furniture Pty Ltd	
23 March 20XX		23 Rupert Street	
		Footscray	
Customer			
Andrew Jones		ABN 95 123 456 789	
147 Lumber Street			
Northcote			
Qty	**Description**	**Unit price**	**Total**
1	Table	$1,500	$1,500
4	Chairs	$200	$800
	Total price (excluding GST)		$2,300
	GST		$230
	Total price (including GST)		$2,530

FIGURE 15-2: Providing the correct details on your tax invoice.

You're not required to have a tax invoice to claim a GST credit for purchases of $82.50 or less (including GST). You don't have to issue a valid tax invoice to a customer where the sale you make is $82.50 or less (including GST). Further, you don't have to withhold tax from a supplier who doesn't provide you with an ABN if the sale is $75 or less (excluding any GST).

If you want to know more about GST and tax invoices, visit the Tax Office website (www.ato.gov.au) and read the fact sheet 'Tax invoices'.

If you purchase goods that you use partly for business and partly for private purposes (for example, a car or computer), you can claim a GST credit only in respect of the business portion. Under the small business concessions provisions, you can make an annual private apportionment election. This rule means you don't need to estimate the private portion each time you prepare your business activity statement (BAS). Rather, you can elect to make one single adjustment at the end of the financial year (refer to Chapter 13).

Examining input taxed sales (supplies)

An input taxed sale relates to financial services and, more particularly, to money transactions (for instance, lending or borrowing money, and share trading transactions) and to residential property for use as residential accommodation (such as a residential rental property). No GST is charged on input taxed sales and you can't claim a GST credit in respect of your acquisitions to make that sale (supply).

You may find helpful the Tax Office fact sheet 'Input-taxed sales', available on its website (www.ato.gov.au).

Checking out GST-free sales (supplies)

GST-free sales (or supplies) means no GST is charged on these transactions and you can claim a GST credit on GST you pay to make a GST-free sale. The following transactions are examples of GST-free sales:

>> Cars for use by disabled people (for more info, check out Tax Office fact sheet 'Tax concessions on cars for people with a disability')

- Certain child care services and certain education courses

- Certain exports (such as Australian goods sold to overseas customers) and international mail

- Certain food for human consumption, including fruit, vegetables, bread, dairy products, meat, fish, tea and coffee (for more info, check out Tax Office fact sheets 'GST-free food' and 'Taxable food')

- Certain medical, health and care services that qualify for a Medicare benefit

- Certain religious services and charitable activities

- Farmland and precious metals

- Services provided by travel agents in arranging overseas travel and overseas supplies, and supplies through inward duty-free shops

- The sale of a business as a going concern (for more info, see Tax Office fact sheet 'Selling a going concern')

- The supply of accommodation and meals to residents of retirement villages by certain operators

- Water and sewerage services

One important GST–free transaction mentioned in the preceding list is the sale of a business as a *going concern*. This transaction can be likened to selling your truck with the engine still running. At the point of sale, you jump out of the driver's seat and a new owner takes over. Generally speaking, for the transaction to be exempt from GST, four conditions must be present — namely:

- The business must still be functionally operating until the date of sale (all things necessary for the continued operation of the enterprise are made available to the purchaser).

- The purchaser must be registered or required to be registered for GST.

- The sale (supply) must be for consideration (for example, you receive a sum of money).

- Both the seller and purchaser must agree in writing that the sale (supply) is of a going concern.

You're best to seek professional advice to ensure that you're complying with these technical issues.

Registering for GST

Under the GST provisions, you're required to register for GST if your annual GST turnover is likely to be $75,000 or more (or $150,000 or more for non-profit entities). If your annual turnover is below the GST turnover thresholds mentioned, you can still elect to register for GST. You also need to apply for an ABN and quote this number when you enter into a business transaction (refer to Chapter 13).

If you have the option to register for GST, before you make your decision you need to weigh up all the pros and cons. For example, a major benefit if you register is you can claim a GST credit in respect of any GST you're charged on your own acquisitions. To claim a GST credit, you need to hold a tax invoice to substantiate your claim for a GST credit. The downside is the red tape and all the headaches that go with the paperwork you need to fill out to comply with the GST rules (which can take hours to complete!).

CHECK THE NET

You may find 'Registering for GST' from the Tax Office website (www.ato.gov.au) and 'Register for goods and services tax (GST)' on the business.gov.au website helpful.

If you cease running a business and/or you're no longer required to register for GST, you can cancel your registration within 21 days of ceasing to trade. You need to contact the Tax Office and complete the form 'Application to cancel registration (NAT 2955)'. For more details see Tax Office fact sheet 'Cancelling your GST registration'.

WARNING

If you cancel your GST registration, you may need to repay some GST credits you claimed on certain business assets (for example, a car) that you purchased when you were registered for GST and still retain after you cancel your GST registration. For more details see the Tax Office fact sheet 'Adjusting for assets retained after cancelling GST registration'.

Paying the GST

If you're registered for GST, you must prepare a business activity statement (BAS) (normally on a quarterly basis). You need to disclose in this document the amount of GST you collect from your customers minus any GST credits you're entitled to claim back, and remit the amount (online or by mail) to the Tax Office. To fulfil this requirement correctly, you need to keep a record of all your sales and purchases, especially all your tax invoices, in order to prepare your BAS and to substantiate your claim for a GST credit. For more details, see the nearby sidebar 'Case study: Preparing a BAS'. See also Tax Office fact sheet 'Completing your BAS for GST' and 'How to lodge your BAS'. You can download them from the Tax Office website (www.ato.gov.au).

If you need help to prepare your BAS, you can get it from qualified bookkeepers who are authorised to prepare GST, BAS and PAYG statements.

REMEMBER

GST is levied only on taxable sales you make. No GST applies to transactions that are classified as input taxed sales and GST-free sales.

TIP

Check out Chapter 22 to discover some common mistakes associated with GST and small business entities. You may also find the following Tax Office fact sheet helpful: 'GST – avoiding common errors'. You can download a copy from the Tax Office website: www.ato.gov.au.

CASE STUDY: PREPARING A BAS

Emma runs a small business and is registered for GST because her annual GST turnover (sales) is $75,000 or more. This means she needs to complete a quarterly BAS disclosing the GST she's legally obligated to collect. Emma uses the cash basis to account for GST (meaning she accounts for GST when she receives it and when she makes a payment).

Her annual GST turnover is less than $10 million, so she has elected to use the 'Simpler BAS reporting method'. This is relatively easy and quick to complete. Under this method, Emma needs only to report on her BAS 'Total sales' at (G1), 'GST on sales' at (1A) and 'GST on purchases' at (1B).

During the March quarter, Emma's total sales (including GST) were $110,000 and she collected $10,000 GST on sales (being one-eleventh of $110,000). She also paid $4,000 GST on purchases amounting to $44,000 (being one-eleventh of $44,000). Under the Simpler BAS reporting method, when Emma lodges her BAS, she needs to pay $6,000 to the Tax Office (being the difference between $10,000 GST collected and $4,000 GST paid). (*Note:* If your annual GST turnover is more than $10 million, you need to use the relatively complex and time-consuming 'Full reporting method' to calculate your tax obligation — not so fun!)

Chapter **16**

Living on the Fringe: Fringe Benefits Tax

Prior to the introduction of the fringe benefits tax (FBT) provisions, you were able to structure your pay packet in such a way that significantly reduced the burden of tax. You could also receive non-cash benefits in lieu of a cash salary or wage, or transfer those benefits to family members. Legislation was introduced in 1986 to put everyone back on an even playing field (subject to certain limited exceptions).

In this chapter, I explain what FBT is all about and how to calculate it, including specific info for cars and salary packaging.

Coming to Terms with FBT

The *Fringe Benefits Tax Assessment Act 1986 (FBT Act)* was introduced to overcome the inability to tax certain benefits paid to employees (or their associates such as a spouse, child or relative) in lieu of receiving a salary or wage. The employer rather than the employee is liable to pay FBT on certain benefits provided to employees (for example, provision of a work car for private use, or paying private expenses such as school fees or membership to your favourite football club). The FBT year begins on 1 April and ends on 31 March. The employer must lodge an annual 'FBT return (NAT 1067)' with the Tax Office by 21 May. Ordinarily, an employer can claim as a tax deduction the cost of providing fringe benefits and the amount of FBT paid. An FBT issue normally arises when an employee receives a salary package.

Ordinarily, three conditions must be present for an FBT liability to arise — namely:

>> **An employer–employee (or associate) relationship must be present.** This condition means the benefit must be paid as a consequence of an employment arrangement. If a payment is made outside an employment arrangement, an FBT issue is unlikely to arise (unless the employee was a past employee or is likely to be a future employee).

>> **The employer must give the employee (or associate) a fringe benefit.** Under the FBT rules, a benefit is broadly defined and includes any rights, privileges or services. For example, you provide a fringe benefit when you

- Allow an employee to use a work car for private purposes. (For example, your employee can take the car home each night and use it to do the shopping.)

- Give an employee a cheap loan for private use (such as help finance the purchase of their main residence).

- Reimburse an expense incurred by an employee, such as school fees and childcare costs.

- Provide entertainment by way of food, drink or recreation (subject to certain conditions and exemptions).

>> **The fringe benefit isn't an exempt benefit.** The FBT Act specifically exempts certain benefits (work-related items) you may give to your employees (or associates). The following are examples of benefits that are exempt:

- An electric car if the price is below the luxury car threshold for fuel-efficient vehicles (at the time of writing $89,332). But you'll need to include the value of this exempt benefit in the calculation of an employee's reportable fringe benefits amount (see Tax Office fact sheet 'Sparks are flying this coming FBT year' for more details).

- Mobile phone or car phone, provided the phone is primarily used in employment.

- Most minor benefits that are infrequent and valued at less than $300 where it would be unreasonable to treat the benefit as a fringe benefit (for example, the annual Christmas party).

- Notebook, laptop (for business use) or a similar portable computer. Exemption is available only if the portable electronic device is used primarily for work-related purposes. *Note:* Small business employees can get an FBT exemption on more than one qualifying work-related portable electronic device that performs a similar function (for instance, a tablet and a laptop).

- Protective clothing, personal digital assistants (PDAs), tools of trade such as briefcases and calculators, and certain relocation expenses.

- Recreational and child-minding facilities and the provision of amenities such as tea-making or coffee-making facilities located on your business premises.

- The first $1,000 worth of in-house benefits in respect of the goods and services that you sell to your customers.

- Work-related, preventative health care.

CHECK THE NET

For more info on benefits that's exempt from FBT, check out Tax Office fact sheet 'Exemptions, concessions and other ways to reduce FBT' on its website (www.ato.gov.au).

These examples show that FBT is so broad that a fringe benefit issue probably arises whenever you give an employee a benefit!

Fringe benefits tax isn't payable in the following circumstances:

>> No car parking fringe benefit arises if you provide car parking for your employees, unless you're located within one kilometre of a commercial car park that charges more than $10.40 for all-day parking (2023–24 FBT year). However, car parking benefits provided by eligible small business employers to their employees are normally exempt from FBT. For more info on car parking and FBT, visit the Tax Office website (www.ato.gov.au) and check out Taxation Ruling 'TR 2021/2DC1' and fact sheet 'Fringe benefits tax – rates and thresholds'.

>> No FBT is payable on salary and wages your employer pays you, and on contributions your employer makes to a complying superannuation fund on your behalf.

In addition to your current employees, the FBT provisions continue to apply to any benefits you provide to your former employees. It also applies to future employees you intend to employ. For example, you may offer an incentive to someone to work for you in the future, such as paying school fees if the person agrees to work for you on completion of studies.

Under the FBT provisions, a principle known as the *otherwise deductible rule* applies to tax-deductible expenses. Under this rule, if an employer pays a tax-deductible expense on behalf of an employee (such as a subscription to a trade union), the taxable value of the fringe benefit is reduced to nil. This interpretation applies because if the employee rather than the employer paid the expense, it would have been a tax-deductible expense to the employee. In other words, the employer claims the expense rather than the employee (for more info, check out Taxation Ruling 'TR 2013/6' and Taxation Determination 'TD 2013/20').

If you provide fringe benefits to your employees and your FBT liability is greater than $3,000, you're required to pay FBT in quarterly instalments. If this situation applies to you, you need to register for FBT. To register you must complete an 'Application to register for fringe benefits tax (NAT 1055)' and send it to the Tax Office. On the other hand, if the amount is less than $3,000, you can pay the tax when you lodge your annual 'FBT return (NAT 1067)'. For more details see the fact sheet 'Register for fringe benefits tax (FBT)' on the business.gov.au website.

For instructions about lodging your annual FBT return, visit the Tax Office website (www.ato.gov.au) and check out the publication '2024 fringe benefits tax (FBT) return'.

Calculating the FBT

If you give an employee a fringe benefit, you need to follow three steps to calculate the amount of FBT you're liable to pay:

1. **Calculate the taxable value.**

   The taxable value depends on the type of benefit you provide to your employee. You need to keep accurate records to calculate and verify its value.

2. **Gross up (increase) the taxable value of the fringe benefit.**

How you gross up the taxable value depends on whether you're registered for GST:

- If you're registered for GST and entitled to claim a GST credit, you multiply the taxable value by 2.0802 (referred to as type 1).

- If you're not registered for GST and you're not entitled to claim a GST credit, you multiply the taxable value by 1.8868 (referred to as type 2).

3. **Calculate the FBT payable.**

Multiply the grossed-up taxable value by 47 per cent for the 2023–24 FBT year.

TIP

If the taxable value of reportable fringe benefits provided to an employee exceeds $2,000, the employer must report the grossed-up taxable value of the fringe benefit on the employee's payment summary. For the 2023–24 FBT year, the minimum grossed-up value is $3,773 if the reportable fringe benefits taxable value is $2,000.01 ($2,000.01 × 1.8868 = $3,773).

Employers must keep proper records to accurately calculate their annual FBT liability. But if you run a small business and your FBT liability is below the record keeping exemption threshold amount ($9,786 for the 2023–24 FBT year) you don't need to keep full FBT records. You can use an alternative way of calculating your FBT liability if you satisfy certain conditions. For more details, see Tax Office publication 'Fringe benefits tax – a guide for employers'.

CASE STUDY: CALCULATING FRINGE BENEFITS TAX ON ELISE'S CHEAP LOAN

Elise's employer gives her a $20,000 cheap loan to buy a car for her personal use. The rate of interest her employer charges her is 4.77 per cent. According to the FBT provisions, her employer must charge her a statutory rate of interest to avoid being liable to pay FBT. The

(continued)

(continued)

statutory rate for the 2023–24 FBT year is 7.77 per cent. Her employer isn't registered for GST.

Because the interest charged (4.77 per cent) is below the statutory interest rate (7.77 per cent), Elise has received a loan fringe benefit to buy a car for her personal use. Her employer is liable to pay FBT on the difference between the statutory FBT benchmark interest rate (7.77 per cent) and the amount of interest charged (4.77 per cent) — that is, $20,000 loan × 3.00% = $600.

Calculate the taxable value.

$20,000 × (7.77% – 4.77%) = $600

Calculate the grossed-up taxable value.

Because the loan isn't a taxable supply, her employer multiplies the taxable value by 1.8868 (type 2):

$600 × 1.8868 = $1132

Calculate FBT payable.

$1,132 × 47% = $532

Elise's employer is liable to pay $532 FBT and can claim a $1,132 tax deduction in respect of the loan fringe benefit ($600 taxable value of FB plus $532 FBT paid).

Determining a Car's FBT

You can calculate a car fringe benefit in one of two ways — the statutory formula method or the operating cost method.

Using the statutory formula method

Under the statutory formula method, you use the following formula to calculate the car's taxable value:

(ABC)/D – E

Where:

A = Base value of the car (cost price)

B = Statutory fraction (0.20)

C = Number of days during the year the car benefit was provided by the employer

D = Number of days in the tax year

E = Your contribution towards the car's running costs

The statutory fraction rate is 20 per cent (0.20) irrespective of the number of kilometres you travel.

Here's an example. Using the following information, you can calculate the taxable value (see the sidebar 'Case study: Tula's salary package' for a more detailed example):

A = $40,000

B = 0.2

C = 365 days

D = 365 days

E = nil

Taxable value:

($40,000 × 0.2 × 365)/365 − 0 = $8,000

Calculate grossed-up taxable value:

$8,000 × 2.0802 = $16,641

The FBT payable is:

$16,641 × 47% = $7,821

Using the operating cost method

Under the operating cost method, you use the following formula to calculate the car's taxable value:

C × (100% − BP) − R

Where:

C = Operating cost for holding period

BP = Percentage of business use (*Note:* You need to maintain a log book over a period of 12 continuous weeks to work out your percentage of business and private use.)

R = Your contribution towards the car's upkeep

If the car is owned by the person providing the fringe benefit, the operating costs include fuel, repairs and maintenance, and registration or insurance charges attributable to the period, plus depreciation (the statutory rate is 25 per cent) and imputed interest (a rate of interest even if you didn't pay any, based on the statutory interest rate).

In this case, the following info is used to calculate the taxable value:

C = $14,000

BP = 50%

R = nil

Taxable value:

$14,000 × 50% = $7,000

Calculate grossed-up taxable value:

$7,000 × 2.0802 = $14,561

The FBT payable using the operating cost method is:

$14,561 × 47% = $6,843

See the sidebar 'Case study: Tula's salary package' for more.

Packaging Your Salary

Under a salary packaging arrangement, your employer may offer you a range of options about how you want to be paid. For example, you can elect to be paid in cash, part cash and benefits, or benefits only. The option you select determines how you're taxed. As far as the Tax Office is concerned, as long as the correct amount of tax is paid in respect of your pay packet, everyone is happy. If you elect to receive the cash-only option, you pay the tax at your marginal rates. If you receive the benefits instead of cash, your employer pays tax on the fringe benefits you receive (see the sidebar 'Case study: Tula's salary package').

One popular salary packaging option is making additional superannuation contributions to your nominated super fund, where extra super contributions are deducted from your gross pay. The benefit in doing this is that extra contributions are taxed in your super fund at the rate of 15 per cent, as against your marginal tax rates plus a Medicare levy (for instance, 34.5 per cent) if no contributions are deducted from your gross pay. However, the trade-off is that you can't access your super fund benefits until you satisfy a *condition of release* such as when you retire (see Chapter 18 for more details). *Note:* No FBT is payable on the extra super contributions that your employer makes to a complying super fund on your behalf.

CHECK
THE NET

To provide more about fringe benefits tax, the Tax Office has issued the following publications, available at www.ato.gov.au:

>> 'Car fringe benefits tax (FBT) guide for small business'

>> 'FBT changes to salary packaged meal and other entertainment benefits'

>> 'Fringe benefits tax'

>> 'Fringe benefits tax – a guide for employers'

>> 'Obligations when people work for you'

>> 'Reportable fringe benefits for employees'

>> 'Salary sacrificing for employees'

TIP

A living-away-from-home allowance (LAFHA) is ordinarily a fringe benefit and not assessable in the hands of the employee. To gain this concession you need to maintain a home in Australia, and you need to be living away from that home while performing your employment-related duties. If this isn't the case, the LAFHA forms part of your assessable income as is ordinarily the case with other allowances you may receive. (For more details, see Tax Office fact sheet 'Living-away-from-home allowance fringe benefits' and refer to Chapter 5.)

TIP

The reasonable amounts for food and drinks expenses incurred by an adult employee receiving a LAFHA fringe benefit within Australia for the 2023–24 FBT year is $316 per week (see Taxation Determination 'TD 2023/2' for more details).

WARNING

If you're a shareholder/employee of your family private company and you receive a benefit as a consequence of being an employee of that company (for instance, the use of the company car for private use), the company is ordinarily liable to pay FBT.

CASE STUDY: TULA'S SALARY PACKAGE

Tula works as a marketing executive for a large manufacturing company. She is offered the choice of receiving a $100,000 cash salary or $50,000 cash salary plus the following benefits:

- $150,000 personal loan to buy her home at an interest rate of 4.77 per cent.
- $1,000 diamond subscription to the Collingwood Football Club.
- Tula's employer to pay her work-related expenses to the value of $750.
- A car for her personal use. The car's cost price is $40,000. During the 2023–24 FBT year Tula travels 24,000 kilometres, of which 12,000 kilometres are for business use. Her total running costs are $14,000 and she makes no personal contributions to the car's running costs. Her employer is registered for GST.

If Tula elects to take a $100,000 salary, her entire income is taxed at her marginal rates. However, after discussing the matter with her tax agent, Tula elects to take the salary package. Tula is liable to pay tax on $50,000 at her marginal rates plus a 2 per cent Medicare levy. Her employer can claim a tax deduction in respect of the $50,000 salary it pays her.

Tula's employer is liable to pay FBT on the benefits she receives, as follows:

- FBT payable on the $150,000 personal loan and the $1,000 subscription to the Collingwood Football Club is calculated in accordance with the three steps mentioned in the section 'Calculating the FBT', earlier in this chapter.

- With respect to Tula's $750 work-related expenses, under the *otherwise deductible rule* the taxable value of the fringe benefit provided is reduced to nil, because the employer claims these expenses rather than Tula.

- For the car provided for her personal use, Tula is best to use the operating cost method to calculate the car fringe benefit.

Tula's employer can claim a tax deduction for all the fringe benefits provided to her, as well as the amount of tax payable.

Chapter **17**

Getting Wealthy: CGT and Small Business

To encourage you to set up and run a small business and employ someone, the federal government has introduced a number of tax incentives. One of the tax incentives relates to capital gains you may make on disposal of business assets.

You may be liable to pay capital gains tax (CGT) on gains you make when you sell or otherwise dispose of CGT assets such as shares, real estate and collectables you acquired on or after 20 September 1985. The tax incentives for small businesses are extremely beneficial if you're contemplating retiring soon and you're sitting on business assets that have increased in value.

In this chapter, I examine these small business concessions and explain what you need to do to qualify for them.

Keeping What You Sow: Tasting the Tax Incentive Goodies

Under the CGT concessions for small business, you may qualify for CGT relief when you dispose of certain CGT assets. These concessions are available to any form of business ownership (that is, individuals who run a business as a sole trader, a partner in a partnership, a company or a trust).

Qualifying for CGT relief

Everyone who runs a business can potentially qualify for CGT concessions. However, before you can taste the goodies, you need to satisfy a number of conditions.

Under these provisions, if you run a small business and you make a capital gain on disposal, the gain can be potentially reduced or eliminated if you satisfy one of the following basic conditions:

>> The $6 million net value of business assets test (the value of your net business assets can't exceed $6 million).

>> If the net value of your business assets exceeds $6 million, your aggregate turnover (your business takings) must be less than $2 million each financial year.

As a general rule, you're unlikely to have any difficulty passing one of the two basic conditions mentioned in the preceding list, especially the $6 million question. If you're on the borderline, you're best to seek professional advice, because you need to satisfy complex technical rules.

TECHNICAL STUFF

For a comprehensive discussion on these conditions, refer to the Tax Office fact sheet 'Small business CGT concessions' available online at www.ato.gov.au. See also 'Taxation for your business' and more particularly the bit dealing with 'Capital gains tax' on the business.gov.au website.

In addition to the preceding two conditions, the CGT assets that you own must be *active assets*. Active assets are assets you own and use (or hold ready for use) in running your business. Active assets can include your business premises, your plant and equipment, and intangible assets such as goodwill or trademarks (see Taxation Determination 'TD 2006/78' for more info).

CGT assets that don't qualify for CGT relief

CGT assets that don't qualify for CGT relief are those that are used to derive passive income, such as a rental property your business may own (for more info, check out Taxation Determination 'TD 2021/2'). Again, if you're not sure about which assets do or don't qualify, you need to seek professional advice because you need to satisfy precise rules.

Businesses operated through a company or trust

If you run a company or trust, in addition to the basic conditions mentioned in the preceding section, you also need to satisfy some additional conditions if the CGT asset is a share in a company or interest in a trust.

You need to satisfy what the Tax Office folk call the 'CGT concession stakeholder' test. The test basically checks to see whether you're a 'significant individual' in a company or trust. It can also include a spouse who may have a small business participation percentage (for example, 1 per cent). The percentage you need to satisfy the Tax Office is 20 per cent or more to gain the CGT small business concession. Because this can get rather complicated, seeking professional advice from a registered agent or solicitor is best.

For more info, check out Tax Office fact sheet 'Additional conditions if the CGT asset is a share or trust interest' on the Tax Office website (www.ato.gov.au).

CGT Concessions for Small Business

If you satisfy the basic conditions for CGT relief, four CGT concessions are available to you under the CGT concessions for small business:

- >> CGT 15-year exemption
- >> CGT 50 per cent active asset reduction
- >> CGT retirement exemption
- >> CGT rollover concession

You can qualify for more than one small business concession. For example, you can take advantage of the CGT 50 per cent active asset reduction concession and then use the $500,000 life-time retirement exemption concession and/or the CGT rollover concession.

WARNING

If you intend to seek relief under the CGT small business concessions, you need to take into account current year losses, prior year losses and any 50 per cent CGT discount you may be entitled to claim on CGT assets held for more than 12 months (refer to Chapter 11).

Checking out the 15-year exemption

The CGT 15-year exemption concession rewards those individuals who have been running a business for a minimum of 15 years. Under this concession, any capital gain you make on disposal of an active (business) asset is exempt from tax.

To qualify for CGT relief you need to satisfy the following conditions:

>> You must have continually owned your active (business) asset for at least 15 years.

>> It must have been an active (business) asset for at least half of the relevant 15-year period (that is, 7.5 years).

>> You must be over 55 years of age and retired or permanently incapacitated.

If you satisfy these conditions, you don't have to consider the other three CGT concessions for small business discussed in the following sections because your capital gain is going to be fully exempt. Further, if you make any capital losses, you don't have to deduct them from the capital gains you made.

TIP

If you put the CGT proceeds from a sale into a complying superannuation fund, you can treat the amount as non-concessional contributions that aren't taxed in the super fund. The proceeds help fund your retirement strategies (for more details see Chapter 18). To fulfil this rule correctly, you need to make a CGT cap election. You have to make this election because eligible small business owners can claim a lifetime $1,705,000 (indexed) CGT cap amount (per 2023–24 tax rates) as well as the non-concessional amounts they can normally make. For more details visit the Tax Office website (www.ato.gov.au) and read Tax Office fact sheet 'CGT cap election'.

Getting a helping hand: 50 per cent reduction

Under this CGT concession, you can get a 50 per cent reduction on the capital gain you make. Ordinarily, if you own a CGT asset for more than 12 months, you also qualify for a 50 per cent discount (for more details, refer to Chapter 11). This concession means that if you own the CGT asset for more than 12 months, you stand to gain a 75 per cent discount. For example, if the gain is $100, the first 50 per cent discount reduces the gain to $50, while the second 50 per cent discount reduces it to $25 (which is an overall decrease of 75 per cent). However, if you don't want to pay tax on the balance of the capital gain you make, you can use the other methods (the CGT small business rollover concession and/or the CGT retirement concession) to gain additional relief.

To use this 50 per cent active asset method, follow these four steps:

1. **Calculate the capital gain you make on disposal of your active (business) asset.**

2. **Deduct any current year capital losses and prior year losses from the capital gain you make (if applicable).**

3. **Claim the 50 per cent CGT discount, if you hold the CGT asset for more than 12 months.**

4. **Apply the small business CGT 50 per cent active reduction concession.**

These steps are also illustrated in the sidebar 'Case study: Using the CGT 50 per cent reduction concession'.

WARNING

If you run your business through a company structure (refer to Chapter 12), a company isn't entitled to a 50 per cent discount on sale of CGT assets that are held for more than 12 months.

Thinking about retiring: Retirement concession

Under the CGT retirement concession, you can claim a $500,000 lifetime retirement exemption on the proceeds of the sale of your active (business) assets. You can get immediate CGT relief if you're over 55 years of age and use this concession. Unfortunately, if you're under 55 years of age, you need to roll over (transfer) the proceeds into a complying superannuation fund, a complying approved deposit fund, or a retirement savings account.

CASE STUDY: USING THE CGT 50 PER CENT REDUCTION CONCESSION

Anita has been in business for ten years. During the financial year, she makes a $25,000 capital gain on sale of an active (business) asset she has owned for the past five years. She also makes a $5,000 capital loss.

The amount of the capital gain liable to tax using the CGT 50 per cent active asset reduction concession is calculated as follows.

Capital gain on active asset		$25,000
Less capital loss	$5,000	
		$20,000
Less 50% CGT discount	$10,000	
		$10,000
Less 50% small business reduction	$5,000	
NET CAPITAL GAIN		**$5,000**

Anita can either pay tax on the $5,000 net capital gain she made, or apply for further relief under the CGT small business rollover concession and/or CGT retirement concession.

Transferring your gains: Rollover concession

The rollover concession allows you to reinvest the proceeds from a capital gain in a replacement asset or make improvements to existing assets. As a general rule, you need to apply the capital gain against assets you buy within one year before the sale or against assets you intend to buy within the next two years.

Identifying Common Tax Mistakes: CGT Concessions for Small Business

To avoid making a tax mistake where CGT concessions and small business are concerned, take note of the most common, including the following:

» Not meeting the basic conditions for entitlement to CGT concessions for small business.

» Using the settlement date for the disposal of a CGT asset rather than the date the contract was signed (refer to Chapter 11).

» Incorrectly classifying 'active (business) assets' (particularly CGT assets used to derive passive income, such as a rental property your business may own).

5

Thinking Long Term

Start thinking long term and plan ahead for any unforeseen contingencies that may pop up.

Discover how to contribute to a superannuation fund and the amount you can legally claim each year.

Prepare for retirement and learn what you need to do to build your retirement nest egg.

Explore pension options that you can access when you retire.

Examine how your beneficiaries are taxed when you're no longer around.

IN THIS CHAPTER

» Selecting your super fund

» Deciding to do it yourself

» Getting some tax deductions

» Adding to your superannuation fund with contributions

» Understanding the conditions of release

Chapter **18**

Preparing for Retirement Using Superannuation

Superannuation is a scheme to help you fund your retirement. If you're an employee, your employer has a statutory obligation to make a superannuation contribution on your behalf to a complying super fund. If you're self-employed, your contributions to a complying super fund are tax deductible. This money is invested on your behalf and can't be accessed until you satisfy a condition of release such as when you retire.

In this chapter, I explain how superannuation works and the benefits you stand to gain when you retire.

Complying and Non-Complying Super Funds

You can contribute money to two types of superannuation funds: non-complying and complying funds.

Non-complying super funds haven't made an election to be regulated under the *Superannuation Industry (Supervision) Act 1993* (SIS Act), or have failed to meet certain standards prescribed by the federal government. These funds don't qualify for any concessions and are liable to pay tax at the rate of 45 per cent (as against 15 per cent for complying funds).

Complying superannuation funds have made an election to be regulated under the SIS Act. Superannuation funds must agree to be regulated to qualify for certain federal government concessions. All the major Australian super funds are regulated funds. Being a complying super fund becomes an issue only if you decide to set up your own super fund. The basic points to note about complying super funds are

>> Complying funds pay tax at the rate of 15 per cent. The amount of tax payable can be reduced further if a super fund receives dividend franking credits (refer to Chapter 9).

>> Pensions payable to individuals who have reached their preservation age and are under 60 years of age qualify for a 15 per cent tax offset (see Table 18-1).

>> Pensions and lump sums paid to members after age 60 are tax free.

>> Income and capital gains to fund pension options are exempt from tax.

REMEMBER

The maximum amount of funds you can transfer to an account-based pension fund (where earnings are exempt from tax) is capped at $1.9 million (indexed for inflation).

WARNING

The federal government has proposed that, from 1 July 2025, if you have more than $3 million in super (for instance, $4 million in your accumulation account), you'll need to apportion your super fund's investments for different tax treatment. The portion that corresponds to $3 million will be taxed at the rate of 15 per cent (as mentioned previously), while the portion that corresponds to the balance above $3 million (in this example, the $1 million bit) will be taxed at the rate of 30 per cent. To add salt to the wound, when calculating your investment earnings you'll need to take into account your super fund balance at the start and end of the tax year and make appropriate adjustments for any contributions and withdrawals you make. This means your investment earnings will include any *unrealised capital gains* on assets you hold (such as shares and property that have increased in value during the tax year — yuk!), along with any interest, dividends and rent you may receive. This additional tax will apply even if you're in retirement phase and you have started a superannuation pension (double yuk!).

TABLE 18-1 **Preservation Age**

Date of Birth	Preservation Age (and tax year you become eligible)
Before 1 July 1960	55 years
1 July 1960 – 30 June 1961	56 years
1 July 1961 – 30 June 1962	57 years
1 July 1962 – 30 June 1963	58 years
1 July 1963 – 30 June 1964	59 years
After 30 June 1964	60 years

Choosing a Goose to Lay the Golden Egg

The federal government introduced choice of superannuation fund legislation. Its purpose is to give you the option to select your own super fund or retirement savings account to help fund your retirement. Under this initiative, you can elect to which fund your employer makes your future compulsory super contributions. If you have no particular preference, your employer chooses a default fund for you (commonly referred to as *MySuper*).

TECHNICAL
STUFF

If you want to know more about the choice legislation, check out the Tax Office website (www.ato.gov.au) and read the publication 'Choosing a super fund: How to complete your Standard choice form (NAT 13080)' and fact sheet 'Offer employees a choice of super fund'.

TIP

You can contribute money to four types of superannuation fund: Public sector funds set up specifically for government employees; industry funds set up for specific industries; retail funds set up by Australia's leading financial institutions (such as banks and insurance companies); and self-managed superannuation funds (SMSFs), set up by individuals who prefer to manage their own super fund.

TIP

With respect to income tax and superannuation matters, same-sex couples and families are treated the same way as other couples and families. For more details see Tax Office fact sheet 'Same-sex relationships and income tax'.

Doing it yourself: Setting up your own fund

Self-managed superannuation funds (SMSFs) are funds you personally set up and run yourself. Under this arrangement, you select the investment strategy to fund your retirement and you can pay yourself a pension when you retire. A significant benefit is you're in total control of your super fund. Although running a SMSF may sound like a great idea, you must comply with a number of restrictive rules.

If you want to transfer benefits you have in other superannuation funds to your own SMSF, you need to complete the form 'Request for rollover of whole balance of super benefits between funds (NAT 75359)'. You can get a copy of this form from the Tax Office website (www.ato.gov.au).

Checking out the rules

If you want to set up your SMSF, you must agree to be regulated (by the Tax Office) in order to qualify for certain tax concessions. Professionals who hold an Australian Financial Service Licence (for instance, financial planners and certain accountants) can help you set up a SMSF.

WARNING

You must make an election to be regulated within 60 days of establishing your SMSF. If you make an election within the prescribed time, you must comply with the following rules:

>> You can have no more than six members in your fund.

>> The sole purpose of running the SMSF must be to provide benefits to members upon their retirement, or provide benefits to dependants in the event of your death.

>> Your super fund must maintain its own bank account (for more info, check out Taxation Determination 'TD 2014/7').

>> Your personal assets can't be mixed with your super fund assets (such as your investment accounts).

>> You must set up an investment strategy regarding your investment holdings, and all your investment decisions must be made in accordance with your investment strategy. *Note:* The initial cost of setting up an investment plan isn't tax deductible, but ongoing costs associated with managing and reviewing an existing plan are tax deductible (see Taxation Determination 'TD 95/60' for more).

>> You must satisfy strict conditions if your super fund invests in certain collectables and personal use assets such as artwork, jewellery, antiques and memorabilia. For instance, your fund must insure them and they can't be stored or displayed in the private residence of any related party of the fund (for more info, check out Tax Office fact sheet 'Collectables and personal use assets').

>> Your super fund can't lend money to you and you can't lend money to your super fund. *Note:* Under the 'in-house asset' rules, loans to, investment in, or lease arrangements between a trustee and related parties is permitted provided the arrangement doesn't exceed 5 per cent of the fund's total assets.

>> If your super fund derives dividends from a private company or discretionary trust, the dividend may be treated as 'non-arm's length income' (also known as 'special income') and liable to a 45 per cent rate of tax.

>> You can't transfer a residential property that you own to your super fund, and your fund can't buy a residential property from a related party (for instance, from a member or member's relative).

>> You can't reside in a residential property that your super fund owns and you can't lease it to a related party.

>> All financial transactions must be done on a strictly commercial basis.

>> Your benefits can't be accessed until you satisfy a condition of release (see the section 'Getting the Money: Conditions of Release', later in this chapter).

>> The maximum amount of funds you can transfer to start an account-based pension fund (where earnings are exempt from tax) is capped at $1.9 million (indexed for inflation). This is called the *transfer balance cap.*

>> You can't make non-concessional contributions once your superannuation fund account balance reaches $1.9 million. This could be a major concern if you have borrowed to buy certain approved investment assets such as a property and you can't make non-concessional contributions to help repay your loan.

>> You must appoint an approved auditor (whose authorised to audit SMSFs) to verify you're complying with all the rules.

You can sell or transfer listed securities that you own (such as shares listed on the Australian Securities Exchange) to your SMSF at their market value. But the bad news is you could be liable to pay capital gains tax (CGT) if you make a capital gain on disposal. This is because under the CGT provisions a change in ownership occurs, because your SMSF then owns the listed securities. (Refer to Chapter 11 for more on CGT provisions.)

If you're running a business, you can transfer your *business real property* (that is, your business premises) to your super fund at market value and lease it back at a commercial rate of rent. These contributions are treated as if you're making cash contributions, and they're taxed in the same way as cash contributions. (For info on what is 'market value', check out the Tax Office fact sheet 'Market valuation of assets'.)

TECHNICAL STUFF

The Tax Office has issued the following publications relating to business real property: 'Business real property' and 'SMSFR 2009/1 Self-Managed Superannuation Funds: business real property for the purposes of the *Superannuation Industry (Supervision) Act 1993*'. You can download these from the Tax Office website (www.ato.gov.au).

As a general rule, your super fund can't borrow money. A SMSF can borrow to buy certain approved investment assets such as property (or a collection of identical assets that have the same market value; for example, a parcel of 1,000 NAB shares). However, strict rules apply. For more details, check out the Tax Office fact sheet

'Limited recourse borrowing'. See also Self-Managed Superannuation Funds Ruling 'SMSFR 2012/1 Self-Managed Superannuation Funds: limited recourse borrowing arrangements – application of key concepts' and Taxpayer Alert 'TA 2012/7 Self-managed superannuation funds arrangements to acquire property which contravene superannuation law'.

If you run a SMSF, you're required to review your fund's investment strategy at regular intervals to check that it meets your objectives, and your fund's assets should be valued at their market value when preparing your fund's annual accounts. (For more info, check out Tax Office fact sheet 'Valuation guidelines for self-managed super funds'.) You also need to consider whether you should take out insurance as a part of your investment strategy.

WARNING

If you fail to comply with these strict rules, the Tax Office may treat your fund as a non-complying super fund, which means you become liable to pay tax at the rate of 45 per cent. Equally, you could incur a financial penalty and the Tax Office may force you to undertake a course of education to improve your ability to run your SMSF (see Tax Office fact sheet 'How we deal with non-compliance').

CHECK THE NET

If you want to know more about setting up and running a SMSF, visit the Tax Office website (www.ato.gov.au) and read the following publications: 'Starting a self-managed super fund (NAT 75397)', 'Ownership and protection of assets' and 'Paying benefits'.

For details on what you must do if you need to wind up your SMSF, see Tax Office fact sheet 'Winding up'. You can download a copy from the Tax Office website (www.ato.gov.au).

Taxing Your Nest Egg

At the end of the financial year, all super funds must lodge an annual superannuation fund tax return disclosing the taxable income (or loss) derived during the financial year by 28 February after the financial year ends, unless otherwise included on a tax agent's lodgement program (refer to Chapter 3). For more details read the Tax Office fact sheet 'Self-managed superannuation fund annual return instructions' online at www.ato.gov.au. When you lodge your 2023–24 super fund tax return, you must provide your super fund's bank account details and pay a $259 (at the time of writing) supervisory levy. Your fund must also be audited by an appropriately qualified auditor before the return can be lodged.

Taxing super funds

A superannuation fund is liable to pay tax on receipts from three major sources:

>> Income derived from the super fund's investment activities

>> Capital gains when the super fund disposes of its investment assets

>> Concessional contributions (before-tax contributions)

If an employer makes a concessional contribution to a complying super fund on behalf of an employee, the contribution is a tax-deductible expense. Under these circumstances, the contributions are treated as assessable income and the super fund is liable to pay tax at the rate of 15 per cent. This rule also applies when a self-employed person makes a concessional contribution to a complying super fund. *Note:* If you earn more than $250,000 and you make a concessional contribution, the rate of tax payable on this contribution increases from 15 per cent to 30 per cent.

The maximum annual concessional contribution an individual who is under 75 years of age can make to a complying super fund is capped at $27,500. If you're 67 to 74 years of age, you need to satisfy a work test to make a concessional contribution (namely, work a minimum 40 hours over 30 consecutive days during the financial year). These contributions are tax deductible. (*Note:* Concessional contributions can't be accepted if you're aged 75 years or over.)

TIP

To help boost your super nest egg if you earn less than $37,000 and a concessional contribution is made to your superannuation fund, a $500 low income superannuation tax offset applies to eliminate any tax payable as a consequence of making a concessional contribution.

TIP

If you're an employee, your employer has a legal obligation to make a concessional contribution on your behalf to a complying super fund. This is called a *superannuation guarantee* (SG) contribution. Employers are required to make SG contributions to complying super funds of eligible employees regardless of their age or how much they earn. However, if you're under 18 years of age, you need to work more than 30 hours in a week to qualify for SG contributions. For the 2023–24 tax year, the SG amount is 11 per cent of your gross pay; this will increase by 0.5 per cent each year until it reaches 12 per cent in the 2025–26 tax year. (*Note:* From 1 July 2026, employers must pay the super guarantee amount at the same time employees are paid salary and wages.)

TECHNICAL STUFF

For a concessional contribution to qualify as a tax deduction, when you make the contribution you must inform the trustee of your super fund that you intend to claim a tax deduction (see the Tax Office fact sheet 'Personal super contributions', particularly the section 'Claiming deductions for personal super contributions'). You must show how much is claimed as a tax deduction and confirm that it wasn't covered by an earlier notice.

Claiming a tax deduction

In Chapter 2, I point out that you can claim a tax deduction in respect of expenses you incur in deriving your assessable income. For an expense to be deductible under the general deduction provisions, you must be able to show a relevant and necessary connection between the expenditure you incur and earning your assessable income. Your super fund can claim expenses such as fees (from accountants, actuaries, advice for audits, investment advice, legal costs and tax agents), and death and disability premiums.

TECHNICAL STUFF

For comprehensive details on superannuation deductions, see Tax Office fact sheet 'Self-managed superannuation funds – deductibility of expenses' and 'TR 2672 Income tax: deductibility of costs of amending a superannuation fund trust deed' all available on the Tax Office website (www.ato.gov.au).

CASE STUDY: CALCULATING THE TAXABLE INCOME

During the financial year, Smithville complying superannuation fund received $40,000 concessional contributions from two self-employed members. The members inform the trustees of the super fund that they intend to claim a tax deduction for the contribution made. Under these circumstances, the $40,000 contributions are treated as assessable income. The fund derives $42,000 dividends that are fully franked from its investment activities and the franking credits were $18,000. (For more details about franking credits, refer to Chapter 9.) It also makes a $21,000 capital gain on sale of shares held for more than 12 months. The fund's deductible expenses are $4,000.

Smithville complying superannuation fund's taxable income is calculated as follows.

Superannuation fund return

Income		
Concessional contributions		$40,000
Dividends	Franked amount	$42,000
	Franking credits	$18,000
Net capital gain (see *Note*)		$14,000
TOTAL INCOME OR LOSS		$114,000
Less deductible expenses		$4,000
TAXABLE INCOME		$110,000
Calculation of tax payable/refund		
TAX PAYABLE (15% of $110,000)	$16,500	
SUPERVISORY LEVY	$259	$16,759
Less dividend franking credits		$18,000
REFUND OF TAX		**$1,241**

Note: Because the shares are held for more than 12 months, just two-thirds of the capital gain is liable to tax ($14,000).

Making a Contribution: Understanding the Rules

The taxation issues associated with making a contribution to a complying superannuation fund depend on whether

>> **The contribution is a concessional or non-concessional contribution.** Only concessional contributions are tax deductible (see the next section for more info).

>> **You're under or over the age of 75 years.** The amount you can put into a super fund each year depends on your age at the time you make the contribution. After you turn 67, you have to satisfy a work test to make a concessional contribution (see Figure 18-1).

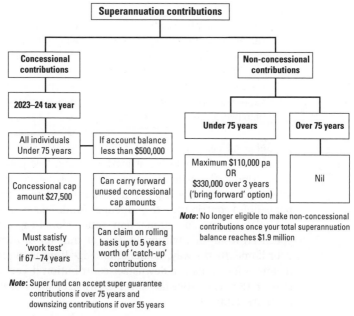

Superannuation contributions

Concessional contributions

Non-concessional contributions

2023–24 tax year

All individuals Under 75 years	If account balance less than $500,000
Concessional cap amount $27,500	Can carry forward unused concessional cap amounts
Must satisfy 'work test' if 67 –74 years	Can claim on rolling basis up to 5 years worth of 'catch-up' contributions

Under 75 years

Over 75 years

Maximum $110,000 pa OR $330,000 over 3 years ('bring forward' option)	Nil

Note: No longer eligible to make non-concessional contributions once your total superannuation balance reaches $1.9 million

Note: Super fund can accept super guarantee contributions if over 75 years and downsizing contributions if over 55 years

FIGURE 18-1: Making a superannuation contribution.

The following rules apply to making a contribution to a complying superannuation fund:

>> All individuals (employees, self-employed, retirees) who are under 75 years of age can make concessional contributions (capped at $27,500 per year). If you're 67 to 74 years of age, you need to satisfy a work test to make a concessional contribution (namely, work a minimum 40 hours over 30 consecutive days during the financial year).

>> All individuals who are under 75 years of age can make non-concessional contributions (capped at $110,000 per annum or $330,000 over three years under the 'bring forward' option). But you can't make a non-concessional contribution once your superannuation fund account balance reaches $1.9 million. (**Note:** Since 1 July 2022, you no longer need to satisfy a work test to make a non-concessional contribution if you're 67 to 74 years of age.)

>> If your super fund balance is less than $500,000, you can rollover (carry forward) unused concessional contribution cap amounts ($27,500 per year) and claim up to five consecutive years' worth of accrued contributions at a later late. This is to allow individuals (such as women who leave the workforce to raise a family) to make additional catch-up super contributions when they recommence employment to help boost their retirement nest egg.

TIP

If you're 55 years or over and you're planning on selling your home that you've held for at least 10 years, I've got some good news. Under the federal government 'Downsizer contribution' scheme, you can make up to a maximum $300,000 (or $600,000 per couple) contribution to your super fund. This is in addition to the existing $110,000 annual non-concessional cap amount. But you need to do this within 90 days of transfer of ownership on your home. By the way, no maximum age limit is in place, which means you can make a downsizer contribution if you're 75 years or over. (See Tax Office fact sheet 'Downsizer super contributions' for more details.)

TECHNICAL
STUFF

If you want more info about super contributions, visit the Tax Office website (www.ato.gov.au) and check out Taxation Ruling 'TR 2010/1 Income tax: superannuation contributions' and Tax Office fact sheet 'SuperStream'.

Figure 18-1 illustrates the rules associated with making a contribution to a complying superannuation fund for the 2023–24 tax year.

Examining concessional and non-concessional contributions

You can make two types of contribution to a complying superannuation fund:

>> **A concessional contribution:** This is a contribution that qualifies as a tax deduction. (**Note:** Concessional contributions as also called *pre-tax contributions*.)

>> **A non-concessional contribution:** This is a contribution that doesn't qualify for a tax deduction. (**Note:** Non-concessional contributions are also called *after-tax contributions*.)

Concessional contributions become assessable income in the super fund and are taxed at the rate of 15 per cent. Concessional contributions that exceed the maximum permitted each year are taxed at your marginal rates plus an interest charge. But you can avoid this if you decide to withdraw your excess concessional contributions (refer to Figure 18-1). *Note:* If you earn more than $250,000 and you make a concessional contribution, the rate of tax payable on this contribution increases from 15 per cent to 30 per cent.

TIP

Individual superannuation fund members can split concessional contributions made in the previous financial year with their (non-income or low-income-earning) spouses or partners. The maximum permitted is 85 per cent of the concessional contributions cap (see the Tax Office fact sheet 'Contributions splitting for members' for more details).

Non-concessional contributions are treated as a capital contribution in a superannuation fund and aren't liable to tax (see the next section for more details).

Making a non-concessional contribution

Non-concession contributions are contributions that don't qualify for a tax deduction and are not liable to a 15 per cent contribution tax (as is the case with concessional contributions). Since 1 July 2022, all individuals who are under 75 years of age can make non-concessional contributions (capped at $110,000 per annum or $330,000 over three years under the 'bring forward' option). But as soon as you turn 75 years of age, you can no longer make a non-concessional contribution to a complying super fund (refer to Figure 18-1).

(*Note:* Since 1 July 2022, you no longer need to satisfy a work test to make a non-concessional contribution if you're 67 to 74 years of age.)

WARNING

You can't make a non-concessional contribution once your superannuation fund account balance reaches $1.9 million.

CHECK THE NET

If you want to know more about non-concessional contributions — especially the bit about the $330,000 'bring forward' option — check out Tax Office fact sheet 'Non-concessional contributions and contribution caps', available at the Tax Office website (www.ato.gov.au).

Helping out the boss: Employee contributions

For the 2023–24 tax year, the SG contribution amount employers are required to make on behalf of employees is 11 per cent of their gross pay. (*Note:* From 1 July 2026 employers must pay the super guarantee amount at the same time employees are paid salary and wages.)

As an employee, you can make additional contributions under a salary sacrifice arrangement, where extra super contributions are deducted from your pay (refer to Chapter 16). You can claim a tax deduction for the amount you contribute.

For the 2023–24 tax year, all individuals (employees, self-employed, retirees) who are under 75 years of age can make concessional contributions (capped at $27,500 per annum). But if you're 67 to 74 years of age, you need to satisfy a work test to make a concessional contribution (namely, work a minimum 40 hours over 30 consecutive days during the financial year). This could benefit employees who work for organisations that don't offer salary sacrificing to their employees and retirees who want to increase their nest egg.

The SG contribution rate for the 2023–24 tax year is 11 per cent. It will then increase by 0.5 per cent each year until it reaches 12 per cent in the 2025–26 tax year.

Being in charge: Employer contributions

An employer can make concessional contributions on behalf of an employee. These contributions are a tax-deductible expense. For the 2023–24 tax year, the maximum an employer can contribute on behalf of an employee is capped at $27,500.

These contributions are taxed in the super fund at a rate of 15 per cent. Contributions that exceed these limits are taxed at your marginal rates plus an interest charge. But you can avoid this additional tax if you withdraw any excess concessional contributions you make to your super fund (refer to Figure 18-1).

REMEMBER

If you earn more than $250,000 and make concessional contributions, the rate of tax payable increases from 15 per cent to 30 per cent.

Working for yourself: Self-employed contributions

A concessional contribution made by a self-employed person to a complying super fund is a tax-deductible expense.

For the 2023–24 tax year, all individuals (employees, self-employed, retirees) who are under 75 years of age can make concessional contributions (capped at $27,500 per annum). If you're 67 to 74 years of age, you need to satisfy a work test to make a concessional contribution (namely, work a minimum 40 hours over 30 consecutive days during the financial year). (*Note:* Concessional contributions can't be accepted if you're aged 75 years or over.)

These contributions are taxed in the super fund at a rate of 15 per cent. Contributions that exceed these limits are taxed at your marginal rates plus an interest charge. But you can avoid this additional tax if you decide to withdraw any excess concessional contributions you make to your super fund (refer to Figure 18-1).

REMEMBER

If you earn more than $250,000 and you make a concessional contribution to a complying super fund, the rate of tax payable on this contribution increases from 15 per cent to 30 per cent.

WARNING

Although making a concessional contribution to a complying superannuation fund is a tax-deductible expense, keep in mind once your taxable income falls below the $18,200 tax-free threshold, no tax is payable.

Getting what's due: Government incentives

The federal government provides two tax incentives to encourage low-income earners to make a contribution to a complying superannuation fund:

>> **Co-contribution scheme:** For the 2023–24 tax year, if your total assessable income is less than $43,445 and you make a non-concessional contribution of $1,000 to your super fund, under the co-contribution scheme the federal government makes a $500 contribution on your behalf (refer to Chapter 5). Taking up this offer is a good way of getting free money for putting $1,000 into your super fund. But this amount reduces as you earn more money and ceases as soon as you earn more than $58,445 per year. (See Tax Office fact sheet 'Super co-contribution' for more details.)

>> **Spouse contribution:** For the 2023–24 tax year, if your spouse's assessable income is $37,000 or less in a financial year, you may be able to qualify for a $540 tax offset if you make a $3,000 spouse contribution to a complying super fund or retirement savings account operated by an approved financial institution. The tax offset is progressively reduced if your spouse earns more than $37,000 per year, and fully phases out if your spouse earns more than $40,000 per year. (See Tax Office fact sheet 'Superannuation-related tax offsets' for more details.)

Getting the Money: Conditions of Release

To access your accumulated benefits, you have to satisfy a *condition of release*. The main conditions are as follows:

>> Compassionate grounds/severe financial hardship

>> Death of member (see Chapter 20)

>> Permanent incapacity/terminal medical condition

>> Retirement (the most common condition of release)

>> Temporary incapacity/physical or mental ill health

Figure 18-2 shows how you're taxed when you receive a lump sum payment from your super fund, and highlights that the amount of tax you're liable to pay depends on your age at the time you withdraw your benefits and whether the payment is a tax-free component and/or taxable component.

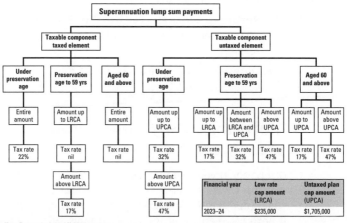

Note: Tax rate includes 2% Medicare levy

FIGURE 18-2: Receiving a superannuation lump sum payment.

When you receive a payment from a super fund, the payment can consist of three components:

>> **Tax-free component:** Payments that are tax free and excluded from taxable income. They include non-concessional contributions and certain other contributions

such as CGT-exempt components and pre-1983 accumulated amounts.

>> **Taxable component — taxed element:** Post-July 1983 accumulated benefits in a super fund that were liable to tax. These payments are liable to tax when distributed, but are tax free when you turn 60 years of age.

>> **Taxable component — untaxed element:** Post-July 1983 accumulated benefits in a super fund that haven't been taxed. These payments normally come from certain federal and state government super schemes that don't pay tax, and proceeds of a life insurance policy, and are liable to tax when distributed.

Three categories are used to describe when you can access your super fund benefits:

>> **Preserved benefits:** Benefits that you can access when you satisfy a condition of release, such as when you reach your preservation age and retire.

>> **Restricted non-preserved benefits:** Benefits that you can access when you retire or satisfy a certain condition of release.

>> **Unrestricted non-preserved benefits:** Benefits that you can access at any time.

Maturing nicely: Under your preservation age

Ordinarily, if you're under your preservation age, you can't access your preserved benefits (the amount that must remain in your super fund) until you reach your preservation age (59 years of age if born between 1 July 1963 and 30 June 1964; see the next section). Meanwhile, your benefits are invested on your behalf until you satisfy a condition of release.

If you receive a superannuation lump sum payment from a taxable component (taxed element — an amount that was previously liable to tax) the entire amount is taxed at the rate of 22 per cent (including the Medicare levy). Payments from this source come from complying super funds that pay tax.

On the other hand, if you receive a superannuation lump sum payment from a taxable component (untaxed element — an amount that wasn't previously liable to tax) amounts up to an indexed untaxed plan cap amount (UPCA) are taxed at the rate of 32 per cent (including the Medicare levy). Payments in excess of the indexed UPCA, which is $1,705,000 for the 2023–24 tax year, are taxed at the rate of 47 per cent (including 2 per cent Medicare levy). *Note:* Taxable component (untaxed element) payments are normally made from certain government-operated super funds that don't pay tax or a life insurance policy.

Reaching your preservation age

Before you can retire and access your funds, you need to have reached your *preservation age* — an age that depends on the date you were born (see Table 18-1 and visit the Tax Office website, www.ato.gov.au, for more info).

Under 60 years

If you've reached your preservation age, are under 60 years of age and want to access your preserved benefits, you need to satisfy the trustee of your superannuation fund that you have no intention to be gainfully employed for more than 10 hours per week. However, you can avoid doing this if you elect to take a transition to retirement pension. Under this option, you can receive a pension while still working (see Chapter 19).

If you receive a superannuation pension from a taxable component (taxed element), your pension is taxed at your marginal tax rates plus a Medicare levy, but you qualify for a 15 per cent tax offset (see Chapter 19).

If you're at or above your preservation age and under 60 years, and you receive a superannuation lump sum payment from a taxable component (taxed element), amounts up to the *low rate cap amount* (LRCA — set at $235,000 for the 2023–24 tax year) are tax free, while amounts above the LRCA are taxed at the rate of 17 per cent (including the Medicare levy).

If you receive a superannuation pension from a taxable component (untaxed element), the pension is taxed at your marginal tax rates plus the Medicare levy (see Chapter 19).

If you receive a superannuation lump sum payment from a taxable component (untaxed element), you're taxed as follows:

>> Amounts up to the LRCA are taxed at the rate of 17 per cent (including the Medicare levy).

>> Amounts between the LRCA up to the UPCA are taxed at the rate of 32 per cent (including the Medicare levy).

>> Amounts above the UPCA are taxed at the rate of 47 per cent (including the Medicare levy).

Between 60 years and 64 years

After you turn 60 years of age, to access your benefits you need only to terminate your current employment and satisfy the trustee that you're no longer contributing to your super fund.

All superannuation pensions and superannuation lump sum payments from a taxable component (taxed element) are tax free after you turn 60 years of age (see Chapter 19).

If you receive a superannuation pension from a taxable component (untaxed element), you're liable to pay tax at your marginal tax rates (plus the Medicare levy), but you qualify for a 10 per cent tax offset (see Chapter 19).

Further, if you receive a superannuation lump sum payment from a taxable component (untaxed element), amounts up to the UPCA are taxed at the rate of 17 per cent (including the Medicare levy), while amounts above the UPCA are taxed at the rate of 47 per cent (including the Medicare levy).

Feeling great: Over 65 years

After you reach 65 years of age, you can open the champagne bottle and start celebrating. You no longer need to retire to access your superannuation benefits. You can choose when to withdraw your benefits and still remain gainfully employed.

Superannuation fund benefits are made up of a combination of tax-free components and taxable components. *Note:* When you turn 60 years of age, all payments from taxable components (taxed elements) are tax free. However, you need to withdraw a combination of any tax-free components and taxable components in proportion to the total amount held in your superannuation fund. This rule applies so that in the event of your death, your beneficiaries are liable to pay tax on any taxable component held in your super fund (see Chapter 20).

If you receive a superannuation pension from a taxable component (untaxed element), you're liable to pay tax at your marginal tax rates (plus Medicare levy), but you qualify for a 10 per cent tax offset (see Chapter 19).

Further, if you receive a superannuation lump sum payment from a taxable component (untaxed element), amounts up to the UPCA are taxed at the rate of 17 per cent (including the Medicare levy), while amounts above the UPCA are taxed at the rate of 47 per cent (including the Medicare levy).

TIP

With respect to superannuation interests as a consequence of a marriage or relationship breakdown, you may find the following Tax Office publications helpful:

>> 'Superannuation and relationship breakdowns'

>> 'Marriage or relationship breakdown'

These are all available at the Tax Office website (www.ato.gov.au).

Chapter **19**

Reaping What You Sow: Receiving a Pension and Government Concessions

The good old days of popping down to Centrelink and lining up to receive the old age pension when you retire are long gone. Unfortunately, no-one gets a free lunch anymore. The federal government has introduced an income and asset test to restrict your capacity to receive the old age pension. To add salt to the wound, the government has increased the old age pension age to 67. Ouch! On the 'carrot' side of the measures, the government provides a number of tax incentives to encourage you to put money into a complying superannuation fund and fund your own retirement.

In this chapter, I discuss the three pension options that are normally offered to self-funded retirees. Each option has particular features that may appeal to you. I also examine the various types of government pension and allowance that you can receive if you satisfy certain conditions. These payments can be either taxable or exempt from tax.

Paddling the Superannuation Stream: Types of Super Pension

Self-funded retirees can purchase three types of superannuation pension (known as *superannuation income streams*) with their accumulated benefits:

>> Transition to retirement pensions

>> Non-account-based (life) pensions

>> Account-based pensions

Keep in mind when you get a superannuation pension that your payment can consist of three components:

>> Tax-free component

>> Taxable component — taxed element

>> Taxable component — untaxed element

The tax issues that you need to consider depend on your age at the time you receive the pension. (Refer to Chapter 18 for more.)

The federal government has introduced a transfer balance cap (at the time of writing, $1.9 million) to limit the amount of assets an individual can transfer to a pension account to fund future pension payments where earnings are exempt from tax. So when you start a super pension, you need to notify the Tax Office of the amount of funds you intend to transfer to your pension account. Stiff financial penalties apply if you exceed your $1.9 million transfer balance cap amount. (For more info, check out fact sheet 'Transfer balance cap' on the Tax Office website — www.ato.gov.au.)

Learning about transition to retirement pensions

To encourage you to keep on working rather than taking the early retirement option, the federal government has set up the *transition to retirement pension* option. A transition to retirement pension allows you to receive a superannuation pension (also known as a *superannuation income stream*) while you're still gainfully employed — the classic Clayton's substitute scenario: 'The retirement you have when you're not contemplating retirement!'

To qualify for the transition to retirement concession, you need to have reached your preservation age and elect to receive a *non-commutable pension*.

Earnings derived in a transition to retirement pension account are liable to a 15 per cent rate of tax (as is the case with earnings derived in an accumulation account). This could adversely curtail the use of this type of pension scheme. Because these funds are liable to tax, no restrictions exist on the amount of funds you can have in a transition to retirement account (which means the $1.9 million transfer balance cap mentioned in the preceding section does not apply).

While you're in receipt of this pension, you can't ordinarily withdraw lump sum payments from your superannuation fund until you reach 65 years of age, or retire. Under this arrangement, your pension must fall between 4 per cent and 10 per cent of the balance in your super fund account. Your pension is recalculated at the beginning of each financial year and the amount you receive depends on the balance in your account.

The taxable component (taxed element) part of the pension qualifies for a 15 per cent tax offset and, after you turn 60 years of age, the pension becomes tax free (see Figure 19-1).

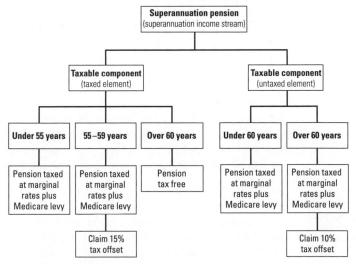

FIGURE 19-1: Taxing your superannuation pension.

For more information on transition to retirement pensions, see fact sheets 'Transition to retirement' and 'SMSF – transition to retirement income streams' on the Tax Office website (www.ato.gov.au).

Your preservation age depends on the date you were born (59 years of age at the time of writing if you were born between 1 July 1963 and 30 June 1964 — which means you can commence this pension during the 2023–24 tax year). Refer to Chapter 18 for more on this.

Understanding non-account-based pensions

If you're a traditionalist at heart and you like some sense of certainty in your life, choosing the option of taking a *non-account-based pension* may be for you. This type of superannuation pension is normally a lifetime pension, which means you're assured of receiving the pension for the rest of your life. In the event of your death, your pension can continue to be paid as a death benefit income stream to a dependent reversionary beneficiary (for instance, your spouse — see Chapter 20 for more).

With this option, you need to exchange a lump sum payment for a non-account-based pension.

The pension payment you receive each year can increase only to counter the impact of inflation. If you're under 60 years of age, the pension qualifies for a 15 per cent tax offset and, when you turn 60, the pension is tax free. Any income or capital gain that your super fund derives during the pension phase to fund your pension payments is exempt from tax. The bad news is you normally can't withdraw any funds or commute (change) the pension to a lump sum payment. Another disadvantage of this type of super pension is you also can't vary your pension payments from year to year except to make an adjustment for inflation.

The federal government has proposed that from 1 July 2025, if you have more than $3 million in super (for instance, $4 million in an accumulation account), you'll need to apportion your super fund's investments for different tax treatment. The portion that corresponds to $3 million will be taxed at the rate of

15 per cent, while the portion that corresponds to the balance above $3 million (in this example, the $1 million bit) will be taxed at the rate of 30 per cent. When calculating your investment earnings, you'll need to take into account your super fund balance at the start and end of the tax year and make appropriate adjustments for any contributions and withdrawals. This means your investment earnings will include any *unrealised capital gains* on assets you hold (such as shares and property that have increased in value during the tax year), along with any interest dividends and rent you may receive. The additional tax will apply even if you're in retirement phase and you've started a super pension.

REMEMBER

If you happen to be a government employee and you receive a super pension paid from a taxable component (untaxed element), the pension is taxed at your marginal tax rates (plus the Medicare levy). Unfortunately, if you're between your preservation age and 59 years of age, you don't qualify for a 15 per cent tax offset because certain government super funds don't pay tax. However, when you turn 60 years of age, you qualify for a 10 per cent tax offset (refer to Figure 19-1).

CASE STUDY: TRANSITION TO RETIREMENT PENSION

Jonathon has reached his preservation age (refer to Chapter 18) and is under 60 years of age. He has $360,000 in his superannuation fund account. He decides to receive a transition to retirement pension. The amount he can take out must fall between $14,400 per year (4 per cent of $360,000) and $36,000 per year (10 per cent of $360,000). He elects to receive $36,000, which is the maximum amount he can withdraw. The pension is liable to tax at his marginal tax rates (plus the Medicare levy) and he qualifies for a $5,400 tax offset (15 per cent of $36,000 — refer to Figure 19-1).

The good news is that when Jonathon turns 60 years of age, the pension is tax free (refer to Figure 19-1).

The bad news is any income or capital gain that the superannuation fund derives to fund this pension is liable to a 15 per cent rate of tax.

CASE STUDY: NON-ACCOUNT-BASED PENSION (LIFE PENSION)

Joanne has reached her preservation age (refer to Chapter 18) and is under 60 years of age. She has $600,000 in her superannuation fund account. She decides to receive a life pension in lieu of the $600,000 balance as a lump sum, because she likes the idea of receiving a guaranteed pension. She's entitled to receive a $36,000 pension per year for life and the pension is adjusted annually to counter the impact of inflation. The taxable component (taxed element) of the pension ($36,000) is liable to tax at her marginal tax rates (plus the Medicare levy) and she qualifies for a $5,400 tax offset (15 per cent of $36,000). When Joanne turns 60 years of age, the pension is tax free (refer to Figure 19-1). Any income or capital gain that the superannuation fund derives during the pension phase to fund the pension is exempt from tax.

Getting familiar with account-based pensions

Under the *account-based pension* option, you need to exchange a lump sum payment for a pension (superannuation income stream).

You have the option to vary your pension payments from year to year, and no set term is specified. You must receive the pension at least annually and continue to receive it until all your funds are extinguished. Therefore, you're best to invest your money wisely. Further, no maximum withdrawals are imposed. However, you must receive a prescribed minimum, which can vary according to your age — from between 4 per cent and 14 per cent each year (see Table 19-1).

For example, if you're under 65 years of age, you must ordinarily withdraw 4 per cent of your account balance, and if you're over 95 years of age, the minimum withdrawal is ordinarily 14 per cent.

The maximum you can transfer from funds held in your accumulation account to start an account-based pension (where earnings are exempt from tax) is capped at $1.9 million. (*Note:* Any income or capital gain derived in an accumulation account is liable to a 15 per cent rate of tax.)

TABLE 19-1 **Minimum Superannuation Pension Payments**

Age	Min. Pension Withdrawals from Account
Under 65	4%
65–74	5%
75–79	6%
80–84	7%
85–89	9%
90–94	11%
95 and over	14%

The good news is no restrictions are imposed on investment growth. This means if your account-based pension balance grows beyond the $1.9 million cap amount (for instance, to $3 million) you can retain the excess amount (where earnings are exempt from tax) to fund future pension payments. But the bad news is you can't make any additional top up payments if investment losses reduce your account-based pension balance below the $1.9 million transfer balance cap amount. So it's important that you invest your money prudently.

By the way, you can progressively transfer additional funds to your account-based pension account if you had not yet reached your $1.9 million transfer balance cap. (*Note:* The $1.9 million transfer balance cap is indexed for inflation and will increase in $100,000 increments.)

The pension is recalculated at the beginning of each financial year and the amount you receive depends on the balance in your account.

WARNING

If you receive a superannuation death benefit pension (for instance, from your deceased spouse), the deceased's transfer balance cap amount is added to your transfer balance cap amount. If the combined balance in your account-based pension account exceeds $1.9 million, you need to transfer the excess bit back to your super fund's accumulation account. Alternatively, you can withdraw the excess amount from your super fund.

CASE STUDY: ACCOUNT-BASED PENSION

Asbel has reached his preservation age (refer to Chapter 18) and is under 60. He has $600,000 in his superannuation fund account. He decides to receive an account-based pension because he likes the flexibility of the various options he can use. The minimum Asbel can receive is $24,000 per year (4 per cent of $600,000).

This financial year, Asbel elects to receive a $36,000 pension, but he has the option to receive more or less next year. The taxable component (taxed element) of the pension ($36,000) is liable to tax at his marginal tax rates (plus the Medicare levy) and he qualifies for a $5,400 tax offset (15 per cent of $36,000). However, as soon as Asbel turns 60 years of age, the pension is tax free (refer to Figure 19-1). Any income or capital gain that the superannuation fund derives during the pension phase to fund the pension is exempt from tax.

WARNING

If you have a SMSF that's in the pension phase and your fund's assets predominantly consist of an investment property, you risk contravening the superannuation rules and regulations if the net rent your fund derives is insufficient to meet your annual minimum pension payments to members and your fund's ongoing expenses. This could become a major problem if the property is untenanted for a substantial period of time. Under these circumstances, you could be forced to sell the property.

TECHNICAL STUFF

For more information on minimum pension payment requirements see the fact sheet 'SMSF minimum pension payment requirements and exception FAQs' on the Tax Office website (www.ato.gov.au).

TIP

Pension payments from a complying superannuation fund (such as a SMSF) must be withdrawn in cash. It's also possible for you to make lump sum non-cash (*in-specie*) withdrawals from a SMSF (such as shares listed on the ASX). Strict rules apply, though, so you're best to seek professional advice. For more details, see Taxation Ruling 'TR 2013/5' and fact sheet 'Super withdrawal options' on the Tax Office website (www.ato.gov.au).

Getting a defined benefit pension

If you receive a pension from a funded defined benefit scheme, you need to multiple the taxable pension payments by 16 to work out the *deemed capital* in this defined benefit fund. This is the amount of capital deemed to fund these pension payments, and you need to work this out to check whether you exceed the $1.9 million transfer balance cap. This will happen once your pension payments exceed $118,750 per annum ($118,750 × 16 = $1.9 million).

Complications can arise if you receive a defined benefit pension and a pension from an account-based pension fund that's in the pension phase (see the sidebar 'Case study: Defined benefit pension and account-based pension').

If you receive a pension from a funded defined benefit scheme, 50 per cent of pension payments that exceed your defined benefit income cap ($118,750 per annum) is liable to tax at your marginal rates.

CASE STUDY: DEFINED BENEFIT PENSION AND ACCOUNT-BASED PENSION

Maria receives a $50,000 defined benefit pension and has $500,000 in a self-managed super fund that's in the pension phase. Maria will need to do the following calculation to check whether she exceeds the $1.9 million transfer balance cap.

Deemed capital in defined benefit fund ($50,000 × 16)	$800,000
Capital in account-based pension fund	$500,000
Total capital	**$1,300,000**

Because the total amount of capital is less than $1.9 million, Maria does not need to transfer any excess amount back to her accumulation account where earnings are taxed at the rate of 15 per cent. On the other hand, if the total capital was, say, $2 million, she would need to transfer $100,000 back to her accumulation account. (**Note:** Any income or capital gain derived in an accumulation account is liable to a 15 per cent rate of tax.)

CASE STUDY: CALCULATING YOUR MINIMUM PENSION PAYMENT

Wai Yee, who is 62 years of age and retired, has a SMSF that's in the pension phase. The market value of the fund's investment assets at the beginning of 1 July 2023 is $500,000.

The annual minimum pension payment for members under 65 years of age is 4 per cent of the market value of the fund's investment assets held at the beginning of 1 July 2023 (refer to Table 19-1).

The annual minimum pension amount Wai Yee must withdraw from her super is $20,000 ($500,000 × 4% = $20,000).

For more info, see the Tax Office fact sheet 'Pension standards for self-managed super funds' and Taxation Ruling 'TR 2013/5 Income tax: when a superannuation income stream commences and ceases'. Both are available at www.ato.gov.au.

If you receive a pension from an unfunded defined benefit scheme (such as certain government schemes that don't pay tax) and your pension payments exceed $118,750 per annum, the 10 per cent tax offset you can claim will be capped at $11,875. For more info, check out Tax Office fact sheet 'Transfer balance cap – capped defined benefit income streams' on its website (www.ato.gov.au).

Getting Help: Government Pensions and Allowances

Once you retire, you may be eligible to receive many Australian government pensions, allowances and other payments. These payments can be either taxable or exempt from tax.

One of the most common payments is the age pension, which is payable to eligible individuals who satisfy an income test and asset test. This pension is liable to tax.

Other examples of government assistance include payments such as the carer payment, Austudy payment, JobSeeker payment, Youth allowance and sickness allowance. These payments are all liable to tax. (For a full list of what's taxable, see Tax Office fact sheet 'Government payments and allowances'.) But the good news is that you may be eligible for a beneficiary tax offset, which means you could end up paying no tax on these payments if this is the only type of assessable income you derive. For more info, check out Tax Office fact sheet 'Beneficiary tax offset'.

If you receive any government assistance payments, at the end of the financial year you may receive a 'PAYG payment summary – individual non-business' statement that sets out the total of your payments assessable for tax (refer to Chapter 3).

CHECK THE NET

If you want to know whether you qualify for government pensions, allowances and payments and whether they're taxable or exempt from tax, you can check out the following websites:

>> Australian Government: Department of Social services (www.dss.gov.au) — go to the Seniors tab and then 'Benefits & Payments'

>> Australian Taxation Office (www.ato.gov.au) — read the fact sheet 'Government payments and allowances'

Getting back what you deserve: Tax offsets

Although the pensions, allowances and other payments mentioned in the previous section are taxable, when you take into account the various tax offsets that you may qualify for (such as the beneficiary tax offset mentioned previously), the amount of tax payable may reduce to nil. This scenario can arise if you're a low-income earner and you qualify for a low income tax offset (where your income is below the taxable income threshold of $37,500 per year), or you receive an age pension and qualify for the seniors and pensioners tax offset (SAPTO), which depends on your taxable income and whether you're single or part of a couple. Refer to Chapter 3 for information about the low income tax offset, and Table 19-2 for the SAPTO.

For the 2023–24 tax year the seniors and pensioners tax offset is $2,230 for a single person and $1,602 for each member of a couple. For more info, visit the Tax Office website (www.ato.gov.au) and read Tax Office publication 'Withholding declaration – short version for seniors and pensioners'. (It's good to know you don't have to read the long version!)

TABLE 19-2 Seniors and Pensioners Tax Offset (SAPTO)

Single	
Financial Year	Taxable Income Threshold
2023–24	Lower limit $32,279
	Upper limit $50,119
Couple (Entitlement for Each Member of a Couple)	
Financial Year	Taxable Income Threshold
2023–24	Lower limit $28,974 each
	Upper limit $83,580 combined

Being allowed to keep it: What isn't taxed

Many Australian government pensions, allowances and other payments are specifically exempt from tax. For a list of what payments are exempt income, check out Tax Office fact sheets 'Taxable, assessable and exempt income' and 'Amounts you do not include as income'.

CASE STUDY: SENIORS AND PENSIONERS TAX OFFSET (SAPTO)

John and Betty are eligible to receive an age pension and qualify for the SAPTO. They also derive investment income. During the 2023–24 tax year, their combined taxable income is $40,000. According to the SAPTO rates, because their combined taxable income is below the taxable income threshold for a couple, they pay no tax on the amount they derived.

The tax offset reduces by 12.5 cents for every dollar above the respective thresholds. If you don't fully use the tax offset, you can transfer the excess to your respective spouse.

Chapter **20**

Death and Taxes: Wills and Asset Distribution

An old saying states that two things are certain in life: Death and taxes. Although you can't predict with certainty your death, you can at least reduce the impact of taxation when you die.

In this chapter, I explain how death benefits are taxed when they're paid to your dependants and non-dependants, and how the capital gains tax (CGT) provisions apply to certain assets that you plan to distribute to your beneficiaries after you die.

Preparing a Will

A *will* is a legal document that sets out your instructions for the distribution of your assets and personal belongings when you die. When you set up a will, you need to choose an executor to administer the will in accordance with your instructions. Because your personal circumstances can quickly change (for example, marriage, divorce, birth of a child, death of a family member or retirement), it's a good idea to regularly amend and update this document.

Preparing a will is an important exercise if you want your assets distributed to specific beneficiaries. Having a will is also essential if you receive a superannuation pension and, on your death, you want payments (death benefits) to go to a specific dependant (such as your spouse) or to several dependants. How your beneficiaries are taxed depends on a number of factors, which I discuss in this chapter.

If you want your superannuation death benefits to be paid to a specific dependant or to your estate, you need to sign a binding death benefit nomination form. If you do this, the trustees of your super fund must comply with your request. Otherwise, you introduce a risk that the fund may not pay the death benefit to the person(s) you nominate or may not even comply with your wishes. (For more details, see Tax Office fact sheet 'Superannuation death benefits'.)

You can get a copy of a binding death benefit nomination form from your superannuation fund.

How your estate is taxed depends on whether your beneficiaries are dependants or non-dependants: Dependants are taxed differently to non-dependants in respect of death benefit distributions. For the purposes of receiving a death benefit distribution (such as your pension), the following beneficiaries are dependants:

>> Spouse, de facto spouse, former spouse or former de facto spouse

>> Child (including stepchild, adopted child and ex-nuptial child) younger than 18 years of age

>> Person financially dependent on the deceased at date of death (for example, a child younger than 25 years of age)

>> Person in an interdependency relationship (such as two people who have a close personal relationship, live together, provide financial support for one another and attend to each other's personal and domestic needs)

Although Australia doesn't have death taxes or an inheritance tax, CGT may have an adverse impact on the distribution of the assets you intend to give to certain beneficiaries. This consequence is because some assets are exempt from CGT (for instance, your main residence and car), while the tax treatment of your other assets depends on whether you acquired them on or after 20 September 1985. CGT was first introduced in Australia on this date. (See the section 'Taxing All Your Treasures', later in this chapter.)

WARNING

Estate planning is complex, so you're best to seek professional advice when preparing your will, especially regarding the steps you need to put into place to minimise the impact of taxation when you die. For more info, check out Tax Office fact sheet 'Estate planning' and 'Wills and powers of attorney' on the moneysmart.gov.au website.

Taxing Your Income

In the event of your death, the executor of your estate takes control of your financial affairs. The *executor* is responsible for the administration of your estate until all your assets have been distributed in accordance with your will. One important duty your executor needs to attend to is your tax affairs. The executor needs to notify the Tax Office of your death, lodge a tax return that discloses the income you derive up to the date of your death, and a trust return for any income you receive after your death (such as income from your investments). The trust net income is liable to tax — to either the beneficiaries who are presently entitled to receive a distribution (meaning they have a legal right to demand payment) or to the executor.

If you're still working when you die, your beneficiaries, especially your dependants and non-dependants, may be entitled to receive a *death benefit employment termination payment* (ETP). Death benefit ETPs include a golden handshake, payment in lieu of notice, unused rostered days off and unused sick leave.

WARNING

A death benefit ETP doesn't include payments for unused annual leave and long service leave. Nor does it include the tax-free part of a genuine redundancy payment or an early retirement scheme payment (refer to Chapter 5).

The following beneficiaries are dependants for the purposes of receiving a death benefit distribution:

>> Spouse, de facto spouse, former spouse

>> Child younger than 18 years of age

» Person financially dependent on the deceased (at date of death)

» Person in an interdependency relationship (such as two people who have a close personal relationship, live together, provide financial support for one another and attend to each other's personal and domestic needs)

How death benefit ETPs are taxed depends on whether the payment is a tax-free component or a taxable component (refer to Chapter 18), and whether the payment is above or below the lower cap amount (LCA) threshold ($235,000 in the 2023–24 tax year).

Taxation of a death benefit ETP is also affected by where the payment goes, as follows:

» **Dependant** (taxable component):

- Tax free up to LCA
- Above LCA — tax rate of 47 per cent

» **Non-dependant** (taxable component):

- Tax rate of 32 per cent up to LCA
- Above LCA — tax rate of 47 per cent

Note: Tax rates include 2 per cent Medicare levy.

CHECK THE NET

If you want to know more about taxation of deceased estates, visit the Tax Office website (www.ato.gov.au) and read the fact sheets 'Recipients of death benefit termination payments' and 'Deceased estates'.

Sharing Your Pension

If you're receiving a superannuation pension when you die, your pension can continue to be paid as a *death benefit income stream* to a *dependent reversionary beneficiary* (a person who can continue to receive your pension after you die until all the money runs out). If your beneficiary is a financially dependent child, your pension can continue to be paid until the child reaches 25 years of age. Your super pension then becomes a tax-free superannuation lump sum death benefit payment. However, if your dependent child is permanently disabled, the payment can continue to be paid as a death benefit income stream to that person.

The amount of tax payable depends on your age when you die, the age of your dependant(s) and whether the payment is from a tax-free component, taxable component (taxed element) or taxable component (untaxed element). Figure 20-1 shows how the death benefit income stream works.

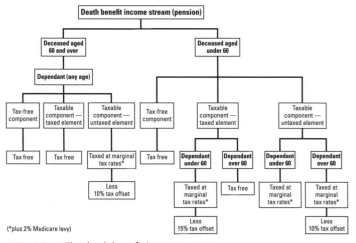

FIGURE 20-1: The death benefit income stream.

The federal government has imposed restrictions on the amount an individual can transfer to an account-based pension account to fund pension payments where earnings are exempt from tax. The maximum transfer balance cap amount you can have is $1.9 million. If you receive a superannuation death benefit pension, the deceased's transfer balance cap amount is added to the surviving spouse's transfer balance cap amount. If the combined amount exceeds $1.9 million, you need to transfer the excess amount back to your super fund's accumulation account where earnings are liable to a 15 per cent rate of tax. Alternatively, you can withdraw the excess amount from your super fund. For more details, refer to Chapter 18.

When you receive a payment from a superannuation fund, the payment can consist of three components:

>> Tax-free component

>> Taxable component — taxed element

>> Taxable component — untaxed element

Refer to Chapter 18 for more information on these three components.

A superannuation death benefit income stream (pension) can't be paid to a non-dependant.

Alternatively, the balance in your superannuation account can be paid out as superannuation death benefit lump sum payments. Under these circumstances, the tax treatment depends on whether your beneficiary is a dependant or non-dependant and whether the payment is a tax-free component or taxable component.

The following sets out the rules of taxing a superannuation death benefit lump sum payment consequently distributed to a dependant and/or non-dependant on your death:

>> **Dependant:** Whole amount tax free

>> **Non-dependant:**

  • Taxed element — taxed at 17 per cent

  • Untaxed element — taxed at 32 per cent

Note: Tax rates include 2 per cent Medicare levy.

The federal government has advised that if a superannuation fund member who's in the pension phase dies, any investment earnings derived will continue to be exempt from tax until the deceased member's benefits are paid out of the fund.

If you want more information about a death benefit paid from a superannuation fund visit the Tax Office website (www.ato.gov.au) and check out fact sheet 'Paying superannuation death benefits'. See also Tax Office Interpretative Decision 'ATO ID 2015/23 Superannuation: member's benefits in a regulated superannuation fund must be "cashed" upon death by being paid – mere journal entries insufficient'.

Taxing All Your Treasures

During your lifetime, you may accumulate many assets. These precious items can include real estate (particularly your main residence), a share portfolio and other assets that you keep for your personal use and enjoyment (such as collectables and personal use assets). Unfortunately, when you die you can't take them with you. Over the centuries, though, many people from different cultures have tried — without success.

Fortunately, Australia doesn't have death taxes or an inheritance tax to worry about. Further, under the CGT provisions, death doesn't constitute a disposal of your assets. Thus, when your CGT assets are distributed to your beneficiaries, no tax liability arises. However, before your beneficiaries open the champagne bottle and start celebrating, the catch is that they become liable to pay CGT when they sell the assets. This rule applies because when you inherit assets you're deemed to acquire them on the date of death of the deceased. The tricky part comes next.

If you (as the deceased) acquired the assets before 20 September 1985, your beneficiaries are deemed to acquire them on the date of your death at their market value. This interpretation means that any increase in their value up to this point in time is ignored by the Tax Office for tax liability. However, your beneficiaries are liable to pay tax on any subsequent increase in value above the market value (this amount is the cost base for CGT purposes). To work out the market value of the assets, you may need to get a professional valuation (such as a sworn valuation).

On the other hand, if you (as the deceased) acquired the assets on or after 20 September 1985, your beneficiaries are deemed to have acquired them on the date of your death at the value you acquired them. This rule means that for the purposes of working out whether your beneficiaries make a capital gain or capital loss, the deceased's cost base is used. So your beneficiaries are personally liable to pay tax on any increase in the value of the assets during the time you (as the deceased) owned the assets, plus any further increase in value during the time your beneficiaries own them.

From a tax planning point of view, you need to be aware of how the CGT provisions apply to assets you intend to distribute to your beneficiaries. The amount of tax payable on disposal of assets you inherit depends on the date the deceased originally acquired the assets (whether they were acquired before, on or after 20 September 1985), and whether they're exempt from tax (for example, main residence and cars).

You can't transfer accumulated capital losses to your beneficiaries in the event of your death. If you have substantial capital losses not yet utilised, it's best — wherever possible — to offset your capital losses against your current capital gains at regular intervals.

The application of the CGT provisions is tricky because different tax rules apply when your beneficiaries sell them. Perhaps the most aggrieved beneficiaries are those who inherit non-exempt assets that were acquired on or after 20 September 1985, because they stand to pay the most amount of tax on a subsequent disposal (especially if the asset increases substantially in value).

In Chapter 6, I point out that under the CGT provisions, owning a main residence is normally exempt from tax. In the event of your death, the good news is that the main residence exemption concession can be transferred to your beneficiaries.

If you inherit a deceased person's main residence, the following rules apply:

>> If you sell the property within two years of the person's death, no CGT applies. This is the case even if you decide to lease the property during this period of time. (By the way, the Tax Office has discretion to extend the two-year period to sell the property, if necessary.)

>> If the property becomes your main residence, the property continues to be exempt from CGT.

If you want to know more about inheriting a main residence, visit the Tax Office website (www.ato.gov.au) and read 'Guide to capital gains tax' and 'Inherited property and CGT'.

CASE STUDY: INHERITING AN ASSET

Chen inherits a parcel of shares from a deceased relative. The deceased bought the shares eight years ago and paid $100,000 for them. Chen is deemed to have acquired the shares he inherits on the date of the death of his relative. The deemed cost base is $100,000 because the shares were purchased on or after 20 September 1985. As at the date of his relative's death, Chen is informed that the market value of the shares is $400,000. If Chen sells the shares, he's personally liable to pay tax on the accrued increase in their value from the date the deceased acquired the shares to the date Chen sells them. At this point in time, Chen indirectly inherits a potential $300,000 CGT liability — ouch!

Chen sells the shares one year later for $450,000. He is personally liable to pay tax on $350,000, being the increase in value from the date the deceased acquired them to when Chen sells them. To help ease the pain, because the shares were owned for more than 12 months (by the deceased and Chen), Chen is liable to pay tax on only half of the gain (that is, $175,000). For more details, refer to Chapter 11.

On the other hand, if the deceased relative had bought the shares before 20 September 1985, the cost base would've been $400,000, being the market value as at the date of death. Under these circumstances, Chen is liable to pay CGT only on any subsequent increase in value above $400,000. When Chen sells the shares one year later for $450,000, he's personally liable to pay tax on the $50,000 gain he makes on sale. Because the shares were owned for more than 12 months, Chen is liable to pay tax on only half of the gain (that is, $25,000).

The Part of Tens

IN THIS PART . . .

Discover a number of ways to minimise your tax bill by the book.

Find out about some common tax mistakes — and how you can avoid making them.

Chapter **21**

Ten Ways to Minimise Your Tax while Keeping the Tax Office Happy

n a federal government inquiry into the media in 1991, Kerry Packer, who was at that time the richest man in Australia, made the following attention-grabbing statement: 'If anyone in this country doesn't minimise their tax, they want their head read' (enough said!). To help you avoid getting your head read, in this chapter I discuss ten ways to minimise your tax bill while keeping the Tax Office happy.

Keep Good Records

Keeping proper records is the first step to minimising your tax bill. Set up a good record-keeping system to keep track of all your assets, income and expenses. If the Tax Office audits your tax return, the onus of proof that your tax affairs are in order rests with you (refer to Chapter 4). Ordinarily, you need to keep your records for five years. A tax agent can help you set up a good system to meet your statutory obligations. The key records you need to keep include

>> A record of all the assessable income you derive and expenditure you incur each year (refer to Chapter 2).

>> Receipts to substantiate work-related expenses that exceed $300 (refer to Chapter 5).

>> A register of all your capital gains tax (CGT) assets, particularly the date of purchase and cost base (refer to Chapter 11).

>> If you own property, the contract of purchase that sets out the property's cost base.

>> A record of improvements you make to your property, because you can add these expenses to the cost base.

>> If you own non-income-producing assets (such as a holiday house) that you acquired after 20 August 1991, a record of all your interest payments, rates, insurance and repairs, because you can add these types of expenses to the asset's cost base (refer to Chapter 10).

>> If you own shares, all your buy and sell contract notes for the purposes of calculating whether you made a capital gain or capital loss (refer to Chapter 9).

>> A record of capital losses that you can offset against current and future capital gains. This may mean that you keep records of your capital loss until the year in which the loss is applied against a capital gain, which may be for more than five years.

Take Advantage of New Developments

Federal governments constantly introduce new tax initiatives to stimulate economic activity and savings to influence your behaviour. These announcements are normally made when a federal budget is brought down or during the lead–up to a federal election. Therefore, you need to be aware of these changes and what you need to do to comply. The changes are normally associated with running a business, super and family benefits. For example, the federal government has introduced

>> Small business tax concessions to simplify running a business (refer to Chapter 13)

>> Small business CGT concessions to reduce or totally eliminate the impact of CGT on your business assets (Chapter 17)

>> Tax incentives to encourage you to fund your retirement (Chapter 18)

>> Incentives to help you buy your first home (Chapter 6)

Failure to take advantage of these initiatives can cost you dearly in the long term.

Get a Helping Hand from the Tax Office

The Tax Office website (www.ato.gov.au) contains a wealth of information you can access free of charge. This library of tax information is useful because the Tax Office regularly issues fact sheets, income tax rulings, tax determinations and ATO interpretative decisions to explain specific tax issues that need to be clarified (as illustrated throughout this book). With a little practice, you can quickly find information that you can use to your advantage.

This website can prove to be a valuable resource if you're running a business or you need some specific details. Further, if you apply for a private ruling, the Tax Office examines your request and gives you a written response about how it would interpret the laws in respect to the issue you raise (free of charge!).

Lose Money the Right Way

While you're building up your wealth, sadly, the strong possibility exists that some of your investment holdings can turn sour. You're not going to win all the time — but if you do manage to never lose money, I'll be first in line to buy your best-selling book.

If your investments decrease in value, you can do two things. You can cry over spilt milk and keep hold of your investments in the hope they come good again, or you can become proactive and turn your bad news into good news. Here's how:

>> If your investments fall in value, you can't claim a capital loss until they're sold. On the other hand, if you sell them, the loss you crystallise can be immediately offset against any current capital gains you may have made.

>> If you make no capital gains during the financial year, the loss can be carried forward for an indefinite period and offset against any future capital gains you may make.

REMEMBER

If you make a capital loss on one category of investment (such as shares), a key rule to capitalise on is that you can offset the loss against a capital gain on another category of investment (for example, real estate). One exception to the rule relates to collectables such as artwork and antiques (refer to Chapter 11). You can only offset a capital loss you make on a collectable against a capital gain on another collectable.

When you apply a capital loss against a capital gain, you save having to pay tax on the gain. Therefore, you're best to keep in mind that a loss has value. The extent of that value depends on your current marginal tax rates.

Contribute to a Super Fund

The federal government has introduced a number of incentives to encourage employees to make a contribution to a complying super fund. Earnings derived by a super fund are taxed at the rate of 15 per cent, and pensions and lump sum withdrawals are tax free after you reach 60 years of age and retire. Refer to Chapter 18 for more information about superannuation contributions.

TIP

If you earn less than $37,000, you may qualify for a $500 low income super tax offset to eliminate any tax payable and help boost your retirement nest egg (see Tax Office fact sheet 'Low income super tax offset' for more details).

Claim a Super Tax Deduction

All individuals (employees, self-employed and retirees) up to age 74 can claim a tax deduction for personal super contributions up to their concessional cap amount (at the time of writing, $27,500). Concessional contributions can include employer contributions and contributions you make under a salary sacrifice arrangement. But you need to satisfy a work test if you are between 67 and 74 years of age. To satisfy this test, you need to work at least 40 hours over 30 consecutive days. Unfortunately, concessional contributions can't be accepted if you're aged 75 years or over.

Take Advantage of the Low Income Threshold

An individual can earn up to $18,200 before being liable to pay tax (or $21,884 when you take the $700 low income tax offset into account — refer to Chapter 5).

If you have a spouse who isn't working or who derives a minimal amount of income, you may take advantage of his or her low income threshold. For example, if you have money to invest, you can consider investing those funds in your spouse's name. Under these circumstances, your spouse isn't liable to pay tax on the investment income derived if the amount is below the low income thresholds. If the investment is in shares that pay fully franked dividends, in addition to receiving a dividend, your spouse also receives a refund of the excess franking credits.

Package Your Salary

One option you can consider to minimise your tax bill is salary sacrificing part of your salary and wages for additional superannuation contributions paid to your complying super fund. This approach may be worth considering if you're a high-income earner and nearing your retirement age. If you follow this route, you gain two significant benefits:

>> You reduce the amount of tax payable on the salary derived.

>> You increase the retirement nest egg that you can access when you retire.

If you salary sacrifice your salary or wage to below $37,000, you pay no tax on the first $18,200 and no more than 19 per cent tax on the next $18,800 you derive. (And you'll also qualify for a $700 low income tax offset!) You pay just 15 per cent tax on the amount of your salary you contribute to super, as opposed to paying your marginal tax rates if the salary were paid to you.

Tap In to Negative Gearing

The Australian tax system can offer you significant tax incentives to help you increase your wealth. One such benefit is commonly known as *negative gearing* (refer to Chapter 10). Using this technique can help you to acquire assets such as investment property and shares that have the capacity to increase in value and pay you regular income.

If you borrow money to buy an investment asset that pays income (such as interest, dividends and rent), the interest you incur is tax deductible. Further, if your total expenditure (being predominantly interest) exceeds your investment income, you can offset the loss against other assessable income you derive, such as your salary and wages, other investment income and business profits. If you take this route, you reduce the amount of tax payable on your other assessable income. In the meantime, if the investment asset increases substantially in value, you're ahead. If you decide to use this strategy, you're effectively using the tax system to help you to finance the purchase and service the debt.

For this strategy to work, five key components must be present:

>> **Assessable income:** You need to be deriving another source of income in order to claim a tax deduction. Negative gearing greatly benefits individuals who pay a high marginal rate of

tax. **Note:** No tax is payable if your taxable income is below $18,200 (refer to Chapter 5).

>> **Cash flow:** You must be capable of servicing the loan repayments. You can use the income you derive to pay your loan.

>> **Interest payments:** Interest payments can be fixed or variable and are tax deductible if the purpose (or use) of the loan is to buy assets that generate income.

>> **Investment growth:** The investment must increase in value — otherwise, you're financing the purchase of an asset of decreasing value. **Note:** You gain no tax advantages by holding an unrealised capital loss.

>> **Income from asset:** You can claim a tax deduction only if the asset generates income.

Account for Income and Deductions

The Tax Act requires you to bring to account on a yearly basis your revenue and expenditure for the purposes of calculating your taxable income. To satisfy this rule correctly, you're required to make timing adjustments with respect to recognising certain revenue and expenditure. When you make end of financial year adjustments, you're able to delay recognising revenue and bringing forward tax deductions. A tax accountant can show you how to take advantage of this rule.

Chapter **22**

Ten Common Tax Mistakes to Avoid

The Tax Office has published a number of common tax mistakes that you need to be aware of. In Chapter 4 I point out that the onus is on you to declare the correct amount of income you derive each year, and the correct amount of tax deductions (and tax offsets) you can legally claim. To keep you honest, the Tax Office performs ongoing tax audits and data-matching checks to verify whether the information you disclose in your tax return is true and correct.

If you breach Australia's tax laws, you incur a financial penalty (a fine) plus an interest charge on the shortfall. If the offence is serious, you could spend some time in the slammer! In this chapter, I identify some common tax mistakes that you need to avoid.

Not Adhering to Small Business Tax Requirements

Each year, the Tax Office conducts routine tax audits and data-matching programs that reveal the following common tax errors relating to running a small business:

>> Not recording every sale

>> Not issuing appropriate tax invoices to customers or clients (refer to Chapter 15)

>> Incorrectly completing BAS statements (refer to Chapter 15)

>> Not lodging a superannuation guarantee charge statement to the Tax Office within the prescribed period — ordinarily on a quarterly basis (refer to Chapter 13)

>> Not paying enough superannuation contributions (or none at all) on behalf of employees

>> Not passing on employee tax file numbers to employees' nominated superannuation funds within 14 days of receiving them

>> Not maintaining a log book if using the operating cost method to calculate a car fringe benefit (refer to Chapter 16)

>> Not paying fringe benefits tax (FBT) if a car is made available to employees (or their associates) for private use (for example, the car is garaged at the employee's home each night — refer to Chapter 16)

>> Failing to pay FBT in respect of certain benefits provided to employees (refer to Chapter 16)

>> Not meeting the basic conditions for entitlement to capital gains tax (CGT) concessions for small business (refer to Chapter 17)

Not Keeping Your Business Records in Shape

If you run a business, you must keep proper records of all your income and expenses (refer to Chapter 13). The Tax Office has identified the following common tax mistakes relating to maintaining proper records:

- Not keeping proper receipts (such as tax invoices) to verify your tax deductions
- Not keeping proper records of your sales and purchases
- Not issuing proper tax invoices to your customers or clients (refer to Chapter 15)
- Not keeping proper records, such as log books, to substantiate motor vehicle claims (refer to Chapter 16)
- Not withholding tax where an Australian Business Number (ABN) is not quoted on a tax invoice (refer to Chapter 15)
- Not keeping accurate employee superannuation records
- Not keeping relevant tax invoices to verify GST credits (refer to Chapter 15)

WARNING

Under Australian tax law, you must retain your business records for a period of five years. Penalties may apply if you fail to comply with this important legal obligation.

Not Registering for (Or Collecting) GST Properly

If you run a business, you may need to register for GST and collect 10 per cent tax from your customers or clients, and remit the amount to the Tax Office on either a monthly, quarterly or annual basis (refer to Chapter 15). The Tax Office has identified the following common slip-ups relating to GST that you need to avoid:

- Not registering for GST if your annual GST turnover (sales) is likely to be $75,000 or more a year (or $150,000 a year if you operate a non-profit organisation)
- Incorrectly classifying taxable sales, input tax sales and GST-free sales
- Incorrectly calculating GST credits
- Incorrectly claiming back GST credits (such as GST on private expenses)
- Not reporting all the GST you collect from your customers or clients to the Tax Office

You may find the Tax Office fact sheets 'Common GST errors – importing or exporting goods and services' and 'GST – avoiding common errors' helpful. Download a copy from the Tax Office website (www.ato.gov.au).

Understating Your Income

The Australian tax system works on a self-assessment basis, so the onus is on you to declare the correct amount of income you derive each year (refer to Chapter 4). The Tax Office has identified the following common tax mistakes relating to not declaring all the income you derive each year:

>> Not recording all your cash sales (see Tax Office fact sheet 'The cash and shadow economy')

>> Not recording every sale you make (see Tax Office fact sheet 'Manual or paper record keeping for businesses')

>> Not declaring capital gains you make on sale of CGT assets (refer to Chapter 11)

>> Not declaring all the interest, dividends and rent you derive (refer to the chapters in Part 3)

>> Not declaring rental income on holiday homes

>> Not declaring profits or capital gains on sale of cryptocurrency (refer to Chapter 11)

If you're planning on not declaring all the income you derive, don't! The Tax Office performs ongoing dividend and interest checks by comparing information you have (or haven't!) disclosed in your tax return with information from external sources, such as companies that pay dividends and financial institutions that pay interest. So the chances are in favour of the system eventually finding you out — and stiff financial penalties apply if your tax return is found to be incorrect (refer to Chapter 4). For more details, see Tax Office fact sheet 'Data-matching protocols'.

Overstating Your Deductions

If you run a small business, the Tax Office uses small business benchmarks (or business ratios) to compare your business performance against similar businesses in the industry (refer to Chapter 4). So if you're planning on cooking the books by overstating your business expenses, don't! You could get audited and found out — especially if your tax deductions appear to be excessive. The Tax Office has identified the following common errors that you need to steer clear of:

>> Overstating your business expenses (refer to Chapter 14)

>> Claiming expenses that are capital, private or domestic in nature (refer to Chapter 2)

>> Overstating your rental expenses if you own an investment property (refer to Chapter 10)

Incorrectly Claiming Certain Expenses

When you incur expenses, you may need to satisfy specific rules before you can claim them (refer to Chapters 2 and 14). The Tax Office has identified the following common errors relating to claiming expenses:

>> Not correctly apportioning business and private use of assets (such as cars and computers) that are partly business-related and partly private

>> Incorrectly claiming the full amount of borrowing expenses in the financial year they're incurred rather than over the term of a loan or five years if the loan is more than five years (refer to Chapter 14)

>> Incorrectly apportioning interest deductions in respect to loans that are partly business-related and partly private

>> Incorrectly claiming prepaid expenses (refer to Chapter 14)

>> Incorrectly claiming certain expenses such as capital works deductions, bad debts and depreciation in accordance with the Tax Act (refer to Chapters 10 and 14)

>> Incorrectly claiming repairs (particularly initial repairs) that are capital in nature and not tax deductible (refer to Chapter 10)

Not Following the Tax Rules for CGT

Specific rules apply when you sell a CGT asset and make a capital gain or loss (refer to Chapter 11). The following list sets out some common slip-ups you need to be aware of:

>> Incorrectly calculating a capital gain or loss — for instance, using the settlement date for the disposal of a property rather than the date the contract was signed

>> Not declaring capital gains on the sale of rental properties, holiday homes and vacant land

>> Incorrectly claiming a main residence exemption — note that a main residence is a place where you and your family normally reside and use for private and domestic purposes (refer to Chapter 6)

>> Not keeping adequate records of your CGT assets to verify information, such as the date of purchase and cost base (refer to Chapter 11)

Not Running a SMSF by the Book

Trustees who run a SMSF must follow strict rules. If you fail to meet certain minimum standards as prescribed in the Tax Act, you could lose your compliance status and miss out on gaining certain tax concessions (refer to Chapter 18). The common mistakes associated with running a SMSF include:

>> Not lodging by the due date (or refusing to lodge) a 'Self-managed superannuation fund annual return (NAT 71226)' disclosing the taxable income (or loss) derived during the financial year (refer to Chapter 3)

- » Trustees making unauthorised loans to members and their relatives (for example, spouse and children) and receiving loans from members

- » Trustees not valuing the fund's assets at market value (particularly real estate) at the end of the financial year — visit www.ato.gov.au and see Tax Office fact sheets 'Valuation guidelines for self-managed superannuation funds' and 'Market valuation of assets' for more

- » Trustees recording the fund's assets in the name of the members

- » Trustees incorrectly receiving contributions from members who are over 75 years of age and no longer working — note also you can't make non-concessional contributions once your superannuation fund account balance reaches $1.9 million

- » Members gaining a personal benefit from SMSF assets before they satisfy a condition of release — for example, your super fund owns a property at a popular holiday resort and fund members stay there when on holidays (wouldn't it be great if you could?!)

- » Acquiring a residential property from a related party (for instance, from a member or member's relative)

- » Leasing a residential property to a related party

- » Residing in a residential property that your SMSF owns

Not Adhering to the Guidelines of a SMSF Pension Fund

Once a member of a SMSF satisfies a condition of release (for instance, retirement) the member can elect to receive a pension (refer to Chapter 19). The Tax Office has identified the following common mistakes associated with running a SMSF during the pension phase:

- » An inability to cash pension assets to meet minimum pension payments to members who have retired. This may become a major problem if your super fund owns a property that can't be readily sold at short notice.

>> Not deriving sufficient income (such as interest, dividends and rent) to pay minimum pension payments to members. This may become a major concern when interest rates are low, if a company does not declare dividends or if you own an investment property that is untenanted.

>> Not paying minimum pension payments to members who have retired.

>> Making contributions to a SMSF pension fund account rather than to an accumulation account. *Note:* Once your fund is in the pension phase, you can't make any further contributions.

>> Transferring funds in excess of the $1.9 million cap to start an account-based pension fund (where earnings are exempt from tax).

REMEMBER

If you receive a pension from a SMSF, the pension must be recalculated at the beginning of each financial year. The minimum amount of pension you can elect to receive depends on the balance in your account and your age at the time you receive the pension.

Not Complying with Tax Rules for Real Estate

When you invest in real estate, you're relying on bricks and mortar for income (rent) and capital growth (refer to Chapter 10). The following are common tax mistakes associated with investment properties that you need to be aware of:

>> Not charging a commercial rate of rent if you lease an investment property to a family member or relative (see Taxation Ruling 'IT 2167') — you need to do this in order to claim all your rental deductions

>> Not apportioning your rental expenses if you use only part of your property to derive rental income (refer to Chapter 2)

>> Incorrectly depreciating items (such as built-in kitchen cupboards) that are deductible under the capital works provisions (see Tax Office publication 'Rental properties (NAT 1729)')

- » Incorrectly claiming capital works deductions (see Taxation Ruling 'TR 97/25')

- » Incorrectly claiming initial repairs (see Taxation Determination 'TD 98/19')

- » Incorrectly claiming capital improvements as repairs and maintenance (see Tax Office publication 'Rental properties (NAT 1729)')

- » Incorrectly claiming interest expenses with respect to loans that are partly investment-related and partly private in nature (see Taxation Ruling 'TR 2002/2' and Taxation Determination 'TD 2012/1')

- » Incorrectly claiming borrowing expenses (refer to Chapter 14)

TECHNICAL STUFF

You may find the Tax Office fact sheets 'Common errors made by individuals that concern us', 'Top 10 tips to help rental property owners avoid common tax mistakes' and 'Tax avoidance schemes to watch out for' helpful. You can download copies from the Tax Office website (www.ato.gov.au).

Appendix A

Taxing the Visitors: Non-Residents

Non-residents of Australia are liable to pay tax only at non-resident rates on income that comes from an Australian source, such as salary and wages, business profits and rental income (see Figure A-1). However, a non-resident isn't liable to pay a 2 per cent Medicare levy and he or she can't claim domestic tax offsets (rebates) and the tax-free threshold.

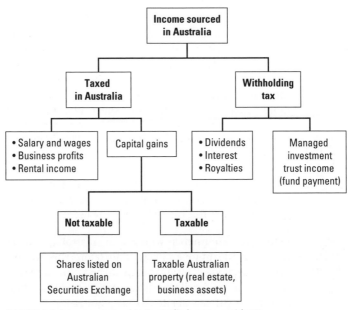

FIGURE A-1: Income sourced in Australia by non-residents.

You can be treated as a tax resident as soon as you're in Australia for more than 183 days. However, this isn't the case if the Tax Office is satisfied that your permanent place of abode is outside of Australia and you have no intention to live here. If you're an overseas student and you enrol at an Australian institution in a course that takes more than six months to complete, you're usually considered a resident of Australia for tax purposes while you're here (refer to Chapter 1).

The income tax rates for non-residents of Australia are shown in Table A-1.

TABLE A-1 **Individual Income Tax Rate for Australian Non-residents, 2023–24**

Taxable Income	Marginal Tax Rates
$0–$120,000	32.5%
$120,001–$180,000	37%
Over $180,001	45%

If you're a tourist on a working holiday visa, the marginal rate of tax payable on the first $45,000 you earn while working in Australia is 15 per cent (colloquially referred to as the 'backpacker tax'). If you earn more than $45,001, the marginal rate of tax payable will increase in accordance to the 'Individual income tax rate for Australian non-residents' as shown in Table A-1. (For more details, see Tax Office fact sheet 'Working holiday makers'.)

REMEMBER

If you work in Australia while on holidays, you need to lodge a tax return disclosing the salary or wages you're paid. If you leave Australia before the end of the financial year, you need to read the Tax Office fact sheet 'Lodge your tax return before leaving Australia', in particular the section, 'How to lodge an early tax return'. You can get a copy from the Tax Office website (www.ato.gov.au).

WARNING

Before you commence working in Australia, you need to apply for a tax file number (TFN) and quote this to your employer. Otherwise, you're automatically taxed at the highest marginal tax rate. For more details see Tax Office fact sheet 'Apply for a TFN' on the Tax Office website www.ato.gov.au.

TIP

If you're a temporary resident of Australia holding an eligible temporary resident visa and you permanently leave Australia, you may be entitled to claim back any superannuation contributions made on your behalf (refer to Chapter 5). For more details visit the Tax Office website (www.ato.gov.au) and read the form

'Applying for a Departing Australia super payment from a super fund or retirement savings account'.

Foreign and temporary residents are liable to pay tax on capital gains tax (CGT) assets that are 'taxable Australian property' and are physically located in Australia. For example, this requirement may arise if you own property in Australia or assets in a business that operates through an Australian branch. You're normally not liable to pay tax on any capital gain you make when you sell shares listed on the Australian Securities Exchange because they're not classified as 'taxable Australian property' (refer to Figure A-1).

WARNING

Non-residents need to seek approval from the Tax Office if they intend to invest in Australian residential property. For more details, visit the Tax Office website (www.ato.gov.au) and read fact sheet 'Foreign investment in residential assets: Our compliance approach'.

If a foreign resident disposes of certain taxable Australian property that's worth more than $750,000 (such as a residential or commercial property), the purchaser must withhold 12.5 per cent of the purchase price and forward the amount to the Tax Office. This is to cover any potential CGT obligations the foreign resident may incur. For more details, check out the Tax Office fact sheet 'Capital gains tax withholding: Impacts on foreign and Australian residents'.

CHECK THE NET

Foreign residents can't claim a main residence exemption from CGT, unless they can satisfy the requirements of the 'life events test'. For more details, see Tax Office fact sheet 'Main residence exemption for foreign residents'. You can download a copy from the Tax Office website (www.ato.gov.au).

REMEMBER

A foreign or temporary resident is ordinarily ineligible to claim a 50 per cent CGT discount on disposal of taxable Australian property owned for more than 12 months. (Refer to Chapter 11 for more details on CGT and check out the Tax Office fact sheet 'Your residency status and GCT'.)

CHECK THE NET

If you want to know more about Australian income of foreign residents, visit the Tax Office website (www.ato.gov.au) to access the following fact sheets:

>> 'Foreign and worldwide income'

>> 'Doing business in Australia'

If you're a non-resident and earn Australian-sourced interest, dividends or royalties, you don't need to lodge an Australian tax return, or include these payments as part of your assessable income. This rule applies even if you do have to lodge a tax return (for example, you earn salary and wages in Australia) because you're liable to pay withholding tax only on the amount you receive (refer to Figure A-1). The rate of tax payable depends on whether an international tax treaty exists between Australia and the foreign country where you reside. If no tax treaty exists, 10 per cent tax is ordinarily withheld from interest payments, and 30 per cent tax is usually withheld from unfranked dividends and royalty payments. No withholding tax applies if you receive a fully franked dividend (refer to Chapter 9). For more details, check out Tax Office fact sheet 'Non-resident withholding tax – interest, dividend or royalty' at www.ato.gov.au.

CASE STUDY: TAXING A NON-RESIDENT OF AUSTRALIA

Franco, who is a non-resident of Australia, earns a $20,000 salary while working in Australia and pays $6,500 PAYG withholding tax. His work-related expenses are $200. He also receives $50 interest on an Australian investment account. The financial institution withholds 10 per cent withholding tax on this payment because he quotes his tax file number and overseas address to it. While Franco is in Australia, he makes a $3,000 capital gain on shares listed on the Australian Securities Exchange. He also receives a $28,000 salary in the country where he normally resides.

Because Franco is a non-resident, he's liable to pay tax only on income sourced in Australia.

Franco is taxed in the following way:

- The $20,000 salary he earns in Australia is liable to tax at non-resident rates.

- He can claim a $200 tax deduction for his work-related expenses.

- A withholding tax of 10 per cent is deducted from the $50 interest, so Franco doesn't have to pay any further tax on this amount, nor include it in his Australian tax return.

- The $3,000 capital gain he makes on his share transaction isn't taxed because it isn't classified as 'taxable Australian property'.

- The $28,000 salary Franco earns in the country where he normally resides isn't liable to Australian tax because the source is outside of Australia.

Franco is a non-resident, so he can't claim the tax-free threshold available to Australian residents. He isn't liable to pay the 2 per cent Medicare levy.

Franco's taxable income (assessable income less deductions) and tax payable are calculated as follows:

Tax return for individuals	
Income	
Salary or wages	$20,000
TOTAL INCOME	$20,000
Less Work-related expenses	$200
TAXABLE INCOME	$19,800
Calculation of tax payable/refund	
Tax payable on $19,800 (see Note)	$6,435
Less tax withheld on salary	$6,500
TAX REFUND	**$65**

Franco's total tax credits ($6,500) exceed the tax payable ($6,435), so the Tax Office refunds the excess ($65).

Note: Calculating tax payable:	
$19,800 × 32.5% =	$6,435
TAX PAYABLE	**$6,435**

Australia has entered into international tax treaties with a number of overseas countries regarding the liability to Australian tax on certain Australian-sourced income derived by a non-resident. So it's possible that a particular tax treaty may exempt the income from tax.

When a resident Australian company pays a dividend to a non-resident, the company must state whether the dividend is fully franked, partially franked or unfranked. Franked means Australian income tax is paid on its Australian profits and this benefit can be passed on to you as a non-resident (for more details, refer to Chapter 9). If the dividends are fully franked, no withholding tax is withheld from your payment. On the other hand, if the dividends are partially franked, some withholding tax may be withheld from your payment and, if the dividends are unfranked, you're liable to pay the full amount of withholding tax (for more info see Tax Office fact sheet 'Dividends paid or credited to non-resident shareholders').

CHECK
THE NET

If you want to know whether Australia has a tax treaty with a particular foreign country, visit the Tax Office website (www. ato.gov.au) and check out the fact sheet 'International tax agreements'. See also the Australian Government Department of the Treasury website (www.treasury.gov.au) and examine the section 'Income Tax Treaties'.

WARNING

If you earn Australia-sourced interest, you need to advise the paying institution of your overseas address. Otherwise, 45 per cent tax is withheld from your payment, instead of 10 per cent.

Appendix B

Leading Tax Cases and Tax Office Publications: Study Guide

The following tax cases and Tax Office publications can be of assistance if you're studying tax law or you need to check out whether a certain receipt or expense is assessable or deductible. You can find these tax cases and publications on the ATO website: www.ato.gov.au.

Leading Tax Cases

The following famous tax cases are often quoted and relied on as being authoritative. You can refer to these tax cases to solve common problems that you're likely to come across.

Income under ordinary concepts

The following tax cases provide core tax principles relating to the general concepts of income, how to account for income and residency issues.

Accounting for income

Arthur Murray (NSW) Pty Ltd v FC of T (1965) 114 CLR 314

FC of T v Australian Gas Light Company & Anor 83 ATC 4800

Ballarat Brewing Co Ltd v DFC of T (1951) 82 CLR 364

Barratt & Ors v FC of T 92 ATC 4275

Brent v FC of T 71 ATC 4195

C of T (South Australia) v Executor Trustee and Agency Co of South Australia Ltd (1938) 63 CLR 108

Country Magazine Pty Ltd v FC of T (1968) 117 CLR 162

FC of T v Dunn 89 ATC 4141

FC of T v Firstenberg 76 ATC 4141

Gasparin v FC of T 94 ATC 4280

Henderson v FC of T 70 ATC 4016

J Rowe and Son Pty Ltd v FC of T 71 ATC 4157

FC of T v Thorogood (1927) 40 CLR 454

Betting and gambling

Babka v FC of T 89 ATC 4963

Brajkovich v FC of T 89 ATC 5227

Evans v FC of T 89 ATC 4540

Graham v Green (1925) 9 TC 309

Jones v FC of T (1932) 2 ATD 16

Martin v FC of T (1953) 90 CLR 470

Shepherd v FC of T 75 ATC 4244

Trautwein v FC of T (1936) 56 CLR 196

Carrying on (running) a business

Ferguson v FC of T 79 ATC 4261

Glennan v FC of T 2003 ATC 4619

Hope v The Council of the City of Bathurst (1980) 144 CLR 1

Southern Estates Pty Ltd v FC of T (1967) 14 ATD 475

FC of T v Stone 2005 ATC 4234

Thomas v FC of T 72 ATC 4094

Compensation payments

Allied Mills Industries Pty Ltd v FC of T 89 ATC 4365

Californian Oil Products Ltd (in liq) v FC of T 52 CLR 28

Federal Coke Co Pty Ltd v FC of T (1977) 77 ATC 4255

Heavy Minerals Pty Ltd v FC of T (1966) 115 CLR 512

McLaurin v FC of T (1961) 104 CLR 381

Fringe benefits tax

Bechtel Australia Pty Ltd v FC of T (2023) FCA 676

FC of T v Virgin Australia Regional Airways Pty Ltd (2021) FCAFC 209

John Holland Group Pty Ltd v FC of T (2015) FCAFC 82

Lake Fox Ltd v FC of T 2012 ATC 10-248

Goods and Services Tax

FC of T v Qantas Airways Limited (2012) HCA 41

FC of T v Reliance Carpet Co Pty Ltd (2008) HCA 22

Income versus capital receipts

Dickenson v FC of T (1957–1958) 98 CLR 460

FC of T v GKN Kwikform Services Pty Ltd 91 ATC 4336

McClelland v FC of T 70 ATC 4115

Memorex Pty Ltd v FC of T 87 ATC 5034

Moana Sand Pty Ltd v FC of T 88 ATC 4897

FC of T v Myer Emporium Ltd 87 ATC 4363

Scottish Australia Mining Co Ltd v FC of T (1950) 81 CLR 188

FC of T v Spedley Securities Ltd 88 ATC 4126

Steinberg v FC of T (1975) 134 CLR 640

FC of T v Walker 85 ATC 4179

Westfield Ltd v FC of T 91 ATC 4234

FC of T v Whitfords Beach Pty Ltd 82 ATC 4031

Partnerships

Cripps v FC of T 99 ATC 2428

Ellis v Joseph Ellis & Co (1905) 1 KB 324

FC of T v Everett 80 ATC 4076

Jolley v FC of T 89 ATC 4197

FC of T v McDonald 87 ATC 4541

Rose v FC of T (1951) 84 CLR 118

Stapleton v FC of T 89 ATC 4818

Yeung & Anor v FC of T 88 ATC 4193

Professional sportspersons

FC of T v Cooper 91 ATC 4396

Kelly v FC of T 85 ATC 4283

Spriggs v FC of T; Riddell v FC of T (2009) HCA 22

FC of T v Stone 2005 ATC 4234

Residency issues: Source of income

FC of T v Applegate 79 ATC 4307

Bayswater Investments Ltd v FC of T (2016) HCA 45

Brookton Co-operative Society Ltd v FC of T (1981) 11 ATR 880

De Beers Consolidated Mines v Howe (1906) AC 455

Dempsey v FC of T (2014) ATC 10-363

FC of T v Efstathakis 79 ATC 4256

Esquire Nominees v Pty Ltd v FC of T 73 ATC 4114

FC of T v French (1957) 98 CLR 398

FC of T v Jenkins 82 ATC 4098

Malaysian Shipping Co Ltd v FC of T (1946) 71 CLR 156

FC of T v Mitchum (1965) 113 CLR 401

Pillay v FCT (2013) ATC 10-324

Sneddon v FC of T 2012 ATC 10-264

Thorpe Nominees Pty Ltd v C of T 88 ATC 4886

Trusts

FC of T v Bamford & Ors (2010) ATC 20-170

FC of T v Carter (2022) HCA 10

Davis v FC of T 89 ATC 4377

Guardian AIT Pty Ltd ATF Australian Investment Trust v Commissioner of Taxation (2021) FCA 1619

Richardson v FC of T 2001 ATC 4058

Taylor & Anor v FC of T 70 ATC 4026

FC of T v Whiting (1943) 68 CLR 199

Zeta Force Pty Ltd v FC of T 98 ATC 4681

Voluntary payment and gifts

FC of T v Blake 84 ATC 4661

FC of T v Cook and Sherden 80 ATC 4140

FC of T v Dixon (1952) 86 CLR 540

FC of T v Harris (1980) 80 ATC 4238

Hayes v FC of T (1956) 96 CLR 47

Kelly v FC of T 85 ATC 4283

Scott v FC of T (1966) 117 CLR 514

Smith v FC of T (1987) 87 ATC 4883

Squatting Investment Co Ltd v FC of T (1953) 86 CLR 570

Deductible expenses

The following tax cases provide core tax principles relating to what is an allowable deduction.

Bad debts

GE Crane Sales Pty Ltd v FC of T 71 ATC 4268

Point v FC of T 70 ATC 4021

Depreciation

FC of T v Mount Isa Mines Ltd 91 ATC 4154

Wangaratta Woollen Mills v FC of T 69 ATC 4095

Yarmouth v France (1887) 19 QBD 647

Employment-related deductions

FC of T v Cooper 91 ATC 4396

FC of T v Edwards 94 ATC 4255

Lodge v FC of T 72 ATC 4174

FC of T v Maddalena 71 ATC 4161

Mansfield v FC of T 96 ATC 4001

Morris & Ors v FC of T 2002 ATC 4404

FC of T v Smith 81 ATC 4114

Westcott v FC of T 97 ATC 2129

General deductions

FC of T v James Flood Pty Ltd (1953) 88 CLR 492

Charles Moore and Co (WA) Pty Ltd v FC of T (1956) 11 ATD 147

Magna Alloys & Research Pty Ltd v FC of T 80 ATC 4542

W Nevill & Co Ltd v FC of T (1936–1937) 56 CLR 290

New Zealand Flax Investments Ltd v FC of T (1938) 61 CLR 179

RACV Insurance Pty Ltd v FC of T 74 ATC 4169

Ronpibon Tin NL and Tongkah Compound NL v FC of T (1949) 78 CLR 47

FC of T v Snowden & Wilson Pty Ltd (1958) 99 CLR 431

Home office deductions

FC of T v Faichney 72 ATC 4245

FC of T v Forsyth 81 ATC 4157

Handley v FC of T 81 ATC 4165

Interest deductions

FC of T v Brown 99 ATC 4600

Fletcher & Ors v FC of T 91 ATC 4950

FC of T v Munro (1926) 38 CLR 153

Placer Pacific Management Pty Ltd v FC of T 95 ATC 4459

FC of T v Roberts and Smith 92 ATC 4380

Steele v FC of T 99 ATC 4242

Travelodge Papua New Guinea Ltd v Chief Collector of Taxes 85 ATC 4432

Ure v FC of T 81 ATC 4100

Repairs

Law Shipping Co Ltd v IRC (1924) 12 TC 621

Lindsay v FC of T (1960) 106 CLR 377

W Thomas & Co Pty Ltd v FC of T (1965) 115 CLR 58

FC of T v Western Suburbs Cinemas Ltd (1952) 86 CLR 102

Revenue versus capital expenditure

British Insulated & Helsby Cables Ltd v Atherton (1926) AC 205

Broken Hill Theatres Pty Ltd v FC of T (1951) 9 ATD 306

Griffin Coal Mining Co Ltd v FC of T 90 ATC 4870

Hallstroms Pty Ltd v FC of T (1946) 72 CLR 634

Herald & Weekly Times Ltd v FC of T 48 CLR 113

John Fairfax & Sons Pty Limited v FC of T (1959) 101 CLR 30

Kennedy Holdings and Property Management Pty Ltd v FC of T 92 ATC 4918

FC of T v Osborne 90 ATC 4889

Softwood Pulp and Paper Ltd v FC of T 76 ATC 4439

Sun Newspapers Ltd v FC of T (1938) 61 CLR 337

Self-education deductions

FC of T v Anstis 2010 ATC 20-221

FC of T v Finn (1961) 106 CLR 60

FC of T v Hatchett 71 ATC 4184

FC of T v Highfield 82 ATC 4463

FC of T v Kropp 76 ATC 4406

FC of T v Smith 78 ATC 4157

FC of T v Wilkinson 83 ATC 4295

Trading stock

All States Frozen Foods Pty Ltd v FC of T 90 ATC 4175

Australasian Jam Co Pty Ltd v FC of T (1953) 88 CLR 23

Farnsworth v FC of T (1949) 78 CLR 504

Lister Blackstone Pty Ltd v FC of T 76 ATC 4285

Philip Morris Ltd v FC of T 79 ATC 4352

FC of T v Sutton Motors (Chullora) Wholesale Pty Ltd 85 ATC 4398

Travel expenses

FC of T v Ballesty 77 ATC 4181

FC of T v Collings 76 ATC 4254

Garrett v FC of T 82 ATC 4060

FC of T v Green (1950) 81 CLR 313

Lunney v FC of T (1957–1958) 100 CLR 478

Case U156 87 ATC 908

FC of T v Vogt 75 ATC 4073

FC of T v Wiener 78 ATC 4006

Capital gains tax

The following are leading tax cases relating to capital gains tax (CGT) issues.

Active assets

Jakjoy Pty Ltd v FC of T 2013 ATC 10-328

Main residence exemption

Erdelyi & Anor v FC of T ATC 2214

Time of CGT event

FC of T v Sara Lee Household & Body Care (Aust) Pty Ltd 2000 ATC 4378

Tax Office Publications

The following Tax Office publications provide excellent summaries of core tax principles and give useful guidelines to help you solve specific tax problems.

Capital gains tax (CGT)

'Capital gains tax'

'CGT concessions eligibility overview'

'Guide to capital gains tax'

Carrying on (running) a business

'Are you in business?'

'Concessions for eligible businesses'

'Income and deductions for business'

'Overview of record-keeping rules for business'

'Personal services income'

'Record keeping for small business'

'Share investing versus share trading'

Companies

'Company tax rates'

'Franking account'

'How to claim a tax loss'

'Incorporating your business – tax implications'

Deductions

'Claiming deductions for personal super contributions'

'Deductions for small business'

'Deductions you can claim'

'General information about prepaid expenses'

'Guide to depreciating assets (NAT 1996)'

'Interest, dividend and other investment income deductions'

'Self-education expenses'

Foreign income

'Australian resident foreign and worldwide income'

'Claiming a foreign income tax offset'

'Foreign and worldwide income'

'Guide to foreign income tax offset rules'

'Tax exempt income from foreign employment'

Fringe benefits tax (FBT)

'Fringe benefits tax'

'Fringe benefits tax – a guide for employers'

'Fringe benefits tax – rates and thresholds'

Goods and services tax (GST)

'GST'

'GST: Helping you understand your GST obligations (NAT 74240)'

Income

'Exempt income from foreign service'

'How dividends are taxed'

'Income averaging for special professionals'

'Income you must declare'

'Taxation of termination payments'

'Your income if you are under 18 years old'

Investing

'Employee share schemes'

'Film industry incentives'

'Forestry managed investment schemes (Division 394)'

'Personal investors guide to capital gains tax'

'Refund of franking credits instructions and application for individuals'

'Rental expenses to claim'

'Rental income you must declare'

'Rental properties (NAT 1729)'

'You and your shares (NAT 2632)'

Residency issues

'Australians living overseas'

'International tax agreements'

'Residency requirements for companies, corporate limited partnerships and trusts'

'Tax on Australian income for foreign residents'

'Work out your residency status for tax purposes'

'Your tax residency'

Superannuation

'Concessional contributions cap'

'Self-managed super funds'

'Self-managed superannuation fund independent auditor's report'

'Starting a self-managed super fund'

'Thinking about self-managed super'

Glossary

accruals or earnings basis: Method of accounting for income that takes into account money due but not yet paid to you. This generally arises when you have a legal right to demand payment, such as when you invoice a client for the services you have rendered.

adjusted taxable income: Your taxable income plus other amounts such as reportable fringe benefits, tax-free pensions or benefits, foreign income, reportable super contributions, losses from negative gearing financial investments minus child support payments.

allowable deduction: An expense you can deduct from your assessable income.

assessable income: Ordinary income and statutory income that's liable to tax.

Australian Business Number (ABN): The number you quote whenever you conduct a business transaction. If you don't quote this number, 45 per cent tax may be withheld from payments made to you.

business activity statement (BAS): A statement under the pay- as-you-go system that's prepared at the end of each reporting period, disclosing certain income liable to tax and any GST collected.

business real property: A business premises such as a shop, office or factory that you use to derive your assessable income.

capital gains tax (CGT): A tax on gains you make on disposal of CGT assets such as shares, real estate and collectables you acquire on or after 20 September 1985.

capital in nature: Expenses that aren't tax deductible because they don't have a direct or relevant connection with deriving assessable income.

cash or receipts basis: A method of accounting for income that recognises income only when a payment is actually received.

CGT asset: An asset that's liable to be taxed under the CGT provisions.

CGT event: Normally arises when a change in ownership of a CGT asset occurs, such as when you sell it. It can also arise if a CGT asset is lost, destroyed or given away.

collectables: Assets such as antiques, paintings, rare books, stamps, coins and jewellery. Collectables that cost more than $500 are liable to tax under the CGT provisions.

complying superannuation fund: A fund that made an election to be regulated under the *Superannuation Industry (Supervision) Act 1993*.

concessional contributions: Contributions you make to a complying super fund that are tax deductible.

condition of release: A condition you must meet before you can access your benefits in a superannuation fund, such as when you retire.

cost base: Under the CGT provisions, the price (and costs) you pay for CGT assets such as shares, real estate and collectables. It may also include sale costs and other associated costs you incur.

derived: Income you have obtained that's liable to be taxed. You're considered to have derived income when you receive a payment or can legally demand a payment for services rendered, or when it's applied or dealt with in any way on your behalf or as you direct.

diminishing value method (DVM): An accounting method whereby you can work out depreciation that you can claim each year — a larger amount in earlier years and a lesser amount in later years.

discount capital gain: A capital gain that arises when you dispose of CGT assets that you have owned for at least 12 months. Just half of the capital gain you make is liable to tax at your marginal tax rates (plus the Medicare levy).

dividend: A distribution of profits by a company to its shareholders.

dividend franking credit: A tax credit you receive from a dividend that's franked. The size of the credit depends on the company tax rate.

exempt income: Certain payments or receipts that are exempt from tax.

financial year: Australia's financial year, commencing 1 July and ending 30 June.

franked dividend: A dividend that carries a franking credit (or tax offset). The credit is applied against the tax payable. If no credit is received, the dividend is unfranked. Partially franked dividends are also possible. This means only a certain percentage of the dividend carries a credit.

fringe benefits tax (FBT): A tax levied on employers for certain benefits provided to their employees or their associates, such as a spouse, child or relative.

fully franked dividend: Means the company has paid tax on its profits. This benefit can be passed on to you.

goods and services tax (GST): A 10 per cent tax on goods and services on purchases and sales.

GST credit: A refund of the 10 per cent goods and services tax you incur on your costs or inputs.

GST-free sales (or supplies): No GST is charged on GST-free sales; you can claim a GST credit in respect of your acquisitions to make that sale.

income from personal exertion: Employment income such as salary and wages, bonuses, commissions and allowances that you earn as an employee.

income from property: Income such as interest, dividends, rent, annuities and royalty payments.

incurred: Point in time when you can legally claim a tax deduction. Normally arises when you're definitely committed and legally obligated to pay for certain goods and services you've received.

input tax supply: A GST term relating to financial services and residential property for use as residential accommodation. No GST is charged on input tax supplies, and you can't claim a GST credit in respect of your acquisitions to make that supply.

log book: Under the car substantiation provisions, a document to record the actual number of business kilometres you travel over a period of 12 weeks. This record is used to calculate a reasonable estimate of the number of business kilometres you're likely to travel during the financial year.

main residence: Place where you normally reside. It can also include up to 2 hectares of land that surround your home. Your main residence is normally exempt from CGT.

marginal tax rate(s): The rate of tax payable on the last taxable income dollar you earn; can vary between 0 and 45 per cent.

Medicare levy: A medical levy based on a percentage of your taxable income (at the time of writing, 2 per cent) to help fund the Australian health system and disability care insurance scheme.

non-concessional contributions: Superannuation contributions you make to a complying superannuation fund that don't qualify for a tax deduction.

non-discount capital gain: A capital gain on disposal of a CGT asset that you have owned for fewer than 12 months. The entire capital gain is liable to tax at your marginal tax rates plus the Medicare levy.

partially franked: You receive a franking credit to the extent the dividend is franked.

partnership: Under Australian tax law, an association of persons carrying on business as partners or in receipt of income jointly.

personal exertion income: Income such as salary and wages, bonuses, commissions and allowances that an employee earns as a consequence of using personal labour and skill.

preservation age: The age you must reach before you can retire and access your superannuation fund benefits.

prime cost method (PCM): An accounting method whereby you can work out a fixed amount of depreciation that you can claim each year.

private company: Under Australian tax law, a company is private if it's not a public company. This is the case if 20 or fewer persons control at least 75 per cent of the company.

private or domestic in nature: Expenses that aren't tax deductible because they don't have a direct or relevant connection with deriving assessable income.

reportable fringe benefits: The grossed-up taxable value of fringe benefits that exceed $2,000 that must be reported on an employee's payment summary.

self-managed superannuation fund (SMSF): A superannuation fund set up by individuals.

superannuation fund: A fund set up to finance retirement strategies.

taxable income: The amount of income that's liable to tax. Taxable income equals assessable income minus deductions.

tax file number (TFN): A number you get from the Tax Office that you need to quote to certain organisations and when you lodge your annual tax return.

tax offset: A tax credit or rebate you can use to reduce the amount of tax payable.

trust: A legal obligation binding a person (referred to as the *trustee*) who has control over certain business and/or investment assets (referred to as *trust property*), for the benefit of certain persons (referred to as *beneficiaries*).

trustee: A person responsible for administering and managing the trust property over which he or she has control for the benefit of the beneficiaries.

unfranked dividend: A dividend that carries no franking credits that you can claim.

Index

C

About the Author

Jimmy Prince is a fellow of CPA Australia and a tax specialist. He is a former lecturer and tutor in income tax law at La Trobe University, Melbourne Institute of Technology and AMI Education, and teaches a number of investment courses for the Centre for Adult Education (CAE) in Melbourne. He is the author of several investment books including *Shares & Taxation*, *Property & Taxation* and *Superannuation & Taxation*. In his earlier years, Jimmy worked for the Australian Taxation Office and also consulted to CPA Australia — Technicall.

Dedication

This book is dedicated to my wife, Maria Rosa Prince.

Author's Acknowledgements

I would like to thank the staff and editors at Wiley Publishing Australia Pty Ltd for helping me complete this new edition.

Publisher's Acknowledgements

Some of the people who helped bring this book to market include the following:

Acquisitions, Editorial and Media Development

Project Editor: Tamilmani Varadharaj

Acquisitions Editor: Lucy Raymond

Editorial Manager: Ingrid Bond

Copy Editor: Charlotte Duff

Production

Proofreader: Susan Hobbs

Indexer: Kevin Broccoli

The author and publisher would like to thank the following copyright holders, organisations and individuals for their permission to reproduce copyright material in this book:

» Cover image: © fizkes/Adobe Stock Photos

» Material from Australian Taxation Office © Australian Taxation Office for the Commonwealth of Australia.

Every effort has been made to trace the ownership of copyright material. Information that will enable the publisher to rectify any error or omission in subsequent editions will be welcome. In such cases, please contact the Permissions Section of John Wiley & Sons Australia, Ltd.